Success Against the Odds
– Five Years On

In 1995 the National Commission on Education carried out a study of effective schools in disadvantaged areas. The findings were published in the highly influential *Success Against the Odds* (Routledge, 1996). Five years on, this book revisits the eleven schools in the original study to assess their fortunes over time.

Success Against the Odds: Five Years On is a unique study of school effectiveness and improvement. Leading educationalists revisit the eleven schools and analyse how they are succeeding in the current educational and political climate. This is a unique opportunity to consider how success can be sustained in the long-term and will be of interest to all those concerned about school effectiveness and improvement.

Reviews of *Success Against the Odds* (Routledge, 1996)

'The schools in this book are an inspiration to all pupils, parents and teachers . . . We must learn what they teach us.'
David Blunkett, Secretary of State for Education

'This book may prove to be the most valuable of all (the National Commission on Education's) influential reports.'
Times Educational Supplement

Professor Margaret Maden is Director of the Centre for Successful Schools at Keele University. She co-edited *Success Against the Odds* (1996) as a member of the National Commission on Education.

SUCCESS AGAINST THE ODDS – FIVE YEARS ON

Revisiting effective schools in disadvantaged areas

Edited by
MARGARET MADEN

London and New York

First published 2001
by RoutledgeFalmer
11 New Fetter Lane, London EC4P 4EE

Simultaneously published in the USA and Canada
by Routledge
29 West 35th Street, New York, NY 10001

RoutledgeFalmer is an imprint of the Taylor & Francis Group

Typeset in Garamond and Scala Sans
by Keystroke, Jacaranda Lodge, Wolverhampton
Printed and bound in Great Britain
by TJ International Ltd, Padstow, Cornwall

British Library Cataloguing in Publication Data
A catalogue record for this book is available from the British Library

Library of Congress Cataloging in Publication Data
Success against the odds, five years on: revisiting effective schools in
disadvantaged areas / edited by Margaret Maden.
    p. cm.
    Includes bibliographical references and index.
    1. School improvement programs–Great Britain–Case studies.
    2. Socially handicapped children–Education–Great Britain–Case
    studies. I. Maden, Margaret

    LB2822.84.G7 S85 2001
    371.01'0941–dc2100   00–068357

ISBN 0–415–25339–X (pbk)
    0–415–253381 (hbk)

CONTENTS

FIGURES

TABLES

CONTRIBUTORS

Introduction – Building for Improvement and Sustaining Change in Schools Serving Disadvantaged Communities

Professor John Gray has been Director of Research at Homerton College, Cambridge since 1994 and is currently a Visiting Professor at the London University Institute of Education and a Fellow of the British Academy. He was previously Professor of Education at Sheffield University.

His main research interests lie in the areas of school effectiveness, school improvement and the dynamics of change. During the course of his career he has directed well over 50 externally funded research projects for a wide range of sponsors including LEAs and their schools, government agencies, research organisations and bodies outside the UK. He has also led several major school improvement initiatives and contributed to their evaluation.

1 Blaengwrach Primary School

Alan Evans has extensive experience of management development at senior level and was a consultant to the School Management Task Force in the early 1990s as well as Wales Education Management. He undertook the evaluation of the implementation of the teacher support programme for the National Curriculum in English, mathematics and science for the Curriculum Council for Wales (1992). He has a particular research interest in small schools and in strategies for countering underachievement, especially in boys. Alan Evans is currently National Co-ordinator of the National Mentoring Pilot Project (DfEE initiative) as well as the Evaluator for the Peripatetic Nursery Teacher Project in Powys.

2 Columbia Primary School

Anne Sofer was the Chief Education Officer for the London Borough of Tower Hamlets from 1989 to 1997. Previously she had been a member of the ILEA and Chair of its Schools Sub-Committee. She has served as a member of the Kennedy (*Widening Participation*) Committee, and the government's advisory committee on ethnic minority achievement. She is a trustee of the Nuffield Foundation and Chair of the National Children's Bureau.

3 Crowcroft Park Primary School

Bill Rogers is head of Manchester School Improvement Service and was formerly head of Inspection Service. He has been a teacher, and senior manager in secondary schools and a sixth form college. He is author of a number of books and articles on careers education, school improvement and action based research and has recently published research on national mentoring schemes. He was founder member of the North West Consortium for the Study of Effectiveness in Urban Schools and is currently LEA lead member for the Manchester and Salford Teacher Training Agency Research Consortium.

4 Fair Furlong Primary School

Agnes McMahon is a senior lecturer in the University of Bristol Graduate School of Education, teaching and researching in the field of education management and policy. Her current research focuses upon the continuing professional development of teachers.

5 Lochgelly North Special School

Professor John MacBeath, OBE, has recently been appointed to the Chair of Educational Leadership at the University of Cambridge. He was previously the Director of the Quality in

Education Centre at the University of Strathclyde and has been involved in research and consultancy for a wide range of bodies, both nationally and internationally, and is currently a Consultant to the Government of Hong Kong on School Effectiveness and Improvement. In June 1997 he was appointed as a member of the government's Task Force on Standards and awarded the OBE for services to education.

Donald Gray is a lecturer in the Department of Maths, Science and Technological Education at the University of Strathclyde. He has a background in science education, curriculum development and research. He has been a research assistant with the Scottish Council for Research in Education and Associate Co-ordinator of the IEA International Survey in Civic Education based at Humboldt University, Berlin.

6 Burntwood School

Professor Kathryn Riley is Co-ordinator of the World Bank's Basic Education Group and Director of the Centre for Educational Management, University of Surrey, Roehampton. She began her career in education in Ethiopia and has been a teacher, governor, local government officer and elected member. Kathryn has written and published widely and her challenging and popular book, *Whose School Is it Anyway?* (Falmer Press, 1998), raises provocative questions about who rules our schools. Her most recent book, co-edited by leading American researcher Karen Seashore, is called *Leadership for Learning: International Perspectives on Leadership for Change and School Reform* (Falmer Press).

Jim Docking is Senior Research Officer in the Centre of Educational Management at the University of Surrey, Roehampton, where he was formerly Head of Education at Whitelands College and Chairman of the School of Education. He is author of several books. Most recently, he edited *New Labour's Policies for Schools: Raising the Standard?* (David Fulton, 2000).

Ellalinda Rustique-Forrester is the lead research officer on the Roehampton Centre's major project on disenfranchised young people, 'Bringing Young People Back into the Frame'. Before coming to the UK, Elle was at Teachers College, Columbia University, New York, where she was a research associate and policy officer, working on the National Commission on Teaching and America's Future.

David Rowles is Deputy Director of the Roehampton Centre and has been its Principal Researcher since 1991. His main areas of work have been on the implications of Ofsted inspections and teacher appraisal. He was Senior Inspector for Schools in the London Borough of Merton, where he concentrated on management issues and professional development of staff.

7 Haywood High School

Valerie Hannon was, until 1999, the Director of Education of Derbyshire County LEA. She was an adviser to the Local Government Association, Chair of the East Midlands Chief Education Officers and an executive member of the Association of Chief Education Officers. Formerly Deputy Director of Education in Sheffield, she has extensive experience of both urban and rural contexts. Before joining local government she was a research fellow in the University of Sheffield exploring aspects of accountability in education. Now an independent researcher and consultant, she works with public bodies in review and development.

8 Hazelwood College

Tony Gallagher is a Professor of Education at Queen's University, Belfast. He worked previously at the University of Ulster Centre for the Study of Conflict and the Northern Ireland Council for Educational Research. His main research interests include the role of education in ethnically divided societies, and education policy for social inclusion. He recently co-directed a major research project into the effects of the selective system of grammar and secondary schools in Northern Ireland, and is currently examining the impact of community-led initiatives to promote education in socially disadvantaged areas of Belfast.

9 St. Michael's School

Gerald Grace is Director of the Centre for Research and Development in Catholic Education (CRDCE) at the University of London Institute of Education. He is currently working on a research study, *Catholic Schools: Mission, Markets and Morality*, which will report the challenges facing Catholic secondary schools in inner London, inner Liverpool and inner Birmingham.

10 Selly Park Technology College

Tim Brighouse has been Chief Education Officer in Birmingham since 1993. From January 1989 until September 1993 he was Professor of Education at Keele University. His administrative career also included Buckinghamshire County Council, the Association of County Councils, Deputy in the Inner London Education Authority and Chief Education Officer in Oxfordshire for ten years from 1978. He was Co-Vice-Chair of the government's Standards Task Force from June 1997 to March 1999 and was appointed as a Member of the Governing Council of the National College for School Leadership in September 2000.

11 Sutton Centre

Jean Rudduck. After teaching in a secondary school Jean Rudduck joined the Schools Council Research Team and later moved to the University of East Anglia's Centre for Applied Research in Education. She was Professor of Education at the University of Sheffield from 1984 to 1994 and is now Director of Research at Homerton College, Cambridge. In recent years she has worked on studies of co-operative learning, disengagement among pupils, gender-related interpretations of discipline, and pupils' secondary school careers. She is currently working on several projects which explore different aspects of the pupils' agenda for improving teaching and learning.

Ian Morrison is currently Director of Undergraduate Studies at Homerton College, Cambridge, combining these responsibilities with teaching science and more general professional issues of schooling. He moved to Homerton College as a physics lecturer involved in the training of science teachers. For many years he has been involved in the initial training of teachers and in in-service courses. He carries these interests over into his writing.

Further Lessons in Success

Margaret Maden is a Professor of Education at Keele University, teaching and researching in the fields of educational effectiveness and the role of LEAs and their equivalents in other countries. She has been a headteacher of an inner London comprehensive school and Director of the Islington Sixth Form Centre. She was chief education officer, Warwickshire County Council, 1989–95. A member of the National Commission on Education, 1991–95, she co-edited *Success against the Odds* (Routledge, 1996).

Research Assistant

Dr Dorothy Harris works as a freelance researcher, lecturer and consultant. She has taught in primary schools and in higher education. She was Co-ordinator for School Governor Training in Cheshire. Her doctoral research was concerned with the teaching and learning of argument and critical thinking in higher education for the professions. She has recently been involved in a national survey of good practice in the provision of education for deaf children conducted by the Universities of Manchester and Birmingham.

PREFACE AND ACKNOWLEDGEMENTS

In 1995, the eleven schools featured here agreed to be visited and included in a collection of case studies of effective schools in disdvantaged areas. On that occasion, the National Commission on Education was the main sponsor and the resultant book, *Success Against the Odds* (1996), was the Commission's second main report, following *Learning to Succeed* (1993).

The schools have again agreed to be the subject of follow-up studies, which are now centred on how schools maintain and sustain momentum and success over the longer term. It is unusual for schools to be re-visited and re-examined in this way and I am grateful to the headteachers, in particular, for agreeing to this request.

The nature of both the 'odds' and the 'successes' has changed over time, as has the balance between the two and the wider political environment in which schools now work.

All of the original lead authors have also returned, with the exception of Michael Barber and Peter Mortimore. I was very pleased that Valerie Hannon and Kathryn Riley agreed to replace them. John Gray is a further newcomer to the project and his Introduction provides an excellent start to the case studies which follow.

On this occasion, the Nuffield Foundation has provided a research grant for the basic expenses involved and for the highly valued services of our research assistant, Dr Dorothy Harris, who compiled the school statistical profiles.

Thanks are also due to Mr Ian Wilkie, education finance officer at Staffordshire County Council, who advised on changes in school budgets and pursued LEAs for additional financial information. LEA officers in all eleven areas have also been very helpful to authors and editor alike. Again, school staff, governors and pupils have been informative and welcoming. Lastly, Mrs Gladys Pye, Education Research secretary at Keele University, has worked very hard and meticulously on the final text, as well as on maintaining contact with the many participants in this project.

I hope all of those headteachers, LEA advisers and School Improvement consultants who expressed real interest in the original case studies in 1995–6 will feel the same about these. Indeed, there have been many questions about these schools and whether they have managed to maintain their 'success against the odds' in the years since the 1995 study.

Here is the answer, with all the variations and 'ups and downs' one would expect amongst any group of schools. Additionally, however, there are valuable lessons and ideas for others to consider adopting, and many of these are summarised in the final chapter.

The Routledge website (www.tandf.co.uk) is a further development for readers. On this, the fuller School Statistical Profiles are available.

Professor Margaret Maden, Editor
Keele University
October 2000

The locations of the case study schools

Lochgelly
(Fife)

Hazelwood
College
(Belfast)

St. Michael's
(Billingham)

Crowcroft Park
(Manchester)

Sutton Centre
(Nottinghamshire)

Haywood High
(Stoke-on-Trent)

Selly Park
(Birmingham)

Blaengwarch
(Neath Port Talbot)

Columbia
(Tower Hamlets)

Fair Furlong
(Bristol)

Burntwood
(Wandsworth)

INTRODUCTION

Building for improvement and sustaining change in schools serving disadvantaged communities

John Gray

Five years have passed since the members of the *Success Against the Odds* team first visited the eleven schools which took part in the original study. Whether five years is a lifetime or a brief moment in a school's natural history is a matter for debate. Time enough, the optimist might argue, for a new head to have arrived, galvanised the staff, performed various 'miracles' and departed. Barely time, a sceptic might think, for a single cohort of students to have passed through their primary or secondary school.

The election of a New Labour government in 1997, clearly committed to raising standards in socially disadvantaged areas, has brought with it the promise of change. Nonetheless, the 'odds still [seem to be] stacked against schools in poorer areas' (NCE, 1996: 5). It would be encouraging to think that policy-makers had somehow succeeded during the last three years in beginning to weaken 'the link between disadvantage and educational performance'. The history of educational reform efforts in this area, however, underlines the extent of the challenges and counsels a degree of caution.

Politicians, meanwhile, have learnt to drive harder bargains. There has been a perceptible shift – change is not merely expected but demanded. In theory, schools which have been 'succeeding against the odds' should be safe from criticism. In practice, memories can be rather short and former laurels may count for little when a fresh inspection is looming. '*Improving* against the odds' is now the name of the game.

The characteristics of 'good' or so-called 'effective' schools have been extensively researched over the last decade and there is consequently much greater understanding and (some would say) agreement about their most salient characteristics. Research on school improvement is, by contrast, still developing. As Barber and Dann has observed: 'being able to describe an effective school does not necessarily indicate what is needed to help an unsuccessful school become successful. The steps required to help a school turn itself around are . . . significantly less researched' (Barber and Dann, 1996: 10).

Some of the reasons for this state of affairs are not difficult to comprehend. As OfSTED has noted: 'Every school's problems are slightly different. No single solution will serve as a panacea to remedy all the ills that befall schools' (OfSTED, 1999: 2). Equally importantly, even the most promising stories will include some false starts, blind alleys and misplaced hopes. Research on school improvement at present amounts to not much more than a sketch map – good enough to note some of the peaks but not particularly clear about the location of rivers and marshes. Only by taking a backward glance can one really discern the path and its general direction.

REVISITING SUCCESS

The original study of 'success against the odds' provided a snapshot of 'successful' schools at a particular point in time (NCE, 1996). Some of them had clearly enjoyed 'success' for a number of years.

Others were more recent arrivals – indeed, their inclusion in the study may have been the first public recognition that they had something to celebrate; their inheritance may consequently have felt less secure. Revisiting the past, moreover, can be difficult. Memories fade, key participants depart, institutions move on and researchers are usually wiser – what looked promising the first time round may require reappraisal.

So what might one expect to find on a return visit? If these schools were already doing well, then simply holding on to their original positions would surely be a significant achievement. We need to remember, however, that generally speaking the odds 'have, indeed, been stacked against' these schools and the communities they have been trying to serve. They owed their positions to mixtures of strength and good fortune. Given what we now know about the ups and downs of school improvement, it would be extraordinary if all (or even most) of them had more or less maintained their original positions. As the Financial Services Authority warns when advising novice investors, 'past performance is not necessarily a guide to future trends'.

For most of these schools, then, the mid-1990s are likely to have represented some kind of peak. Only a handful are likely to have replicated their earlier success. The rest will have been concerned to hold on or to consolidate, depending on how they got to their positions in the first place. Expecting them to embark on new phases of *intensive* development in the intervening years may be neither realistic nor reasonable. Continuing to live with the fractures and stresses of social deprivation may be challenge enough. Indeed, several are likely to have had quite a bumpy ride in the meantime. Much of this, however, is merely informed speculation. The honest answer to questions about what I anticipate may have happened in these schools is that I simply don't know. Too few researchers go back and, despite the obvious advantages of doing so, hardly any school improvement studies have been designed to revisit the same schools a number of years later.[1]

NATIONAL TRENDS

The headline statistics relating to schools' performance show a fairly continuous pattern of gains over time. In 1992 some 35 per cent of pupils were obtaining 5 or more A*–C grades at GCSE; by 1999 this figure had risen to around 47 per cent (see Figure 0.1). Give or take a few minor fluctuations, the performances of boys and girls rose in equal measure with the achievement gap between them remaining fairly constant for most of the decade.

Performance in primary schools on Key Stage 2 literacy tests also rose quite dramatically from just under 50 per cent getting over the level 4 hurdle in 1995 to somewhere around 70 per cent in 1999 (see Figure 0.2). A similar pattern emerged with respect to the numeracy tests although there was a slight fall in the results between 1997 and 1998 before the marked recovery in 1999. Owing to some early boycotting of the tests and changes to their construction, however, strict comparisons over time are difficult for both literacy and numeracy.

Whilst Figures 0.1 and 0.2 provide some indication of upward trends in performance in both primary and secondary schools, they do not give much sense of the extent to which the changes varied from one year to the next. Figure 0.3, therefore, recasts the data in Figure 0.1 to show the rate of change. It suggests that in the period

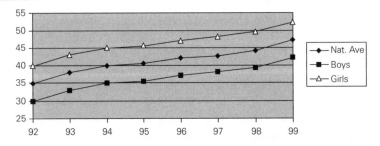

Figure 0.1 Changes in performance over time (% scoring 5+ A*–C grades), 1992–9

Source: DfEE statistics

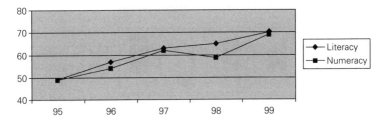

Figure 0.2 Progress in primary schools on literacy and numeracy tests (% reaching level 4 or above), 1995–9

Source: DfEE statistics

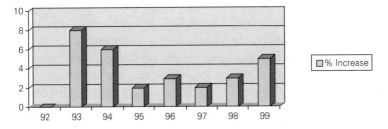

Figure 0.3 Annual year-on-year rates of change in percentage scoring 5+ A*–C grades

Source: Reworking of DfEE statistics; all percentages have been rounded to the nearest whole number

Note: The base year for this run of figures is 1992, so no rate-of-change calculation is appropriate

immediately after the introduction of so-called 'league tables' in 1992 the rate was almost double that which prevailed during the second half of the decade. Whereas at the beginning the figures were running at between 6 to 8 per cent, by the end they had dropped to between 2 and 5 per cent.

Figure 0.4 shows the same information relating to rates of change in primary schools where year-on-year changes were running at much higher levels than in secondaries. Primary schools experienced a much bumpier ride, especially in relation to numeracy. The annual

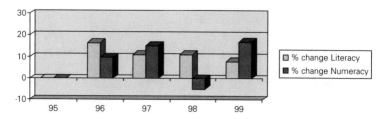

Figure 0.4 Annual year-on-year rates of change in percentage scoring level 4 or above

Note: The base year was 1995, so no rate-of-change calculation is appropriate

rates of change in literacy averaged out at some 10 per cent a year over the period but varied from as little as 3 per cent to as much as 16 per cent. Changes on numeracy tests also averaged out at broadly similar levels but ranged from a 5 per cent drop to a 17 per cent increase. Changes of this order suggest that the steady state that seemed to have emerged within the secondary sector by the end of the decade had yet to be experienced in primary schools.

National statistics on other outcome measures are in short supply but Figure 0.5 shows the proportions of lessons which OfSTED inspectors rated as 'satisfactory' or better during the middle years of the decade. These rose from just over 80 per cent to around 95 per cent over the period in question.

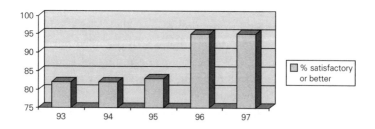

Figure 0.5 Trends in teaching as judged by OfSTED inspectors, 1993–7
Source: Annual reports from OfSTED

The figures might, at first glance, suggest a possible causal reason for some of the changes in performance outlined above. However, their stepped nature (with a sharp rise between 1995 and 1996) rules this out. The most likely explanation for the recorded improvements in classroom teaching over this time scale is simply OfSTED's decision to alter the scale employed to judge it, which was implemented around this time.

NATIONAL AND LOCAL FACTORS DRIVING CHANGE

Trends in national statistics suggest the entire educational system is on the move. A variety of factors are likely to be driving these changes although some may be more influential than others (see Table 0.1).

First, and possibly most importantly, there are the various effects of national initiatives. So-called 'league tables', the introduction of target-setting and the National Literacy and Numeracy strategies are examples of this kind – almost all schools respond to them and almost all 'improve' their performance as a result, albeit to a greater or lesser extent. Within a year or two of the introduction of league tables, for example, large numbers of schools had decided to enter their pupils for at least one more GCSE examination – higher

Table 0.1 Types of influence on improvement

Major influences?	Modest influences?
National initiatives, developments and changes of framework	'Catching up' with the pack; schools' belated implementation of strategies other schools have already put into practice
LEAs and schools paying (more) attention to particular indicators of 'performance' (possibly at the expense of others)	Schools' and teachers' own efforts to find innovative routes to improvement

performance seems to have resulted (see Gray *et al.*, 1996). Schools vary in their understanding of the national changes and the speed with which they explore and exploit their implications but, within a relatively short period of time, most seem to have caught on and caught up.

Second, there has been a trend in recent years for most schools to pay greater attention to certain measures of their outcomes and spend (a good deal) more time preparing their pupils for them, either because they have been motivated to do so or, in many cases, because they have felt obliged to. However, if other outcome measures are either not measured or seen as less important, rises in one area might be at the expense of performance in others.

Third, there seems to have been a good deal of 'catching up' going on. Such 'opportunities' are, of course, only available to relatively ineffective schools which have fallen behind others similarly placed. There is some fairly straightforward scope for improvement in these instances. The widespread introduction of mentoring arrangements for individual pupils and the revamping of behaviour policies provide examples of these kind of initiatives.

Finally, there are the specific innovations a school may adopt as a result of their own analysis and evaluation of their situation. Some of these are likely to be quite adventurous and may put a school out on a limb for a while. A decision to encourage teachers to explore and implement changes to the ways in which they teach might fall into this category; encouraging pupils to take greater responsibility for aspects of their own learning might be another. Of necessity, such developments are likely to be more tentative and exploratory but their long-term pay-off may be greater.

All the activities listed in Table 0.1 could be counted as forms of 'improvement' and all are likely to be experienced by schools as things they have themselves initiated. National initiatives and a narrowing of focus appear to have been the more influential drivers in terms of the headline statistics (see Gray *et al.*, 1999 for a fuller discussion). In due course, however, schools' own initiatives may begin to have greater force. A school which wants to continue 'improving' will probably need to spread its efforts and take some risks.

IN SEARCH OF DEFINITIONS

What, then, is an 'improving' school? There is a semblance of agreement amongst researchers and practitioners as to what constitutes 'school improvement' but still some fuzziness about when a school may legitimately be referred to as an 'improving' one.

As part of an international project van Velzen and colleagues (1985: 34), for example, defined school improvement as: 'a systematic, sustained effort aimed at change in learning conditions and other related conditions in one or more schools with the ultimate aim of accomplishing educational goals more effectively'. Following in this tradition, Hopkins and colleagues have argued that it is 'a distinct approach to educational change that enhances student outcomes as well as strengthening the school's capacity for managing change' (1994: 3). Both definitions, in their different ways, attempt to link processes to outcomes.

One might expect it to follow from these definitions that schools which are engaged in such *acts* of school improvement are somehow 'improving', but clearly there are some potential flaws in the logic here. First, one must assume that they have actually implemented the desirable activities rather than merely begun to do so. And, second, that the specific activities the schools are engaged in have well-established records for delivering 'improvement'; in default of such evidence their status is more debatable. Such evidence, it turns out, is quite difficult to come by – much of what is launched in the name of improvement is initially (and necessarily) based on intuitions and hunches about what *might* work rather than what will.

These definitions place the emphasis on the taking of *deliberate* steps to secure change – schools can't, they appear to be saying, simply fall into the habit of school improvement. Both definitions, however, fit the project contexts within which they were constructed rather better than the more general improvement scene. Recently, in an attempt to embrace a broader definition, Mortimore (2000: 1) has defined 'school improvement as the process of "improving" the way the school organises, promotes and supports learning . . . It includes changing aims, expectations, organisations (sometimes people), ways of learning, methods of teaching and organisational culture.' There are echoes here of an earlier era of research in which aims, expectations, teaching methods and so on contributed to the 'effective' school. If low expectations are part of the problems facing a less 'effective' school, then it makes sense to change them; if a school is poorly led then it may require new leadership and so on. Probably but not necessarily – the emphasis again seems to be on the activities a school undertakes rather than what emerges as a result.

In recent years OfSTED has also entered the fray. In his 1998 Annual Report the Chief Inspector identified some 70 schools which had been identified as 'good and improving' (OfSTED, 1999). A wide range were included. No precise criteria for judging a school to be 'good and improving' are specified, and there seem to be several anomalies, but a close reading of a dozen or so reports suggests that two dimensions were central to the judgements: first, that there had been an improvement in the schools' exam results which ran ahead of national trends; and second, that there had been a marked increase in the lessons rated as 'satisfactory' or better.

Other factors which may have contributed to the overall picture formed by inspectors included whether (most of) the school's action plan from the previous inspection had been implemented and whether there had been a change of head. The schools' 'commitment to improvement' may also have been important. One report, for example, commented that there was 'an ethos of school improvement', another that 'there were frequent testimonies to a school which [was] undergoing a transformation in ethos and culture'.

Harris has recently suggested that 'what distinguishes the school improvement movement from other school reform efforts is the understanding that it is necessary to focus upon student outcomes in academic performance as the key success criteria, rather than teacher perceptions of the innovation' (2000: 6). As a description of an orientation amongst influential contributors this is probably increasingly true. However, it does not, as yet, accurately reflect the criteria employed in most school improvement studies.

In recent years the concern to find ways of linking research on school effectiveness and school improvement has undoubtedly contributed to the development of more rigorous definitions. Building upon and extending the approaches adopted in earlier studies of school effectiveness, Gray and colleagues (1999: 48) have argued that an 'improving' school is one 'which secures year-on-year improvements in the outcomes of successive cohorts of "similar" pupils . . . in other words, it increases in its effectiveness over time'. On this definition both 'effective' and 'ineffective' schools which are 'improving' are of equal interest; what matters is how much progress they make from their respective starting-points.

Whilst the shift towards 'changes in effectiveness' as the defining dimension of the 'improving' school provides a more rigorous definition, it does so at some cost. In theory 'effectiveness' may be broadly construed. It *could* connote changes in students' attitudes and motivations towards learning as well as trends in their academic performance. In practice, empirical realisations of 'effectiveness' tend to be more bounded. Few educational systems to date have collected data over time on anything more extensive than academic performance and, sometimes, attendance.

Difficulties of definition are familiar territory, already extensively trawled in the course of debates about what constitute 'good' or 'effective' schools. As historian Harold Silver (1994: 102) remarks: 'The effective schools movement did not replace the ways in which previous judgements about schools had been made; it added another ingredient to them'. To express an interest in 'improvement' may simply be to add a further one.

THE DIMENSIONS OF 'IMPROVEMENT'

What do schools achieve when they embark on school improvement? Unlike the now relatively well-established field of school effectiveness there is little agreement as yet as to what matters, nor does most of what there is lend itself to easy summary. Furthermore, given the range of views about what should count, reports of what has happened vary widely. Sometimes the variations can be explained by reference to the range of strategies tried out; on other occasions it is more difficult to grasp why they have occurred. Nonetheless, there are some recurring themes. The studies discussed here took account of periods ranging from two to five years.

Louis and Miles (1992) researched developments in urban high schools during the 1980s. They contacted the principals of institutions which had attempted to implement so-called 'effective school' programmes and asked them what improvements had resulted. The principals judged that a good deal of 'improvement' had, indeed, taken place, most notably with respect to students' attitudes and behaviours (see Table 0.2). Around a quarter (24 per cent) also reported changes in the area of 'student achievement'.

Sammons and colleagues (1997) asked London headteachers similar questions during the early 1990s. The heads mentioned

Table 0.2 Reported outcomes/effects of 'effective schools' programmes on participating students in North America

Area of outcomes	% of principals reporting 'greatly improved'
Employment of graduates	12
Student dropout rate	15
Student achievement	24
Student attendance	38
Student attitudes	43
Student behaviour	49

Source: Louis and Miles (1992), Table C6.

some twenty areas of activity where they had had success or achievements. Reflecting their main areas of responsibility, nine out of ten (89 per cent) mentioned their school's 'improved organisation' whilst over eight out of ten reported improved record-keeping and student monitoring (see Table 0.3).

Around seven out of ten heads also mentioned improved exam results and better student attendance. The study accepted the heads' evaluations at face value and did not seek to probe the extent of the changes. What is perhaps most interesting about their replies, however, was the extent to which they were likely to cite changes in management practices (see column 1 of Table 0.3) as often as (if not more often than) changes to students' performance and experiences (see column 2).

Management-led reforms also dominated perceptions in the schools studied by Gray and colleagues (1999). They asked teachers about the extent of changes in their own institutions over the previous five years since the early 1990s (see Table 0.4). The proportions of teachers reporting 'substantial' change varied considerably from school to school and from area to area. What is clear, however, is that teachers themselves noted considerably greater changes in areas to do with their schools' management and organisation than in ethos, culture or teaching. Indeed, whilst almost two thirds reported changes in the former area, only 17 per cent said there had been 'substantial' changes in the quality of teaching and learning. As reported by their own colleagues, classroom-level 'changes' were far less frequent than school-wide initiatives.

Earl and Lee (1998, 2000) evaluated the changes in 15 Canadian senior high schools in the state of Manitoba.[2] Using a wide range of sources of data, they attempted to reach summary judgements about the extent of improvement across several dimensions. They then grouped together the items on their list into a notional School Improvement Index. However, as this index summed very different kinds of outcomes, they have been kept separate in Table 0.5.

Table 0.3 Heads' descriptions of major successes/achievements of their school over the last five years

Area	% of heads	Area	% of heads
Improved organisation	89	Higher expectations for student performance	77
Improved record-keeping/student profiles	83	Improved exam results	75
Improved monitoring of student performance	83	Improved student behaviour	68
More effective and cohesive senior management team	72	Better student attendance	66
More effective leadership by most heads of department	66	General improvement in quality of teaching in most cases	62
		Better relationships between staff and students	62
Improved homework policy and practice	57	Greater student motivation	55
Reduction in staff shortages	57	Focus on equal opportunities	55
		Improved staff morale	51
Helpful OFSTED inspection	36	Greater opportunities for student responsibilities in school	45
		Greater parental and community involvement	40

Source: Sammons et al. (1997), Table 6.5; evidence from the original table has been reorganised into columns 1 and 2.

Table 0.4 Teachers' reports of the extent of 'substantial' change in their school over the last five years

Area of change	% teachers reporting change was 'substantial'
Ways school is run and organised	62
Ethos, culture or climate of school	31
School's attitude and approach to planning	50
School's curriculum organisation and delivery	44
Quality of teaching and learning in the school	17

Source: Gray *et al.* (1999), Table 9.3.

Table 0.5 Areas where there was judged to be 'improvement' in the senior schools in the Manitoba School Improvement Project

Area in which evidence collected	% of schools in which there was 'evidence of improvement'
Student learning	33
Progress towards project goals	47
Increased student engagement	47
Process factors	
Focus on student learning (progress towards)	36
Engagement of school community (progress towards)	50
Connection to the world outside school (progress towards)	40
Ongoing inquiry and reflection (progress towards)	50
Coherence and integration (progress towards)	43
Internal capacity for change (progress towards)	40

Source: Earl and Lee (1998), Tables 6, 9, 11 and 13a–f. The percentages combine the schools where Earl and Lee felt there was 'evidence of improvement' with those where they judged there to be 'solid evidence'.

On none of the nine dimensions they explored did Earl and Lee judge more than half the schools in the Manitoba project to have shown 'solid evidence' or 'evidence of improvement'. Around half their schools showed signs of change in relation to two process factors: progress towards the 'engagement of the school community' and progress towards 'ongoing inquiry and reflection'. However, only 33 per cent showed 'evidence of improvement' in the outcome area of student learning; furthermore, in only 13 per cent (2 out of 15 schools) was the evidence judged to be 'solid' (table not shown).

Earl and Lee felt that there was some consistency across the three outcome areas they considered. They claim that 'schools seemed to progress on all dimensions simultaneously' (1998: 47). However, closer inspection of the relationships between their outcome measures (student learning, progress towards project goals and increased student engagement) suggests a rather different and more complex position. Improvements in student learning and the school's progress towards its project goals were highly and positively correlated. This correlation is broadly in line with the 'movement on all fronts' position. However, improvement in terms of student learning was only weakly related to improvements in student engagement: schools which progressed in one of these two areas were only slightly more likely to progress in the other. Furthermore, schools' success in securing their own goals and improving student engagement were fairly strongly but *inversely* related. In other words, the more successful a school was in securing its goals, the *less* likely it was to have enhanced student engagement. The Canadian evidence, in short, suggests that developments with respect to some outcomes may be at the expense of others.

School improvement takes time and it can be difficult for governments to mandate change. The case of so-called 'failing' schools in England, however, presents a situation where questions about the speed and extent of improvement have become crucial to schools' survival. These schools have typically been given only a two-year window to secure a turnaround. In fact, evidence from a recent review of the experiences of schools put on Special Measures (Gray, 2000) suggests that the vast majority (9 out of 10) do eventually manage to pull through within this sort of time-frame although some take several months longer than the 24 months officially allowed.

Schools on Special Measures have usually secured 'measurable progress' in several areas of their functioning, including teaching, attendance and exclusions (see Table 0.6). At the same time they must also demonstrate that they have managed to improve their pupils' academic performances. Inspectors are specifically asked to look for 'increases, year on year, in the proportion of pupils [achieving particular levels of performance] . . . with an emphasis on trends, for example, over three years' (OfSTED, 1997: 2). Unfortunately, whilst inspectors have doubtless been able to convince themselves that changes have occurred in specific cases, more systematic evidence on this topic across large numbers of schools has yet to be published.

There is a further area in which schools on Special Measures are supposed to improve, namely the extent to which they have developed 'the capacity (that is the commitment, strategy and systems in place) to secure further improvement' (OfSTED, 1997: 3).

Table 0.6 Areas of 'measurable progress' among schools on Special Measures

Area of progress	Nature of changes
Proportion of lessons judged 'satisfactory' or better	Up by 10 to 20% overall
Attendance	Up by 2% in secondary and 1% in primary schools
Pupil exclusions	Down from 8% to 1% in secondary schools and from 2% to almost nothing in primaries

Source: Gray (2000), pp.13–14.

Since the vast majority of schools put on Special Measures eventually emerge from them, one must assume that they have made progress in this respect and that such 'capacities' are in place. Again, however, evidence on what it is that has actually impressed inspectors is harder to come by.

Given the diverse nature of school improvement studies to date, it is no easy matter to summarise the main lines of advance. Nonetheless, some observations may be worthwhile.

First, there is, as yet, no clear view about the limits and possibilities of school improvement. Most of the literature simply asserts that 'improvement' has taken place. Estimates of the proportions of schools which have 'improved' over any particular time period range widely from study to study. Furthermore, much of the evidence stems from the rather special circumstances of school improvement projects – to date there have been relatively few naturally occurring experiments.

Second, the extent to which improvement is reported to have taken place is heavily dependent on whose perceptions are given greatest weight. Heads and teachers engaged in implementing changes may discern more 'improvements' than students, external evaluators or inspectors.

Third, although many schools attempt simultaneous improvement on several fronts, the relationships between these developments are not well understood – progress in one area may well be at the expense of progress in others.

Fourth, there is as yet little agreement about the timescales over which *major* improvements take place. Some changes can be brought about quickly, others take longer. In particular, measurable changes in students' performance which do not simply involve focusing to a much greater extent on the easily measurable appear to take time.

Fifth, changes to school management and organisation seem easier to secure than changes to classroom practice. Whether there is an invariable sequence here, however, is unclear. Most schools engaged in improvement efforts seem to start work at the top – on the organisational conditions. Few, in practice, have started elsewhere – consequently knowledge about the sequences is limited.

Sixth, notwithstanding the widespread interest in improving performance, most studies to date have been rather short on evidence of *measured* improvements over time, whether in terms of pupils' academic progress or of such things as pupils' attitudes, motivations and engagement. They are largely premised on the assumption that if they work on the conditions for learning progress will (eventually) follow. As a hypothesis this may be useful but only if the circumstances within which it holds true can be established.

Seventh, some researchers have argued that it is more difficult for schools serving socially disadvantaged areas to make progress on many of the traditional indicators than others more favourably placed. More evidence on this issue is needed.

Finally, there is a shortage of evidence about the extent to which schools manage to sustain improvement. Is continuous improvement a realistic ambition or merely some kind of holy grail?

THE SEARCH FOR CONTINUOUS IMPROVEMENT

Schools' fortunes may vary from one year to the next but central to the idea of continuous improvement is the notion that schools are on some kind of 'improvement trajectory' which, viewed over the medium term, evens out the ups and downs. Databases on schools' performance over several years may help to identify such institutions. To date, however, there has been little serious study of such trajectories. The reasons are not difficult to fathom. Runs of data on several cohorts are needed along with a conceptual framework to analyse them. Until recently neither has been available.

Figure 0.6 shows the trajectories of three hypothetical schools all starting out from the same point in 1994 in terms of the proportions reaching the 5+ A*–C hurdle. School B has been basically tracking the national average. School A, by contrast, has been improving at a faster rate and the gap between it and School B has been perceptibly growing over time. School C, for its part, has improved its results over the years but has not managed to keep up with School B – as a result of its slower rate of improvement an increasingly large gap has emerged between it and the national average. All three schools can say that they have been 'improving' but, in the context of rising national performance levels, the implications are clearly different.

If all the schools in Figure 0.6 had similar intakes to each other and their intakes did not vary significantly from year to year, then interpretation of the trends would be straightforward – all the changes and improvements could be attributed to the schools' own efforts. However, these assumptions are unlikely to hold true in a number of different circumstances – intakes vary across schools and, in some schools, from year to year. Just as school effectiveness researchers have developed the idea of needing to take intakes into account, so school improvement researchers have increasingly realised that they need a conceptual framework which pays regard to changes in intakes. Gray and colleagues (1999) have attempted to provide one.

The most influential determinants of students' academic performance are the characteristics they bring with them to school related to their home backgrounds and prior levels of performance. Nonetheless, as numerous school effectiveness studies have shown,

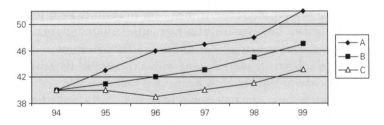

Figure 0.6 Hypothetical improvement trajectories of three schools over time

the school a particular pupil attends also makes some difference to how well they do. Pupils attending a school which is especially effective can be expected to perform somewhat better than 'similar' pupils attending other, less effective, schools. If schools were consistently effective or ineffective from year to year there could be no school improvement or decline – some element of instability is necessary for changes to take place. We term the latter the 'improvement' dimension whilst bearing in mind that it also connotes declines in performance. Until recently, the relative sizes of these two components (the stable and the unstable) were unknown.

For any given starting point in terms of a school's effectiveness there are (at least) three different possibilities:

(1) that the school stays at roughly the same level in terms of its effectiveness from one year to the next;
(2) that it increases in its effectiveness over time, adding more value to successive cohorts of pupils; or
(3) that it decreases in its effectiveness and goes into decline.

Consequently a framework is needed for thinking about schools' performances which locates them in two dimensions: in terms of their effectiveness at any one point in time; and in terms of their changes in effectiveness (i.e. their improvement or decline). Figure 0.7 describes the positions of nine hypothetical schools in terms of these two elements. A score of plus 2 means they were of 'above-average' effectiveness, a score of minus 2 of 'below-average' effectiveness whilst the lines on the graph linking these scores give some feel for each school's 'improvement trajectory'.[3]

Schools A, B and C were all, given their intakes, of average effectiveness in 1994. School B basically stayed in this position for the next five years. In 1999 it was still judged to be of average effectiveness. School A improved its effectiveness over the years; by 1999 it was a good deal more effective than it had been and was on

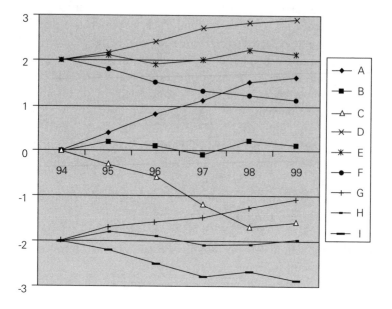

Figure 0.7 Hypothetical improvement trajectories of nine schools in terms of their effectiveness and changes in their effectiveness (improvement/decline) over time

Notes: A positive score means the school is more effective, a negative score that it is less effective; scores of +2 and −2 mean that the schools are respectively of above-average effectiveness and below-average effectiveness. The lines linking each school's scores provide a general indication of their 'improvement trajectory'

the verge of being seen as of above-average effectiveness. School C, by contrast, declined somewhat from its 1994 position; by 1999 it was in danger of being viewed as a school of below-average effectiveness.

Figure 0.7 also shows the position for several other schools: D, E and F, which started off being of above-average effectiveness, and G, H and I, which were all initially of below-average effectiveness. Schools D and G improved over the time period from their initial starting points whilst F and I declined.

Returning to the notion of continuous improvement, we find that only three of the schools in Figure 0.7 have trajectories which approximate to this position (Schools A, D and G). How many such schools will be thrown up in practice depends on two things. First, the relative importance of the twin dimensions of 'effectiveness' and 'improvement': if the latter dimension turns out to be relatively large then the potential for finding schools on markedly different improvement trajectories is increased. Second, the extent to which schools actually succeed in stringing together several years of year-on-year improvement: there could, in theory, be a considerable amount of instability from year to year without any clear trajectories being revealed.

Using a sophisticated statistical technique known as 'multi-level modelling' Gray *et al.* (1996) partitioned the schools' contribution into two parts – one part related to the stable components of schools' effectiveness, the other to the unstable or changing component of schools' effectiveness.

They report that the schools in their study did not vary much in their general levels of effectiveness from year to year – a school which was pretty effective one year was likely to be pretty effective the next year. Conversely, a school which was pretty ineffective one year was likely to be pretty ineffective the next. The partitioning of the schools' contribution into these two components did, however, suggest some evidence of changes over time (see Figure 0.8); just under one-seventh of the variance was attributable to the so-called 'improvement' dimension.

The findings of this study provide some encouragement for those engaged in the search for *continuous* school improvement but they also establish some limits. The procedures and criteria adopted to establish 'improvement' were particularly stringent. Fewer than one in five schools were on trajectories which generally went up (or down) several years on the run. Of these only around ten per cent were on improvement trajectories which were consistently rising. These figures are considerably lower than those discussed earlier in

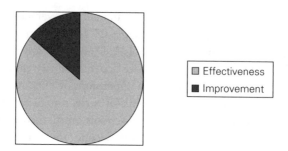

Figure 0.8 The relative influences of variations in schools' effectiveness and changes in schools' effectiveness over time on pupils' performance at GCSE

Source: Gray *et al.* (1996)

this chapter where, using less rigorous criteria, estimates that up to one-third of schools were securing success in improving their students' learning seemed plausible.[4]

A second finding is of interest because it injects a sense of realism into schools' efforts to improve over time. After a period of movement schools seemed to plateau. Three years of year-on-year improvement represented 'a good run' for a school, four years an exceptional one.

The frustrating feature of this finding, if we return to Figure 0.7, is that it suggests it is quite demanding for schools to change their general levels of effectiveness. When the size of the yearly steps schools which were 'rapidly' improving were taking is combined with the distance between schools at differing levels of effectiveness, four or five years of consistent improvement would seem to be necessary for a 'less effective' school to join the pack or for an 'averagely effective' one to move ahead of it. The experiences of Schools G and A respectively in Figure 0.7, both of which managed to keep going on a fairly continuous basis over five years, turn out to be fairly exceptional.

Recently Thomas and Smees (2000) have replicated and extended the initial estimates provided by Gray and colleagues.

They are rather less optimistic about the extent to which schools have been securing systematic improvements over time. Using a range of data-sets from different LEAs, they conclude that 'irrespective of schools' apparent improvement in raw league table performance, few schools are able to improve substantially in their effectiveness – *relative to that of other schools*' (2000: 6, their emphasis). In other words many of the changes in performance that schools claim in the name of improvement are probably best attributed to national developments eventually affecting the vast majority of schools to a greater or lesser extent or, alternatively, to changes in schools' intakes rather than to the ways in which they have tackled their improvement agendas.

Recent evidence from the experiences of schools on Special Measures tends to support the view that 'improvement' takes place in bursts which are not necessarily sustained. In the year immediately following their entry into Special Measures a spurt in primary schools' scores on literacy and numeracy tests appears to have occurred (table not shown).[5] Their rate of improvement at this point seems to have been considerably above that prevailing nationally. In subsequent years, however, further improvement rapidly tailed off; the increased rate of change was not sustained. A similar phenomenon occurred amongst secondary schools on Special Measures although here the narrowing of the gap with the national average has been a good deal less marked. Furthermore, and worryingly, many secondary schools in this position seem to have subsequently had difficulty even in keeping up with national trends and developments.

Whether one takes the more optimistic or more pessimistic view of these findings, the policy implications are considerable. A school which is committed to substantial improvement (and crucially to improving its pupils' performance) will be very fortunate indeed if it can reach its desired destination in one concerted push. It will almost certainly need two or more attempts, each sustained over two or three years, to be truly confident it has changed its level of effectiveness. Nor should we be particularly surprised if apparently promising improvement efforts seem to fizzle out or lose their potency. To succeed in *sustaining* improvement is the exception rather than the rule.

SCHOOL CULTURES AND SCHOOL IMPROVEMENT

The search for continuous improvement through the analysis of schools' trajectories is relatively new. The more-established tradition seeks to identify the organisational and cultural characteristics of 'improving' schools. What do they actually do to make things happen?

When asked why their school has improved, the first and almost universal response given by those most closely involved is to say that it resulted from 'hard work' and 'determination'. Instilling a sense of 'urgency' and 'commitment' into colleagues also receive frequent mentions. Whilst such 'people factors' undoubtedly help to get initiatives moving, few researchers (or practitioners for that matter) think that they are sufficient to keep improvement going.

Probe a little deeper and references to various institutional characteristics may start to emerge – such things as leadership, vision, planning and organisation, and the need for some external pressure and support. Again, however, something seems lacking. Does the successful pursuit of school improvement require some means of making the whole add up to more than the sum of the parts? A number of key players have argued that this is the case.

What improvement initiatives are really up against, they argue, is a school's 'culture'. Cultures vary – some are more receptive to change, others less so. Schein, in a now much-quoted definition, describes culture as the 'deeper level of basic assumptions and beliefs that are shared by members of an organization, that operate unconsciously, and that define in a basic taken-for-granted fashion an organization's view of itself and its environment' (1985: 6). Culture, in short, is 'the way we do things round here'. Changing schools, the argument runs, must mean engaging with and changing cultures.

In the more recent school improvement literature 'culture' has given way to 'capacity'. There are doubtless several reasons for this conceptual shift but one particularly obvious one is that cultures, by their nature, are extremely difficult to change – 'capacities' may be more malleable and lend themselves to development. As a result the school's 'capacity to improve' has increasingly emerged as the engine-room of change. There are, nonetheless, some difficulties in grasping what is at the core of such constructs.

The relationships between 'improvement' and 'capacity' are of relatively recent origin. Interestingly, neither term appears in the index of Fullan's *The New Meaning of Educational Change* which covered the literature until the end of the 1980s. However, both are there in embryonic form. Suggesting reasons why so many innovations appear to have 'failed', Fullan argues that a different perspective is required:

> Instead of tracing specific policies and innovations, we turn the problem on its head and ask what does the array of innovative possibilities look like, if we are on the receiving or shopping end. Thus, institutional development – changes that increase schools' and districts' *capacity and performance for continuous improvement* – is the generic solution needed.
>
> (Fullan, 1991: 349, my emphasis)

A similar theme featured in Louis and Miles's study of urban high schools. What particularly distinguished institutions making considerable progress, they argued, was the extent to which they had developed 'deep-coping' strategies. 'Deep-coping', they suggested, included such things as: 'vision-building and sharing, rolling planning, substantial restaffing, increasing school control over the environment, empowering people and redesigning the school organisation' (1992: 281). At first sight the idea of 'deep coping' seems attractive. Whether the range of factors listed by the authors amounts to a coherent set of cultural characteristics, however, seems more questionable.

BUILDING THE CAPACITY TO IMPROVE

The IQEA (Improving the Quality of Education for All) school improvement project is one of the longer-established change efforts in this country (Hopkins *et al.*, 1994). Its originators argue that the best way to bring about cultural change is to focus schools' 'development strategies [on ways] which operate both on the conditions and the culture of the school' (Hopkins *et al.*, 1996: 25). Efforts to build 'capacity', they suggest, are needed in six areas relating to the school's:

- commitment to staff development;
- practical efforts to involve staff, students and the community in school policies and decisions;
- approaches to 'transformational' leadership;
- strategies for effective co-ordination;
- attention to the benefits of enquiry and reflection; and
- commitment to collaborative planning activity.

The project maintains that this 'list of conditions . . . represents [their] best estimate of what the important factors are at present, rather than a definitive typology'. All these things are probably worth doing in their own right. However, the team argue that if a school could succeed in developing all (or even most) of them, then its emerging 'capacity' would eventually enable it to lock into continuous improvement.

The IQEA list of development priorities is relatively short. Stoll has recently attempted to take a wider-ranging look 'at the internal dynamics and potential of a school: what can help or hinder it from starting and sustaining the process of learning' (Stoll, 1999: 515). She justifies her focus on process factors by arguing that 'students will learn best when their teachers and schools do', but warns that 'the activities that follow [from this position] are not necessarily those that would raise test or examination scores the quickest'.

Stoll's review, in short, eschews the 'quick fix' in favour of strategies with longer-lasting potential. It underlines the extent to which developing capacity is an 'extremely complex and long-term enterprise'. Table 0.7 summarises no fewer than 13 strategies which she believes schools have adopted (or might adopt) to generate changes in their 'internal capacity' to improve.

There is considerable evidence that schools embarking on cultural change operate on several fronts at the same time. Some of the areas outlined in Table 0.7, however, may not 'fit' and most schools will probably select and prioritise. Given what we currently know about how to influence and change cultures, arguing that schools should start in one place rather than another would probably be unhelpful.

The *Improving Schools* research (Gray *et al.*, 1999) suggests that a school's approach to its own development may be crucial to its long-term chances of success (defined in this particular case as

Table 0.7 Strategies to develop schools' internal capacity

- Challenge low expectations
- Pay attention to people's feelings about change
- Establish a positive climate
- Develop understanding of the change process
- Cultivate development-friendly norms
- Model, promote and support professional learning
- Work between and beyond schools
- Change structures where necessary
- Broaden leadership
- Give inquiry and reflection pride of place
- Listen, especially to students
- Seek connectedness between the various influences
- Promote collective responsibility

Source: Stoll (1999: 526)

'increasing its effectiveness' over time). Schools, they argue, have particular ways of working for change which come to be their main (if not necessarily preferred) styles. Time and again they will approach change issues in the same sort of way. These approaches are likely to be mainly at one of three levels: the 'tactical', the 'strategic' or the 'capacity-building'.

Most schools operate at the 'tactical' level for some of the time but some tackle change this way most of the time – this approach constitutes the limit of their efforts and thinking. Such schools 'focused (possibly for the first time and certainly more than previously) on outcome measures and identified some "obvious" things they needed to do to improve their pupils' performances . . . in the process they had begun to respond to the dictates of what more than one head called "the improvement game"' (Gray *et al.*, 1999: 145). This approach to school improvement is essentially a *series* of 'tactics' or 'quick fixes', each of which is launched on its own and (probably) has some short-term pay-off. After a while, however, there is a distinct danger that schools pursuing it will simply run out of ideas, suffer from innovation-fatigue or give up exhausted. In reality, 'most of their initiatives involved sustaining teachers' commitment over lengthy periods. Furthermore, as other schools picked up on the same agendas, the competitive edge attached to them began to diminish' (Gray *et al.*, 1999: 145–8).

Schools involved in 'strategic' approaches were in a minority. They

> had almost invariably pulled a variety of the tactical levers but were also more aware of their limitations. They focused more systematically on particular areas of weakness. At the same time they were reviewing the various approaches which might help to raise achievement levels across the institution. Their agendas had begun to include some of the links between classroom practice and pupils' learning.
>
> (Gray *et al.*, 1999: 145–8)

Only a very small minority of schools in this study had got to the 'capacity-building' stage. They had

fairly sophisticated views about how to undertake change and 'pull all the relevant levers'. They were knowledgeable about the problems they faced, believed that they had engaged with issues of teaching and learning for some time and were able to put forward fairly coherent rationales for the next steps . . . [furthermore] they had shown a willingness to go beyond merely incremental approaches to change . . . and engaged in organisational restructuring with enhanced learning as an intended outcome.

(Gray *et al.*, 1999: 145–8)

Commenting on the school improvement strategies being contemplated for schools in difficulty, David Hargreaves has suggested that there is probably 'too much emphasis on the symptoms of failure and too little understanding of its pathology'. Such approaches will undoubtedly generate lists of things to be fixed but may not produce much coherent action. In the rush for school improvement it is easy to forget that schools' 'capacities' for significant change are embedded within cultures with long-established traditions.

Using a simple two-dimensional framework to analyse schools' cultural features, Hargreaves (1995) shows how many of the resulting 'types' of school culture cohere around norms and values which are antithetical to change. Even in the process of committing themselves to school improvement, key players will act from deeply rooted positions which (intentionally or otherwise) negate, frustrate or resist reform. By ignoring such forces, the scale of the problems of 'repositioning' schools in cultural terms is routinely underestimated. Action is mistaken for progress.

The herd instinct in school improvement represents another danger. Whilst acknowledging that each school's position is different, schools that are into 'improvement' frequently jump on to each bandwagon as it comes along. Better to try out what others are recommending and fail, they seem to be saying, than strike out on our own. In the process they run the risk of forgetting that there are several routes to 'success' and that these may be in competition with each other. Gray and colleagues (1999), for example, found that the more 'rapidly improving' schools in their sample had either adopted one set of initiatives or another but not both. Schools may need help and support from 'critical friends' in deciding which routes to follow to supplement self-evaluation (MacBeath, 1999).

The realisation that long-term school improvement is about capacity-building and the institutionalisation of an 'improvement culture' does not, of course, rule out the need to decide what specific actions will be taken next week and what initiatives will be launched over the coming months. It is not unusual for schools to have launched more than a dozen sizeable initiatives over the last five years. With the benefit of hindsight, many feel they could have chosen more wisely. Nor should it be assumed that schools operating at the capacity-building level ignore 'tactical' opportunities – they are as quick to spot the potential of 'quick fixes' as the next one. What distinguishes them is the extent to which they are developing longer-term approaches alongside.

THE CONSTRAINTS OF CONTEXT

There is a strong feeling amongst those working in schools serving socially disadvantaged areas that school improvement is more difficult than in other schools more favourably located. To what extent is this view backed by the research evidence?

Early studies of school effectiveness were fairly naive about the effects of a school's context on its performance. It was assumed that once pupils' own backgrounds and prior attainments had been taken into account, no further controls for a school's circumstances were necessary. More recent studies, however, have shown that there is often a collective effect of 'social' mix over and above that which would be indicated by individuals' characteristics alone.[6]

Criticising earlier research for being blind to this kind of effect, Thrupp (1999), for example, argues that the backgrounds and communities from which pupils are recruited play a crucial role in defining a school's culture and holding it in place. He argues that:

> the issue of school mix highlights powerful social inequalities in the provision of schooling. For policy-makers it will mean grappling with the possibility that technical solutions will never be enough, that schools and teachers in low-SES (Social-Economic-Status) settings may only be held partly responsible for addressing poor achievement and that educational quality in low-SES settings will not be able to be substantially improved without redistributive policies of various kinds.
>
> (Thrupp, 1999: 183)

Thrupp's main concern is to inject a greater sense of realism into what he sees as sociologically naive debates about school effectiveness and improvement. The honest answer is that we don't really know *how much* more difficult it is for schools serving disadvantaged communities to improve because much of the improvement research has ignored this dimension – that it is more difficult, however, seems unquestionable. As Gray and colleagues (1999) note, even some of the more successful schools in their study serving disadvantaged areas 'experienced significant changes in the composition of their catchment areas, problems with their local communities, difficulties in managing falling pupil numbers, budget restraints and the threat of closure'. These were not pressures to which schools in more prosperous areas were exposed.

The evidence points to the difficulties disadvantaged schools may have in even getting to the starting gate for improvement (Gray, 2000). It costs more, for example, to keep a teacher in front of a class in such a setting – teacher turnover and staff recruitment difficulties may conspire to make the retention of more experienced teachers a constant problem. Whatever a school's 'philosophy', more effort may need to be put into getting pupils to school in the first place – such activities seldom receive the public recognition they deserve. And once schools have begun to secure their pupils' engagement they may have to stage their improvement efforts – an initial phase during which they create the basic conditions for a safe and orderly learning environment followed by a subsequent one in which they work on more systemic conditions (Wimpelberg *et al.*, 1989). Furthermore, such phased development may extend to the need for different leadership styles at different times (Teddlie and Stringfield, 1993).

Equitable frameworks for judging school improvement would give equal reward to equal effort. Unfortunately, a sense of what it is realistic to expect from schools in socially disadvantaged areas has yet to be fully embraced, even by some of those who are closest to the school improvement process. As Robertson and Toal (2000) have remarked in relation to Scottish schools:

> Generally, a school struggling against a background of social and economic disadvantage, *even when performing significantly beyond expectation*, may still be seen by its own teachers as not succeeding. Evaluating the discourse of teachers against numerous indicators of school quality suggests that, in general, they do not implicitly convey a (contextualising) perspective.
>
> (My emphasis)

In short, many teachers themselves may be co-conspirators, albeit unwittingly, in the undervaluation of what schools like their own have been achieving. There is an uncomfortable but salutary lesson here for everyone interested in helping schools 'improve against the odds'. Teachers' own morale and perceptions are crucial.

CREATING SOME CONDITIONS TO BREAK THE MOULD

Writing about the impact of research on school *effectiveness*, historian Harold Silver reminds us that its 'ability to influence policy and judgements depends on the nature of the research, the communication context within which it operates, and the direction and balance of popular and political opinion' (Silver, 1994: 153). The most recent push for school *improvement* post-dates Silver's account but the message still seems apt. Over the past few years, however, a tension has emerged between those who insist that performance should be raised quickly and those who argue that tomorrow's gains could be at the expense of longer-term strategies.

The pressure to improve is not confined to educational systems in the United Kingdom. Around the world politicians are busily committing schools to ever-higher targets and inventing strategies for getting there. Unfortunately, many seem to be suffering from restricted vision about what school improvement involves and how it works. Simply raising test scores by whatever means, for example, has become a preoccupation in the state of Texas.

Faced with statistics which suggest wide gaps in performance between rich and poor and white and black, Texas educators are apparently responding in ways which revolve round variants on a single strategy: holding pep rallies and 'camps' to familiarise students with test drills; making extensive use of what are referred to somewhat euphemistically as 'test preparation' materials; organising Friday night 'lock-ins' in the gym to do test drills; laying on pizza parties and trips to the ballpark for students who score well on practice exams; and displaying banners in their foyers counting down the number of days to the tests (see *International Herald Tribune*, 22 April 2000). Helpfully, at least for the rather narrow purposes of boosting scores, the measures used to assess progress have remained pretty similar from one year to the next. Furthermore, teachers and administrators have been increasingly 'encouraged' to see their careers as being dependent on keeping the figures on the move. Other state governors, meanwhile, have been exploring the introduction of financial rewards for teachers and their leaders. The governor of California, for example, was reported at a recent conference in the USA to be contemplating $25,000 bonuses – 'teacher of the month' and 'school of the year' prizes seem on the cards.[7]

Even if such accounts are only half the story their messages are potentially worrying for schools in the UK – there is undoubtedly a 'logic' at work here, if not necessarily an educational one. Since its election the government has introduced two major programmes of support for schools serving disadvantaged communities in England – Education Action Zones (EAZs) and Excellence in Cities (EiC). As the EiC prospectus clearly states, 'no school will be allowed to drift' (DfEE, 1999: 16). In both programmes participating schools have been encouraged to draw upon promising innovations and to experiment with alternative ways of raising achievement that suit their circumstances – furthermore, and encouragingly, significant numbers have been given sufficient resources to enable them to at least make a start.

There are already clear indications that many teachers in this country want to 'break the mould' and tentative signs that some are beginning to do so. Taking stock of a school's position in relation to an emerging body of knowledge can nonetheless be uncomfortable. Several plausible routes to improvement may be beckoning, and hard choices need to be made.

Schools which have already been 'succeeding against the odds' should be relatively well placed (and perhaps more skilled than most) to identify potential areas of inertia and overcome resistance. Just two questions, however, should be uppermost as they plan the next steps in their strategies to sustain what they have already achieved and build for the future. If we pursue this course of action, will our students take learning more seriously? And will anything in our *own* classrooms and about the ways we teach change as a direct result? One lesson, above all, cries out from research on school improvement to date – it is all too easy to mistake innovations for change and changes for improvement.

NOTES

1 The study of Louisiana elementary schools by Teddlie and Stringfield (1993) is probably the longest-running project in this field; these researchers have now sustained their interest in the same schools for well over a decade.
2 Seven middle schools were also involved but these have been excluded from the reworking of the analyses presented here.
3 Readers of school effectiveness studies who are familiar with the notion of school 'residuals' will doubtless recognise this scoring scale. The scale is used here, however, simply for heuristic purposes and should not be interpreted too literally.
4 A decade after they were first selected eight of the sixteen elementary schools followed up in the Louisiana study were judged to have retained their original positions as either more or less effective. Of the remaining eight, two were judged to be improving and two declining in their effectiveness whilst the remainder fluctuated over time with no clear trends emerging.
5 Communication from the DfEE.
6 See Chapter 5 of Teddlie and Reynolds (2000) for a fuller review and discussion of context-related issues in school effectiveness research; this review confirms that relatively little work has been done on the effects of context in relation to school improvement issues.
7 Reported at a session on some of the consequences of so-called 'high-stakes' testing on schools and teachers held at the Annual Conference of the American Educational Research Association, New Orleans, April 2000.

REFERENCES

Barber, M. and Dann, R. (1996) *Raising Educational Standards in the Inner City: Practical Initiatives in Action*, London: Cassell.

DfEE (1999) *Excellence in Cities*, London: Department for Education and Employment.

Earl, L. and Lee, L. (1998) *Evaluation of the Manitoba School Improvement Program*, Toronto: International Center for Educational Change at OISE/UT.

Earl, L. and Lee, L. (2000) Learning for a change: school improvement as capacity building, *Improving Schools*, 3, 1, 30–8.

Fullan, M. (1991) *The New Meaning of Educational Change*, London: Cassell.

Gray, J. (2000) *Causing Concern but Improving: A Review of Schools' Experiences*, London: DfEE (Research Report RR188).

Gray, J., Goldstein, H. and Jesson, D. (1996) Changes and improvements in schools' effectiveness: trends over five years, *Research Papers in Education*, 11, 1, 35–51.

Gray, J., Hopkins, D., Reynolds, D., Wilcox, B., Farrell, S. and Jesson, D. (1999) *Improving Schools: Performance and Potential*, Buckingham: Open University Press.

Hargreaves, D.H. (1995) School effectiveness, school change and school improvement: the relevance of the concept of culture, *School Effectiveness and School Improvement*, 6, 1, 23–46.

Harris, A. (2000) What works in school improvement? Lessons from the field and future directions, *Educational Research*, 42, 1, 1–11.

Hopkins, D., Ainscow, M. and West, M. (1994) *School Improvement in an Era of Change*, London: Cassell.

Hopkins, D., West, M. and Ainscow, M. (1996) *Improving the Quality of Education for All: Progress and Challenge*, London: David Fulton.

Louis, K. and Miles, M. (1992) *Improving the Urban High School: What Works and Why*, London: Cassell.

MacBeath, J. (1999) *Schools Must Speak for Themselves: The Case for School Self-Evaluation*, London: Routledge.

Mortimore, P. (2000) Paper delivered to a conference of the International School Improvement and Effectiveness Centre, London Institute of Education, May.

NCE (National Commission on Education) (1996) *Success against the Odds: Effective Schools in Disadvantaged Areas*, London: Routledge.

OfSTED (1997) *School Inspections: Removal from Special Measures*, London: OfSTED.

OfSTED (1999) *Annual Report of Her Majesty's Chief Inspector of Schools 1997/98*, London: HMSO.

Robertson, P. and Toal, D. (2000) Extending the quality framework, in J. MacBeath and P. Mortimore (eds) *Improving School Effectiveness*, Buckingham: Open University Press.

Sammons, P., Thomas, S. and Mortimore, P. (1997) *Effective Schools and Effective Departments*, London: Paul Chapman.

Schein, E. (1985) *Organizational Culture and Leadership*, San Francisco: Jossey Bass.

Silver, H. (1994) *Good Schools, Effective Schools: Judgements and their Histories*, London: Cassell.

Stoll, L. (1999) Realising our potential: understanding and developing capacity for lasting improvement, *School Effectiveness and School Improvement*, 10, 4, 503–32.

Teddlie, C. and Reynolds, D. (2000) *The International Handbook of School Effectiveness Research*, London: Falmer Press.

Teddlie, C. and Stringfield, S. (1993) *Schools Make a Difference: Lessons Learned from a Ten-year Study of School Effects*, New York: Teachers College Press.

Thomas, S. and Smees, R. (2000) Dimensions of secondary school effectiveness: comparative analyses across regions, paper presented to the Annual Conference of the American Educational Research Association, New Orleans.

Thrupp, M. (1999) *Schools Making a Difference – Let's Be Realistic*, Buckingham: Open University Press.

van Velzen, W., Miles, M., Ekholm, M., Hameyer, U. and Robin, D. (1985) *Making School Improvement Work*, Leuven: Acco.

Wimpelberg, R., Teddlie, C. and Stringfield, S. (1989) Sensitivity to context: the past and future of effective schools research, *Educational Administration Quarterly*, 25, 1, 82–107.

1

BLAENGWRACH PRIMARY SCHOOL

Neath, West Glamorgan

Alan Evans

INTRODUCTION

In the book *Success against the Odds* (Routledge, 1996) a study on effective schools in disadvantaged areas, under the auspices of the National Commission on Education, the account of Blaengwrach School concluded with the following remarks:

> In Blaengwrach School there is a commitment to excellence, to high expectations and to partnerships with parents, the community and local industry. This commitment is consistent with government aims to raise standards in schools and to increase parental choice as set out in the education legislation enacted between 1980 and 1993 which brought into being national frameworks for the curriculum, assessment, inspection and appraisal. However, Blaengwrach school expresses that commitment in the form of its own particular alchemy.
>
> The headteacher and the staff have a contagious enthusiasm for learning, a sense of mission and a commitment to raising standards, enhancing quality and using the school's resources efficiently and effectively. They are committed 'school improvers' who realise that without the help and support of the parents,

Table 1.1 Blaengwrach County Primary School, Neath, Port Talbot

	1995–96	1999–2000
Headteacher	David Davies (apptd 1990)	David Davies
Number of pupils	163	153
% white pupils	N/A	N/A
% pupils for whom English is an additional language	0	0
% pupils entitled to free school meals (FSM)	21.5 *Welsh average: 25.1*	30.1 *Welsh average: 21.8 (1)*
No. of pupils with Special Educational Needs Statements	2	3
Pupil/teacher ratio, incl. head and nursery classes	20.5 *Welsh average: 22.5*	19.7 (1) *Welsh average: 22.3 (1)*
Support staff per teacher (2)	14.2	10.4
Key Stage Two: level 4+ in core subjects: total score (3)	248 *Welsh average: 177*	270 (1) *Welsh average: 212 (1)*

Key:
N/A : Not available
(1) 1998–99
(2) Full-time-equivalent (f.t.e.) support staff hours per week, per f.t.e. teacher
(3) 300% = maximum score for Standard Assessment Tasks (SATs) maths, English and science combined

community and local industry they would, at best, succeed only partially. They also appreciate that there is much to be gained from this approach. The pupils receive a challenging, enriching and developing quality education. The teachers benefit from increased motivation and job satisfaction. Parents and governors become increasingly involved and gain greater confidence in the school.

The headteacher has taken professional risks to invest in the vision he has for Blaengwrach School. He shares with Bruner the sentiment that 'we have yet to discover the treasures of the minds of young children' and is deeply committed to that educational odyssey. Nothing will detract him from this enthralling prospect. Quite properly, all those interested in and committed to Blaengwrach School have their own sense of why it is such a happy and successful school. It is above all a school where children are treasured and cherished, where quality learning is given primacy but is also fun, and where the contributions of teachers, parents, governors and friends of the school are recognised and celebrated. It is a school where all those involved, in whatever way, work for its development and enrichment.

In June 1998 the school was inspected and in the main findings of the report produced by the inspectors the following comment was made: 'Blaengwrach Primary is a very good school which contributes greatly to the academic and social development of its pupils and enriches their lives significantly.' In its remarks on key issues for action the report concludes: 'There are no significant weaknesses. The school needs to maintain its current high standards and further disseminate the very good practice.'

Nevertheless, despite the fact that the inspectors did not require that the school should draw up an action plan, the governors' annual report to parents in December 1998 commented that 'the school felt it beneficial to do so'.

The action plan identified the following issues as priorities to which the school should address itself:

1 External provision of information to parents
2 Enhanced provision for the teaching of gymnastics
3 Development of a consistent style of handwriting throughout the school
4 Further improvement of attendance figures

5 Maintenance of current good practice and its dissemination throughout the school

In the five years since the National Commission report little has changed in the demographic and socio-economic structure of the area. Blaengwrach (with a population of some 2000 and situated in the upper part of the Vale of Neath, to the east of the new Merthyr to Swansea trunk road) remains predominantly a working-class community in which unemployment is considerably in excess of the national average. There has, however, in recent years been a small influx of professional people into the community.

The school is smaller than it was five years ago with 153 f.t.e. (full-time-equivalent) pupils on its roll compared with 163 in 1995. This decrease in number has led to the loss of one teacher. Of the seven full-time members of staff in 1995 three remain and, of those, one at present is on secondment to an ITT centre. Since 1995 three new teachers have been appointed. There has also been an appointment of a part-time nursery teacher to meet the targets which the government has set for nursery education. Notwithstanding the changes in the composition of teaching staff, Blaengwrach has maintained its educational momentum and is still a school which is succeeding against the odds.

This is the message contained in the inspectorate report and is supported by the evidence contained in the local authority's report on the performance of pupils in their Key Stage One (KSI) and Key Stage Two (KS2) assessments. In 1999, 100 per cent of the pupils attained level 2 or above in KS1 in English and mathematics and 86 per cent attained level 2 and 14 per cent level 3 in science. The comparable results in schools across the local authority were: in English 66 per cent level 2 and 16 per cent level 3, in mathematics 65 per cent level 2 and 20 per cent level 3, and in science 75 per cent level 2 and 11 per cent level 3. At KS2, however, the school consistently exceeded the overall authority results in English, mathematics and science. In science 94 per cent of the children attained level 4 or above in both teacher assessment and tests, which is considerably above the local authority averages. The question needs to be considered of how the school has maintained its reputation as a successful school.

HEADTEACHER'S PHILOSOPHY AND COMMITMENT

The headteacher, whose enthusiasm and commitment were so apparent in the 1995 report, maintains that despite staff changes the mission, vision and philosophy remain the same. He sums up the aim of the school as making pupils successful and he firmly believes that success is achieved by encouraging all the pupils in the school to achieve in something, whether that achievement is in the academic work of the school or in any other of the many activities which the school provides for its pupils. Wherever success is originally located it soon becomes apparent in the improved attitudes which pupils adopt to their academic work. Success in sporting activities, particularly in badminton (the headteacher is an international and Olympic umpire in badminton) has been perceived as having an effect on attitudes to school. The establishment of a drama club also serves to enhance the self-acceptance of the pupils by giving them the opportunity to perform in plays and concerts. The breadth of this wider view of learning and the development of the whole person were also key factors in the winning by the school, situated in a predominantly deprived urban area, of the schools' section of 'Wales in Bloom' in 1998.

The teaching and non-teaching staff share the head's enthusiasm and commitment and the teachers fully support the emphasis which is placed on children's experiential learning. The success of the school in teaching science, which is seen in the high attainment in the subject at KS2 (94 per cent with test scores of level 4 or above), rests on the fact that the children learn by activity. Science lends itself to this hands-on approach and the school uses primary experiences and activities to promote children's insights and experiential skills. Confident that this approach to science is beneficial to children's learning, the headteacher considers that it is not necessary to prepare pupils for SATs. In fact, the core subject indicator for the pupils in the school (i.e. three level 4's or above in English, maths and science) is some 90 per cent, which is almost 30 per cent above the Welsh national average and is considerably above the local authority average, and demonstrates the significant added value that the school, in partnership with parents, contributes to the attainment of its pupils.

Figure 1.1 Learning the recorder

PROFESSIONAL DEVELOPMENT AND THE QUALITY OF TEACHING AND LEARNING

The teachers have a heightened sense of their professional development needs and afford a high priority to professional growth both within and outside of the school. Information technology and rich and varied experience in sport, drama, music, art and the rural and urban landscape are seen to be important to child development as well as the core areas of the National Curriculum. Accordingly, the teaching and support staff are committed to extending their pedagogic and skills repertoire in order to offer pupils quality experience in the curriculum areas just mentioned.

This approach is subsumed into the overall philosophy of the staff about what constitutes quality teaching and learning. They believe that good teaching involves an openness to new ideas and methods for engaging children in their learning and in so doing promote a culture of self-worth and love of learning. The staff, with appropriate leadership from the headteacher, have developed a similar and coherent philosophy about children and how they learn. It involves supporting children, encouraging success in many aspects of the overt and hidden curriculum, and then challenging them to go even further down the path of discovery and achievement.

Over time the staff have acquired a common set of values and beliefs which are communicated in their teaching, in their approach to assessments, in communications with parents and in their dealings with the community. The teachers at Blaengwrach are known for their professional commitment, their optimism, their high aspirations, their belief and trust in their pupils, their pervading view that nothing is too good for their children. This climate of a vibrant learning community is not, however, serendipitous: it is something the teachers strive for on a daily basis, and target-setting, monitoring, review and evaluation are essential components. As one teacher put it, 'It's what we do to meet our own expectations'.

For the appointment of a new member of staff the job description is specific about the philosophy of the school and about what is expected of applicants. Intending applicants are encouraged to seek information about the school. In assessing the suitability of the applicants for a post their letters of application are all-important, requiring the applicants to show what they have done in teaching practice, or in their teaching career, what they have done with children, and how they have involved themselves in the life of a community. The appointment process is in three stages. After drawing up a long short-list consisting of about ten applicants, the headteacher speaks to these candidates and then consults with his senior staff on the priorities which should govern the appointment. A short-list is drawn up of four to six applicants. These are interviewed during a whole day, the morning being devoted to informal interviews with the headteacher, the deputy headteacher and subject co-ordinators. A formal interview by an appointing panel of three governors and the headteacher takes place in the afternoon. At that interview the questions are based on answers received in the morning meeting and revolve mainly around the teacher's philosophy.

This careful system of appointment is to ensure that the person appointed is keyed into the vision, philosophy and aims of the school. When present members of staff were asked what qualities they would look for in a teacher newly appointed to the school their response was that the person appointed should be enthusiastic about what he or she does. Such enthusiasm would involve constant evaluation of practice, taking on ideas and developing them. As one member of staff said, it was a process of making the familiar strange by looking at what needed to be done in a new light. That teacher considered that this process of constant evaluation had practical manifestations in teaching children in the classroom because it had to do with paying attention to the needs of each individual child. That such a philosophy has had an effect on children might be summed up in the remark of one boy: 'The teachers are always there for me'.

ENGAGING AND CHALLENGING CHILDREN

Within this caring environment there is, however, a steely side which has to do with inculcating into children a concern for raising levels of achievement by teachers insisting that they work to their highest potential. Poor or indifferent work is not accepted. In their work children are constantly referred to their best performance in a particular subject or aspect of the curriculum. This also extends to the presentation of their work. The teachers are aware that in any period of time it is necessary to overcome the troughs which inevitably occur in children's learning rates. Their answer is to keep the children going by 'injections of enthusiasm'. This injection may take many forms both in the curriculum offered in school and in the many extra-curricular activities provided by the school, all of which serve to broaden the range of experiences for children.

This encouragement of children to perform to the best of their ability is helped by generous amounts of praise, although one teacher referred to the fact that though over a given period of time every child has a measure of praise, there were occasions when children were 'called to account' for failing to achieve their best. There does not exist a set formula for rewards and incentives; however, informal methods, such as giving children the responsibility of using photocopying facilities or answering telephones, are interpreted by children as measures of praise and affirmation, and these are seen to have positive effects on teaching and learning. There are, however, formal symbols of rewards such as reward stickers, and these are worn by the children or placed alongside the work being commended.

The use of pupils' portfolios continues to play an important part in the education of the children, providing evidence not only of the progress and development of the children in particular areas of the curriculum but also of the standards of which the children are capable. Each half-term in the school year provides an opportunity for the assessment of children's work in a specific area, for example in music. In this way during the course of the school year it is possible to give a focus to children's performance in every area of the school curriculum. An interesting dimension to this approach is that in Year 6 each pupil produces a Memory Book which is a selection by the pupil, suitably referenced and annotated, of the work they liked best over their years in the school. The Memory Books are a treasured part of school life and the pupils keep them as mementoes on leaving at the end of the primary stage.

Assessment is not seen by the head and the staff as a chore but as a pivotal instrument in effective teaching and learning. All members of staff are involved in fashioning, shaping and refining the assessment process in the school. The headteacher provides guidelines on assessment to reaffirm the understanding of the process and outcomes of assessment in the school and its powerful impact on pupil learning and development. The portfolios support the judgement of the teacher in the assessment and in the recording and reporting of achievement. They monitor progress and promote continuity and progression.

As children mature and become more senior members of the school community they become more knowledgeable about the assessment process and become good judges of quality against a range of criteria which in turn helps them to strive for improvement in several academic and practical areas of the curriculum. For their part the staff are aware that whilst the school policy provides the working framework, the nature of assessment does and will vary according to the needs of each individual child. In this way assessment is used successfully for formative and summative purposes and is a major instrument for improving the quality of learning.

PARTNERSHIP IN LEARNING

The culture of success in this school inevitably depends upon a partnership between parents, pupils and teachers. The message to parents is that they are necessary for ensuring the success of the children. The receipt of this message by parents has led to increased support for the aims and aspirations of the school for its pupils. This is seen in the number of parents, particularly mothers, who actively support the school by acting as classroom assistants, listening to children read and taking part in other activities. Although still a small group, fathers also are becoming involved in the life of the school.

The attitude of parents to their duty to fulfil their obligation to support the school in the education of children is apparent. This is helped by the 'Keep in Touch' (KIT) system, established in the school, which ensures effective liaison with parents, particularly with regard to the setting of homework which is logged in 'KIT' books in the possession of the children. The KIT approach is much more than a homework recording instrument: it is seen as a major vehicle of communication with parents about their children's learning. It conveys the message that learning is a partnership between the school and the parents, that all children could attain level 4 in the core subjects and that parental support on a nightly basis (preferably before the children go out to play) would realise such a target.

The importance of the involvement of parents and of the community generally is seen in their participation in activities and events which aim to provide and enrich the experiences of pupils and set a climate of high expectations. Many of the extra-curricular activities, such as snorkelling, sub-aqua and canoeing, are activities in which parents and other members of the community participate, thus anchoring within the community activities which provide its children with wider experiences of life outside that community. With these strongly developed links, the school is able to reciprocate the interest which the community takes in it by participating in and enriching the cultural life of the area. The pupils of the school regularly perform in concerts which are held in the community and outside.

CONCLUSION

In the five years which has elapsed since the publication of the National Commission on Education report, what has pleased the headteacher is the fact that his staff has continued to share the school's philosophy and aims and has made them its own. What has displeased him is the growth of unnecessary bureaucracy which takes time away from children, for what children need most from teachers is time. What has concerned him most is the length of time which it took the staff to recover from what was perceived to be a good inspection. It suggested to him that there was something amiss with the inspection process. This feeling is shared by those members of staff who were at the school during the inspection. One teacher spoke of the pressure of the inspection as 'leading in a sense to the stifling of one's normal activity'. It was the same teacher who considered that the best part of the five years was 'being in the classroom with children' and that she was happy in her job and 'not thinking of teaching in another school', sentiments shared by other teachers interviewed.

Blaengwrach is a school which wants the best for all its pupils and is willing to strive to realise such a goal. Many primary schools have computers in all (or most) classrooms or have a computer suite. Blaengwrach insists on both. Some schools excel in sport, or music and drama. Blaengwrach excels in all three curriculum areas. The sceptic may ask 'why?' and the headteacher, the staff and parents of Blaengwrach say 'why not?'. This is a school in pursuit of excellence. It has experienced hard knocks on the educational journey but the commitment, resilience and resourcefulness have prevailed. The headteacher provides inspirational leadership for the school, but the success of the school is testimony to a team effort. More than half the staff were not working in the school five years ago: yet the vision, contagious enthusiasm for learning, high expectations and a profound belief in and commitment to the children in their care have endured. Standards have continued to rise and pupils and parents have direct experience of the richness of educational, cultural and sporting achievement. The school is changing the way the community thinks about itself and is helping to ensure that the educational and technological revolution that Wales is experiencing will not bypass Blaengwrach.

2

COLUMBIA PRIMARY SCHOOL
Tower Hamlets, London
Anne Sofer

I had not visited Columbia Primary School and its neighbourhood for more than three years and I had expected, somehow, to
see a change. This is how I described it five years ago in *Success
against the Odds* (1996):

> Columbia [Primary School] . . . a red brick galleon moored beside
> the famous Columbia Sunday flower market . . . is surrounded
> by the remains of the warren of streets of two-up, two-down
> houses built for the artisans of Bethnal Green in Dickens' time:
> most of them were cleared away in the 1950s to make way for
> tower blocks. On Sundays the area is flooded with market
> customers from far and wide, including tourists and wealthier
> Londoners from north and east. During the week, it reverts to
> reality: a neighbourhood which has never, since it was absorbed
> into London in the early nineteenth century known affluence or
> economic security. In the immediate post-war years, aspiring
> working-class familes, third-generation Jewish families and
> members of the thriving East End criminal sub-culture lived here
> cheek by jowl. Now the same space is shared by first-generation
> families from rural Sylhet, a beleaguered and ageing working-
> class white community and a paper-thin layer of middle-class
> gentrification.

Table 2.1 Columbia Primary School, London Borough of Tower Hamlets

	1995–96	1999–2000
Headteacher	Penny Bentley (apptd 1986)	Penny Bentley
Number of pupils	440	427
% white pupils	11 (1996–97)	23 *English average: 86.0 (1)*
% pupils for whom English is an additional language	92	77
% pupils entitled to free school meals (FSM)	73 (1994–95)	61 *English average: 18.9 (1)*
% pupils with special educational needs, incl. those with Statements	28.3 (1994–95) *English average: 17.2*	23.4 *English average: 20.8 (1)*
Pupil/teacher ratio, incl. head and nursery classes	19.3 *English average: 23.2*	19.7 *English average: 23.3*
Support staff per teacher (2)	11.8	10
Key Stage Two: level 4+ in core subjects: total score (3)	88 *English average: 107.7*	241 (1) *English average: 215.8 (1)*

Key:
(1) 1998–99
(2) Full-time-equivalent (f.t.e.) support staff hours per week, per f.t.e. teacher
(3) 300% = maximum score for Standard Assessment Tasks (SATs) maths, English and science combined

The ward in which the school is located is called Weavers, recalling an even earlier group of settlers, the Huguenot refugees who set up their looms here in the eighteenth century. The 1991 census provides a profile of this ward which seemed little changed at the time I wrote this: 7.8 per cent of adults had a higher education qualification, compared to 13.5 per cent nationally (for the UK); 11.6 per cent of children were in 'high social class households' (31 per cent nationally); 67.8 per cent of children were from ethnic minorities (10.1 per cent nationally); 61 per cent children lived in overcrowded households (10.5 per cent nationally).

Superficially, there is little change in the way the area looks. There has been some improvement work to the council estates, one or two more trendy shops fronting the market, but the feeling of a 'poor neighbourhood' is still strong – litter, out-of-order parking meters, and very old people shuffling to the corner shop.

Under the surface, however, things are changing. Even in the space of five years, no London neighbourhood stands still. The Bangladeshi community, for instance, can hardly be described as 'first-generation' any more. An exaggeration even then, it now immediately jars with anyone who knows the area. Increasingly, Bangladeshi parents will have had at least some of their education in this country, and many probably now confidently identify themselves as Londoners (if not yet as English). And the 'paper-thin' middle-class layer is a little thicker now, with consequences for the school as we will see below. Although unemployment levels in the borough are three times the national average, and twice those of inner London, there is anecdotal evidence of more parents (particularly more mothers) working at least part-time than was the case a few years ago.

The 2001 census will prove an interesting check on these impressions, but it is safe to predict that they will reveal only incremental changes over the last decade, not a transformation. This is still a very deprived area. The fact that it is within spitting distance of the multi-million designer offices and *pieds-à-terre* of the expanding City of London only throws that reality into sharper relief.

With the school, it is the same. Physically it is unchanged – and I am surprised by this. There have been no great capital improvements. And the changed educational climate – targets, literacy hour, league tables, etc. – does not seem to have changed the look of classrooms. What I described then as 'classrooms . . . built for sixty children in tiered seating but now barely manag[ing] to accommodate a class of thirty, with their book corner and technology display and science gear and paintings' were pretty much the same today. ('No, we haven't got them all in rows facing the blackboard', said the head sardonically.) There is perhaps more evidence of stacks of test papers and less of flamboyant artistic creativity, but you would have to look a lot more carefully than I was able to to be sure of this impression.

The atmosphere of the school also, reassuringly, feels the same – which, with the same head and a core of many of the same experienced staff is not surprising.

However, below the continuities and similiarities, there *are* significant changes. Let me try to tease them out.

First, the children. What I particularly noticed from the statistics, even before I revisited the school, was that the proportion of children of Bangladeshi origin has dropped. It was 84 per cent five years ago and is now only 67 per cent. White children, 7 per cent five years ago, are now 23 per cent (about a third of these are non-English-speakers). The other 10 per cent is made up of other ethnic minorities, the largest single group being Africans. In other words what was almost a mono-cultural school five years is now multi-cultural, and apparently becoming more so. Children admitted in recent weeks come from Colombia, Sierra Leone, Azerbaijan and Kosovo. As compared to five years ago, English, rather than Sylheti (a distinctive dialect of Bengali, spoken by the vast majority of local families from Bangladesh), is the predominant language of the playground, though 77 per cent of the children speak English as an additional language (85 per cent five years ago).

Columbia is also, possibly for the first time in its history, becoming multi-class. The reputation of the school has persuaded some middle-class parents, both from the immediate area and from further afield, to trust their children to this school rather than to local church schools or the private sector. This trend is so far confined largely to the younger age groups, but is moving up the school.

Figure 2.1 Columbia Primary School – a Year 2 classroom

Despite this evidence of increasing popularity the roll is about 5 per cent down on five years ago, probably as a result of the decreasing pressure on places from the Bangladeshi population whose family size is stabilising. The proportion of pupils eligible for free school meals has dropped from 73 per cent to 61 per cent – though it is worth noting that this is still more than three times the national rate (for England). The number of children with Statements of special educational needs has remained stable at around the national level (1.6 per cent), but children with un-Statemented special needs are a higher proportion (27 per cent compared to a national 21 per cent in 1998/99). There have been no permanent exclusions since 1995. Unauthorised absence is at exactly the national average (0.5 per cent), though attendance overall is lower (91 per cent compared to 94 per cent). The causes of this may be a poorer child health (there is plenty of corroboratory evidence from the Area Health Authority) and extended holidays in Bangladesh. Mobility, a threat to continuity in many inner-city schools, is not a major issue at Columbia, though in some classes as many as half the class may have joined the school after Year 1.

WHAT ABOUT STAFF?

The most significant continuity is that the same headteacher, Penny Bentley, is still in post. During the five years since *Success against the Odds* (1996) she has had a one-term secondment as an adviser working with failing schools in another inner London borough. She found this experience stimulating and enjoyable ('and not nearly such hard work as being a head'). She is glad to have done it, and to have reassured herself that other career possibilities are open. But in the end she decided to return to Columbia.

In my previous report on Columbia I did not say much about Penny. I quoted in full the comments of my two co-authors on her vision and management style which made clear how impressed they were, but there was no picture of her as an individual. Given the key role she has played this is an omission which needs to be put right this time round. Penny is now 57. She originally trained and worked as a secondary teacher, then left teaching to bring up three sons. Her husband is an Anglican clergyman, based during this period in Tower Hamlets, where the children attended their local primary school. She started teaching part-time at this school and found herself hooked on primary teaching. During this period she was also active in the community. She became the chair of governors of the church secondary school which her boys went on to – a position she resigned from when the school decided to go for grant-maintained status. Over the years she has become an important opinion former within the education community in Tower Hamlets and beyond – assertive and articulate, highly principled but pragmatic and close to the chalkface. She possesses a wonderful combination of wisdom, wit and total engagement.

The school at which Penny started her primary teaching career, John Scurr, has the distinction of having produced no fewer than four Tower Hamlets headteachers. In her turn, she has fostered future school leaders among her staff. Over the last five years, two have moved on to headship and one to a Tower Hamlets advisory position. But there is still a large core of eight experienced staff who have been at Columbia for more than five years. The strength of the school management team (head, deputy, head of early years and head of humanities) is, in the head's view, a very important factor. There is a high level of trust and shared responsibility which acts as a model for other teams in the school. Penny takes pride in the fact that the school has run smoothly in her absence, most recently through a difficult time which included the traumatic death of a child in a road accident.

Below this senior cadre, however, things are very different. Five years ago the school was filling its two or three vacancies every year with newly qualified teachers, often those they had 'talent-spotted' during teaching practice. Now the annual vacancy rate is much higher – eight last September – and the newly qualified are very thin on the ground. Most of these eight vacancies were filled by temporary teachers from the Antipodes and Canada, some of whom stayed only a few weeks. These teachers are generally both competent and adaptable (a history remains to be written of the debt which London education owes to supply teachers from the former British colonies) but continuity has become a serious problem. This picture is typical of east London generally.

The drop in pupil numbers has meant a reduction in full-time teachers over the last five years from 23 to 21. This includes an allocation of 4.2 full-time-equivalent teachers funded by EMTAG (Ethnic Minority and Travellers Achievement Grant – what was Section 11). The school has chosen to spread this allocation over nine teachers – so the responsibility, and developing expertise, for this work is spread more widely. The deputy head teaches two days a week and the head one day a week.

As far as support staff are concerned, there is a growing number of bilingual assistants recruited from the local community, making an increasingly valued and confident contribution. There are six classroom assistants (one training to be a nursery nurse), three learning support assistants for Statemented children, and two nursery nurses. This group were described five years ago as having had, typically, 'three or four' years of education in this country. Now that period will be longer, but these young women are still not, by and large, making the leap to teacher status. According to the head, some of them are able enough, but would have a lot of ground to make up academically in order to qualify as teachers. Unfortunately, it appears that very few of the much larger numbers of young people of Bangladeshi origin now doing well in examinations and going on from school to higher education are aiming at teaching. It is not proving easy to recruit a more ethnically diverse teaching force.

There are two staffing innovations since five years ago. The school has appointed a counsellor and a home–school liaison worker, both for one day a week and both from the delegated budget. This is evidence of the growing concern for the children's emotional well-being – an issue discussed later in this chapter.

Columbia seems to sit comfortably within its own structures of governance. The governing body is described as 'still very supportive and involved'. A large majority are parents, though the Bangladeshi community is still under-represented. The LEA provides good support through its provision of data and advisory service.

STILL A SUCCESS?

Five years ago, when I was still Director of Education in Tower Hamlets, I felt I had to justify the selection of Columbia with some sensitivity. After all, most Tower Hamlets schools are working against pretty heavy odds, and many of them are successful. As I explained then I based the choice on both quantitative and qualitative data. The quantitative data then was the London Reading Test scores (SATs were not yet established and publicly available). The qualitative data was inspection evidence –at that time our local LEA review process, since the school had not yet had an OfSTED inspection.

One of the interesting facts five years on is the explosion of available data – a battery of SATs for the last four years, benchmark data, national comparators, and the OfSTED 'PANDA', which provides contextual data. In terms of tested performance in English, maths and science we now know far more about how schools are doing, both in absolute terms and in comparison with similar schools. There is also now, for Columbia, an OfSTED report.

Another interesting fact, five years on, is the difference – in both message and impact – of the two different types of monitoring. It is the opposite of what one might have expected a decade ago before any of these systems were in place. Then it was the hard quantitative test data that was feared and the qualitative judgements of HMI that were accepted and respected – now it is the other way round.

Let me take the SATs results first. Although the 1996 results did not confirm the pre-eminent position of Columbia among Tower Hamlets schools the annual improvement since then has vindicated my choice of this school as one which is succeeding against the odds. By 1999 the Key Stage Two results were above the national average in all subjects.

The OfSTED PANDA document sets these results in the context of the results of similar schools. The definition of 'similar schools' is not generous to schools like Columbia. Schools are grouped in five categories, each representing roughly 20 per cent of the total, and as a result all schools with more than 50 per cent of children entitled to free school meals are considered to be 'similar schools', even though there is a body of evidence indicating the cumulative effects of deprivation at higher levels. Similarly, schools with over 50 per cent of children learning English as an additional language are all considered together.

Analysis of the OfSTED PANDA's detailed figures indicates that Columbia is in the top 3 per cent of England's schools in terms of deprivation – and therefore near the extreme end of the spectrum of the so-called 'similar schools'. Nonetheless, Columbia's Key Stage Two results are shown to be all Grade A ('well above the average for similar schools') in all subjects, with results in English earning A* (the 95th percentile, 'very high in comparison with the average for similar schools'), and the results in Science only just missing that bracket by one point.

The results at Key Stage One are not quite as outstanding, though no grading falls below a B ('above the average for similar schools'). An important factor must be the high proportion of children learning English as an additional language. By Key Stage Two they have had an extra four years.

The SATs results and the SATs process seem now to be accepted as an enduring fact of life by the school, not any longer as an irritant or an imposition. In fact, the school has opted this year to take the additional yearly SATs for the intervening years between the two key stages – 'mostly to improve the accuracy of teachers' assessments'. I came across a Year 3 teacher going through some scripts in her classroom in the lunch hour. 'Did the children get stressed about it?', I asked. 'No, not at all'. I asked the head about the effects of 'teaching to the test'. She answered by describing the school's approach to science. 'We do lots of creative and practical work, involving investigations and scientific thinking, all the way up the school. Then in Year 6 we concentrate on making sure they have all the necessary vocabulary for the SATs.' We discussed a recent *TES* article both of us had read by the children's author Anne Fine, who was commenting on the greatly improved standards of correctness in children's writing over the last five years, an improvement which, Fine judged, had not been achieved at the expense of creativity. Penny agreed. The effects of SATs on all-round academic achievement had been positive. Her worry was that other aspects of children's development – particularly emotional development – were being neglected.

SATs results clearly mattered to all the staff, both in terms of external perceptions of the school and as a vital tool for monitoring progress. There was anxiety about volatility from year to year. For instance, Penny was predicting that the 2000 results would see a dip – because of the make-up of that particular year. (There was a dip – but only a small one.) In many inner-city schools, mobility both in and out can play havoc with predicted results: Penny was laughing ruefully about the case of a high-flyer whose family was rehoused just before the SATs. Nonetheless, overall, the whole SATs package and the huge change in the public exposure and accountability of schools which it has brought about seem to be accepted.

With OfSTED, it is very different. The school's experience was an unhappy one and there is a feeling of anger and apprehension about what the future may bring. This may in part be due to a fact of timing. The OfSTED report was undertaken in June 1997, during the period when the directive to inspectors was that standards should be reported against national averages, with no concessions to context. The opening statements concentrate on 'low standards of attainment', 'standards below national expectations' and 'slow progress' – all this only weeks after pupils had been taking SATs which subsequently proved to have shown improvement faster than the national rate.

This was felt by the school to be grossly unfair, and there was still – when I raised the matter with teachers – indignation about it. There was also strong disagreement with some of the judgements and resentment about what was felt to be the overlooking of some evidence.

Now, of course, there has been a change in the reporting requirements of OfSTED inspection. Contextual data is quoted more prominently and the grading system comparing with 'similar schools' is used. But there is a new worry about OfSTED – now it is the directive that any school with more than 10 per cent of unsatisfactory lessons will be deemed to be in the category of 'serious weaknesses', regardless of other strengths. Additionally, the new criteria for 'unsatisfactory' make it very easy to acquire this label. With the chronic teacher shortage and the high proportion of temporary and supply teachers, the risks are obviously high, and this too is seen as unfair.

As it happened, I heard all these comments before I read the OfSTED report, and I was surprised when I did come to read it to find that large sections of it were highly complimentary. The leadership and vision of the head, management, standards of behaviour, relationships, links with parents, value for money, special educational needs – all of these come in for the whole-hearted praise which they deserve. But none of this compensates for the perceived under-rating of the academic achievements of the school. The head's overall verdict is that the OfSTED process as an instrument of improvement is wasteful and inaccurate. And the work required to rebuild morale and energy in the following year at Columbia actually made the improvement more difficult.

However, Penny Bentley is nothing if not fair-minded, and she commented:

> If I am really honest I have to admit they were right about some things – for instance our tracking of individual pupils needed strengthening. The report also said – correctly – that we should be making better use of data. We have been taking this seriously and have welcomed the move towards school self-evaluation. We have become much more effective at analysing data (of all kinds, not just numbers!), setting targets, and evaluating progress.

THE NEW EDUCATIONAL SCENE

We scanned the educational landscape. First, what about the literacy and numeracy strategies?

The literacy strategy was overall a positive development. 'Of course, you'd been a Real Books person, hadn't you?', I reminded her. 'And I'm still a Real Books person', she came back sharply. There was a risk with the literacy strategy that whole books were no longer read, only extracts, and that opportunities for children to read, and be read to, for sheer enjoyment were reduced. Children's love of books, always fostered at Columbia (and praised by OfSTED), is still central to this school's approach. Nonetheless, she and her staff accepted some years ago that a more prominent position needed to be given to a structured approach to phonics and this was in place before the literacy hour insisted on it.

A few teachers at Columbia had resisted the imposition of the literacy hour on principle but these teachers have gone. Penny feels the strategy was too hastily introduced and she is still critical of some of the material which has been issued. Overall, however, she is sure that standards of teaching have improved as a result. 'Though perhaps we've lost some of the real star quality we used to get.'

There are no such reservations about the numeracy hour. 'It's wonderful! – much more carefully and professionally prepared and introduced.'

The ICT strategy, and this area of work generally, is a 'huge burden in terms of anxiety'. Very few of the children have access at home to a computer and there are doubts as to whether, even with two computers now in each classroom, they will get the sustained regular experience and expert guidance they need to become proficient. 'We are running to catch up all the time.' Penny worries about relying on the notion of 'ICT across the curriculum'. Will the skills actually be learned this way? (This recalls the old debates about the teaching of reading!) She wishes she could afford a properly staffed dedicated computer suite. Failing that, she thought that a better national strategy might be to concentrate resources and expertise on an intensive three-week course at the end of Year 6 for all children in schools like Columbia.

The children who *are* benefiting from specialist IT teaching are the ten particularly able Year 6 pupils who, under the 'Gifted and Talented' strand of the Excellence in Cities programme, are spending two afternoons a week in the IT suite of the neighbouring comprehensive school, now a specialist Technology College. Although she acknowledges the benefit to this minority, Penny has questions about this programme as well. The timing means that they regularly miss lessons on writing and science.

Time pressures on the curriculum are obviously still a problem, and looming large again with the new National Curriculum for the foundation subjects. Not only the staff but some of the new middle-class element among the parents are particularly alert to the risk of the creative subjects being squeezed out of the mainstream. And it is true that more art and music activities are now being pursued in extra-curricular time. Despite the added workload on teachers, they are giving more time (unpaid) to after-school clubs.

In the last two years particularly, the concept of 'learning beyond the classroom' has been promoted. New Opportunities Fund moneys (and some of the school's own resources) have been used to pay parents and community groups to run a whole range of after-school activities – clubs for reading, writing, quiet games, French, sewing, basketball, football, drama, art and environmental studies, and a study centre.

In my last account of Columbia, I commented that the school appeared to be reluctant to get involved with business – unlike many other Tower Hamlets schools which even then were benefiting from strong business links built up by the Tower Hamlets Education Business Partnership. Now, the head reports:

> We have overcome our reluctance! We now have a strong link with ABN-AMRO Bank, who provide 20 reading partners visiting once a week, and a governor. They also give every class a Christmas present each year, have provided sponsorship for our Millennium activities and this term are organising visits to the bank for Year 6 classes.

Columbia is not in an Education Action Zone – though Penny would welcome one, not just for the extra money but for the boost to inter-school collaboration – 'always a good idea'. She reminds me that this particular geographical patch, despite its socio-economic profile, has always missed out on regeneration initiatives. But her great hope is now in winning lottery cash to establish a 'Healthy Living Centre' in the former schoolkeeper's house. This would be a base for the services she feels many parents badly need – mental health, child guidance, basic skills. Both she and her SEN co-ordinator find co-ordination with other services, especially social services and health, a constant challenge. Cuts and turnover of staff have worsened (from an already dire situation) over recent years. The school has been without a school nurse for almost a year. The speech therapy waiting list is eleven months.

It is in this area of work – the emotional well-being of children – that Columbia seems most in tune with the government's thinking, indeed racing ahead of it. There was more excited talk about innovations and possibilities here than anywhere else. The school has introduced 'Quality Circle Time', a highly structured programme teaching self-understanding and respect for others, and 'Golden Time', a weekly period of optional activities, with time lost from the latter as a sanction. Year 6 volunteers are trained as a 'Friendship Squad', with special white baseball caps, to befriend children who are new or lonely and to organise games in the playground.

The 'moral and spiritual' area was a strength commented on in *Success against the Odds* (1996), and also in the OfSTED report – so it is not an area in which the school was under any pressure to improve. Yet it is here, in their own judgement, that more investment is most urgently needed. The more heterogeneous nature of the school seems to have brought with it more troubled children and families. Also, the nature of the Bangladeshi community is changing fast. With westernisation has come a greater prevalence of teenage pregnancy, gangs, drugs and crime, these in their turn strengthening a reaction in favour of Islamic fundamentalism. These conflicts are not left at the school gates. Hence, Columbia's conviction that, for the school to be able to contribute to its pupils' chance of becoming creative, confident and responsible adults, it needs to be able to do more – much more – than turn out good SATs results. It recognises and applauds the government's inclusion agenda and wants to be part of it.

I asked about the new structure of the teaching profession – a hot topic as my visit was only days before the applications to cross the threshold were due to be submitted. Penny was giving guarded approval to the process and her staff a somewhat weary – and wary – acquiescence. The amount of work involved in making the application was seen as unduly burdensome, but it was accepted that this would become easier as the system became embedded. One teacher expressed admiration for more militant union members who were boycotting the scheme ('but I need the money!'); another apprehension was about divisiveness.

The issue of 'red tape and bureaucracy' was definitely a live one. 'These days every teacher needs a secretary', said the head of SEN. 'Accountability gone mad', exclaimed the head. The latter comment related particularly to the arrangements for the Standards Fund, the writing of bids and the making of claims for seemingly scores of small pots of money, and the ludicrous pretence that every extra £1000 could be credited with a precise and quantified test-score improvement outcome. (Only days after my visit David Blunkett, Secretary of State for Education and Employment, announced a simplification of this system – so this is perhaps one complaint that has been heard.)

Columbia's reaction, then, to New Labour's stewardship of education is mixed: positive on the literacy and numeracy strategies, education out-of-school and the inclusion agenda, negative on OfSTED's continuing role and central bureaucracy. And the jury is still out on the new structure for the profession and ICT.

It is noticeable that many of the government's most important initiatives pass Columbia by, or touch it only peripherally. The nursery education guarantee and the maximum of 30 in infant classes have had no impact, since these were both the norm throughout Tower Hamlets before 1997. Education Action Zones to the north and east (for schools no less deprived, it has to be said) do not touch this particular school. Excellence in Cities has had only a minor (and doubtful) impact. The school's budget has not increased beyond the rate of inflation and the pupil–teacher ratio remains the same.

If the increased resources for education have not yet been felt here, the greater demands certainly have. And this does cause resentment. The head summed it up in four words: 'More work, less trust'.

COMMENTARY

In *Success against the Odds* (1996) I commented in conclusion about three issues – minorities within the school, the nature of good

........g and the 'political' climate. It may be interesting to touch base again with all of these.

Minorities within the school

My concerns last time were about the lack of male role models and the possible isolation of the white minority of children. The former is now recognised as a national problem for which no solution is in sight. The latter is now, at Columbia, not exactly the same problem. The reversal of 'white flight' in any inner-city school is an achievement and it is a tribute to the school that they have achieved it. What none of us expected five years ago was that many incoming immigrant groups would themselves be white. This undoubtedly changes the racial and social dynamic of the school.

The nature of good teaching

Five years ago I commented on the great range of styles and groupings used by Columbia teachers:

> Usually it was working. Sometimes it wasn't, but that was inherent in a philosophy of teaching which was open to new techniques. As long as there is constant evaluation and revision, as it appears there is, this diversity of method is a considerable strength. . . . Whether it could be replicated in schools with a less committed and experienced team is a difficult question.

Well, the team – though still led by an experienced group – is less experienced on average than it was five years ago; and while it may be no less committed, the high proportion of temporary teachers must have made an impact on the quality of this commitment. Coincidentally, national pressures are bringing about a far greater uniformity of teaching method. I would guess – though this is only a guess, not based on observation – that there is less diversity and experiment in teaching styles than there used to be. For schools notable for their creative buzz – as Columbia has been – this may be a loss.

It is worth quoting in full Penny's comments on the above paragraph which she saw in draft:

> Teachings styles **have** become more uniform, especially in the Literacy and Numeracy Hours. But that's not necessarily a bad thing – you could argue that they've become more consistent, which is good for children. And Columbia teachers are still encouraged – and still seize the opportunity – to be creative and innovative by using visits, visitors, special projects in art or music and contacts in the community to support teaching and learning in the classroom. We also have a whole-school topic once a year when Inset for staff, special events for pupils and parents, and permission to spend extra time on one subject (this year science) always leads to a rush of enthusiasm and creative energy.

Columbia is definitely still a 'learning institution' – this was evident from the number of references the head and teachers made to shared training and experiences and ideas and information they had passed on to each other. Some of this has undoubtedly been encouraged by the emphasis now placed by the DfEE and OfSTED on planning, targeting and tracking progress; and some of it stems from the philosophy of the school itself.

The political climate

Five years ago, this heading covered the reaction of the head and teachers to the abolition of the Inner London Education Authority and the introduction of OfSTED and the National Curriculum. I described their underlying commitment to 'the "progressive" platform: child-centred primary education, comprehensive secondary education, anti-racism, equal opportunities', and the head's determination to hold fast to these ideals.

> Her strategy, however, is to colonise whatever structures present themselves in pursuit of these aims. . . . Externally she and the teachers appear to have embraced the 'reform' of the last ten years. Yet in reality they are profoundly antipathetic to much of its thrust.

Penny reminded me of the word 'colonising', which she liked and had adopted. She felt that this still described what she was doing. Yet this passage does not seem to be an entirely accurate description of her attitude now. 'Profound antipathy' sounds too strong. That mood has passed – perhaps with the departure of the group who resisted the literacy hour so strongly. Much of the infrastructure of accountability – externally marked tests, precise targets, published results – all of these seem to have been accepted as an inevitable part of the zeitgeist and (yes) thoroughly colonised and domesticated.

But there is a new mood – a mixture of bafflement and bitterness – which was not there before. This is caused less by the substance of New Labour's policies than by its style. Most inner-city teachers, whether they are politically active or not, feel themselves to be on the left. When national policy was being made by a Conservative government they knew where they stood. They would carry out their work as best they could within the constraints of a politically alien culture, but would hope for something better come the next election. That 'something better' would not just mean better pay and more resources. Far more important than these it would mean (they hoped) more understanding and trust from government and some acknowledgement of the challenges they face. Instead they have been slapped in the face with 'naming and shaming', damning comments on 'these inner-city schools' and the mantra of 'poverty is no excuse'.

CONCLUSION

As I left Columbia I found it hard to predict what the next five years would bring. When Penny talked about her idea for a 'Healthy Living Centre' I had a vision of Columbia becoming a pilot for the 'full-service school' model which is being discussed at national level. Adult literacy, career guidance, baby clinic and community centre, would all be centred round the neighbourhood primary school – a focus of excellence, in terms of both academic standards and community vision. This is what this school deserves and what, I believe, it could deliver. A return visit in five years' time could be an inspiring example of 'joined-up' inner-city regeneration and the current apprehensive mood could be nothing but a fleeting memory.

On the other hand, it could be an entirely different and more depressing picture. There are some more ominous indicators, in particular the growing crisis in teacher recruitment. Columbia in five years' time could be clinging on by its fingernails to the standards it has reached today, afflicted by all the 'inner-city' demons it is currently holding at bay – high turnover of staff, poor teacher morale, community tensions, fragmented and overstretched public services.

Penny herself, reflecting on the future, poses the issue in a self-questioning way which provides, I think, an insight not only into the thinking of experienced and successful inner-city teachers, but also into the stresses and strains they have been living under:

> Maybe it's also important to wonder whether the school has the capacity within itself to sustain success. Regeneration doesn't just require government support, although of course that's important. It would also require the school itself to change its thinking, to consider doing things in different ways, to be a different kind of school. Part of the question is, do we have the vision and energy to do that?

In the summer of 2000, with the results of the government's Public Expenditure Review eagerly awaited, it is possible, on balance, to be optimistic. This is a school that has proved itself ready to change and improve and which has a vision for the future. If given the opportunity to draw breath, and with the assurance of support, I feel sure it could take on new challenges. But those two preconditions are not trivial considerations. The government needs to take note.

POSTSCRIPT

At the very end of the summer term, a week after this chapter had been finished, I was contacted by the headteacher of Columbia who had just heard that the school was to get a major new resource – a Learning Support Unit funded through the Excellence in Cities programme. This would be one of two such units in the borough, intended for children with behavioural difficulties and/or at risk of exclusion. It will work only with pupils from Columbia. There are to be two teachers and an assistant for the unit and a learning mentor working across the whole school – in addition to resources for building adaptation – 'as soon as we can spend it'.

The reaction of the staff, and in particular the head and the SENCO (SEN co-ordinator), was elation. Instead of the normal exhausted wind-down, the last day of term was spent planning the details. The goal of the Healthy Living Centre had not been abandoned by any means. It can, says the school, easily be accommodated alongside the Learning Support Unit in the former schoolkeeper's house. Clearly a lot of synergistic thinking is going on – itself an answer in the affirmative to Penny's own question 'Do we have the vision and energy?'

It seems churlish to comment in any way other than appreciatively on this happy ending, but it acts as a final illustration of two of the themes of this chapter: the attachment of successive governments to a top-down model of improvement, and the school's talent for 'colonisation'. The Learning Support Unit is not exactly what either the school or the LEA wants – there are particular concerns about how it fits with a philosophy of inclusion. But that is what is on offer, and the LEA in choosing Columbia to host the unit is demonstrating its confidence that this school will be able to bend the model to suit the philosophy, rather than the other way round.

One cannot help wondering, however, about the last day of the summer term 2000 in all the other schools struggling against the odds – where there wasn't such an unexpected boost to morale. The number of inner-city primary schools benefiting from the new initiatives is still a minority. From 2001 onwards the new increases in public expenditure announced by the Chancellor will be coming on-stream and should spread the resources more widely. It won't be a moment too soon.

3

CROWCROFT PARK PRIMARY SCHOOL

Manchester

Bill Rogers

THE SCHOOL'S ACHIEVEMENTS IN ITS SETTING

Crowcroft Park is a county primary school for pupils aged 3 to 11 situated approximately two miles to the south-east of Manchester city centre. The school was built in 1935 and is located just off the main Manchester to Stockport road sandwiched between a small park and an area of terraced houses the majority of which are rented on short-term leases from private landlords. The majority of pupils are drawn from the Longsight Ward which has seen a steady influx of families from the Indian subcontinent and in particular from Bangladesh and Pakistan; 42.5 per cent of the pupils have English as an additional language. The main first languages of pupils in the school are English, Urdu, Bengali and Punjabi although many more languages and cultures are represented.

The official figures for the percentage of pupils eligible for free school meals at the time of my visit was 54 per cent but the number of claims awaiting processing suggests that the real figure is significantly higher. The school has also experienced a high level of pupil transience, averaging 31.4 per cent as families move in and out of the district. Also, 18.3 per cent of the pupils are on the Special

Table 3.1 Crowcroft Park Primary, City of Manchester

	1995–96	1999–2000
Headteacher	Heather Stemp (apptd 1983)	Heather Stemp
Number of pupils	234	241
% white pupils	50.0	52.5 *English average: 86.0 (1)*
% pupils for whom English is an additional language	37.9	42.5
% pupils entitled to free school meals (FSM)	54.7	53.5 *English average: 18.9 (1)*
% pupils with special educational needs, incl. those with Statements	N/A *English average: 17.2*	18.3 *English average: 20.8 (1)*
Pupil/teacher ratio, incl. head and nursery classes	20.4 *English average: 23.2*	25.4 *English average: 23.3*
Support staff per teacher (2)	10.3	16.2
Key Stage Two: level 4+ in core subjects: total score (3)	91 *English average: 107.7*	194 (1) * *English average: 215.8 (1)*

Key:
N/A : Not available
(1) 1998–99
(2) Full-time-equivalent (f.t.e.) support staff hours per week, per f.t.e. teacher
(3) 300% = maximum score for Standard Assessment Tasks (SATs) maths, English and science combined
* The school has sought assurances from OfSTED that, in future, the publication of Key Stage Two scores and related grades should take account of the number of children in Year 6 who have very limited knowledge of English (especially recently arrived immigrants).

Education Needs Register and two pupils have Statements of Special Need. Unemployment in families of children attending the school is much higher than the catchment-area figure of 21.5 per cent. The school is now heavily oversubscribed. Twice as many applications are received in the nursery and reception as there are places available.

Although the external features of the school and its immediate environment have not substantially changed in the past five years there have been small but important developments which have impacted on school improvement.

A gradual turnover of staff has provided a good balance of new blood and experience. New staff have been selected for their skills and experience to complement specific needs in the school and all new staff, other than newly qualified teachers, were observed by the headteacher teaching in their own classrooms prior to their appointment.

During the last visit we commented on the difficult nature of the school building, given that it is an open verandah-style building built in a V-shape. Little has changed in recent years, although extensive work is now taking place to renew rotting verandahs. The school has also set up its own computer suite to facilitate its delivery of the National Grid for Learning (NGfL). Apart from the geography of the building the difficulties caused by so small a playground, limited storage, the lack of a separate dining room and generally cramped accommodation remain.

The most significant change to the admissions procedures is that the nursery is now full-time only and has a long waiting list. At the time of the last visit we noted that pupil turnover due to a transient population was becoming an issue. By 1999 the level of transience had risen to 31 per cent but in the last twelve months has plummeted. Although the reasons for this turn-around are not clear, it seems likely that it is partly to do with an urban regeneration project in the A6 and Longsight corridor area on the edge of the school's catchment. The most obvious signs of this are improvements to the exterior walls of the houses, significant improvement to the pavements, traffic calming schemes and improved security to houses which includes the fitting of new doors. There is no doubt that the area is becoming one where people would feel both safer and happier to live and it may be that more settled families are moving into the area. Nevertheless the area is still one with a large proportion of private landlords and the issue of transience remains one of concern to the school.

Through the Single Regeneration Budget and funding from the Progress Trust the school has established a transience project involving the employment of a nursery nurse and a teacher to focus on this particular issue. This work is concentrating on initial assessment, the settling in of children, liaison with families, making connection between those families and other key services, the development of pupil records during their time at the school and at transfer stage to secondary school and, then, tracking the further destinations of pupils. A relatively high proportion of children from the Indian subcontinent return home for extended periods and sometimes due to problems with tickets or the funds to be able to return, these extended periods can go on for up to three months and in extreme cases for six months. Whilst seeking to reinforce with parents and their community groups the importance of continuity of education – and in no way wishing to condone long-term absence – the school is considering the development of learning packs for these children while they are absent from school and also for accelerated learning on their return. The project will connect with other such initiatives throughout the United Kingdom as part of a research project led by King's College at the University of London.

A DESCRIPTION OF THE LIFE AND WORK OF THE SCHOOL

When we last visited the school the strong positive leadership by Heather, the head and her senior staff was identified as a key

Figure 3.1 Reception class numeracy lesson

strength, and nothing has changed in that regard. At that time the head had introduced the notion of two co-ordinators for each subject, working across key stages of the National Curriculum. This has become embedded in the school processes and has had a very powerful effect on standards through greater consistency of teaching and learning. Decisions are arrived at primarily through discussion and the headteacher continues to actively encourage initiative among all staff, teaching and non-teaching alike. It was evident from discussion with staff that the good atmosphere and spirit in the school is a result of strong commitment to shared aims and values. Relationships are characterised by enthusiasm, professional talk and leadership by example. It's quite clear that staff are inducted carefully into the school and their continued development is influenced by role-modelling. As before, the ethos and the behaviours within the school are very much 'caught, not taught'.

The school has no insurance for teacher absences, but, as the headteacher pointed out, 'staff are so professional', and no teacher absence was recorded in the past term despite the fact that this was one where flu and other forms of sickness were prevalent in the city. The headteacher's primary intention is to improve the educational attainment and wider achievements of the pupils by making this a school where people want to be and 'a school which is all about the children'. This is evident in relationships throughout the school. Passion in the school is all about the children: as the headteacher constantly reminded me, 'our children come first'. She senses that there is a feeling of missionary zeal but one which is very much grounded in common sense, practicality and good practice.

Children come from a wide variety of ethnic communities and mutual respect is evident. The school seeks to celebrate differences and to recognise the way in which those differences are special, but within a family atmosphere. Much of this was encapsulated in the assembly which I observed where the children entered quietly and chose where to sit, regardless of age, in a mixture of friendship and family groups. The way in which this then contributed to the children's participation and, in particular, the part which involved celebrating each other's achievements, birthdays and birthplaces, was remarkable.

The school clearly has high expectations of all of its pupils. The headteacher's consistent message both to pupils and staff is 'do your best, then do even better'. There is a clear and continuing focus on teaching and learning. The headteacher reviews the yearly plan and half-termly teacher plans for all teachers, and gives oral and written feedback. Staff have improved their capacity to identify the skills, knowledge and understanding which they are targeting in lessons and in their short-term plans for both classes and individual pupils. In the lessons I observed, the objectives were consistently reinforced through the introduction to the lesson, the direct teaching and the plenary sessions.

The head regards the national literacy and numeracy strategies as having played a significant role in improving the focus of teachers and in the targeting of children's learning programmes. In a school with a large percentage of children with English as a second or other language and at the early stages of English language acquisition, the Manchester Ethnic Minority Achievement Service was having a dramatic effect in moving pupils forward, in line with the strategies within the literacy hour. Nevertheless, the headteacher and staff were concerned that the necessary focus on literacy and numeracy was squeezing out foundation and arts within the curriculum, and a range of curriculum organisational approaches are being used to mediate this.

The procedures for identifying how pupils are progressing have developed considerably. There is a much greater emphasis on linking assessment to National Curriculum levels within Key Stage One and then in Year 6 and Year 7 for transition to the high school. The school uses Key Stage Two optional tests but is also looking at the pupils' key skills. The main area for development is a major focus on the individual child and the senior managers are working hand in hand with the Key Stage One co-ordinator to target this approach. As part of this strategy, teachers share in the moderation of pupils' work, with a particular push on Years 3 and 4. Pupils have increasingly been drawn into taking responsibility for their own learning with the setting of 'bite-size' pieces of work as targets. Year 5 and 6 pupils are well aware of what levels mean and work towards them, and this is exemplified in the dispays and notices on classroom walls. Overall, there is a lot more analysis of pupils' prior attainments and progress and this has been linked systematically at both key stages to 'booster' classes for those pupils who are likely to benefit.

On our last visit we commented on the high level of responsibility which pupils were encouraged to show and their participation in the life of the school. The picture is much as it was before and the headteacher reminded me that the children understand that their first responsibility is to be responsible themselves and then to be responsible for each other. The school is introducing 'buddy' and peer mentoring and this will play a significant role within the life of the school.

As one might expect in a school which has high expectations for pupils there is a wide range of rewards and incentives to encourage pupils to succeed. Despite the fact that Crowcroft Park has its share of pupils capable of very challenging behaviour, I saw very little evidence of the use of correction of inappropriate behaviours – basically because there was little need for it. On the other hand I did see a consistently high use of praise. Pupils were regularly praised in classes and non-class contexts for their behaviour.

PRESS FOR ACHIEVEMENT

Positive reinforcement for behaviour, improvement and excellence is evident through the use of certificates, stickers, weekly record cards and extra special certificates which are given out at assembly. This positive reinforcement is not only for individuals but extends to classes and teams within classes. Rewards for very focused intensive work with high-quality outcomes can result in rewards of blocks of time from five to ten minutes where pupils can choose the nature of the work of a lighter 'fun nature'. Although there are many formal means of rewarding and encouraging pupils and providing incentives, the most commonly observed were the hand on the shoulder and the word in the ear. During a conversation with the head she suddenly said, 'I've just thought of another catch-phrase – it's cool to be clever at Crowcroft Park'. I have no doubt that catch-phrase will have become part of the motivational culture within a week. But don't let that deceive you – this is no culture of slick spin and short-term measures. If my re-visit has proved anything, it is that all of the improvements have been hard-won on the back of consistent application of hard work, ingenuity and common sense, coupled with an openness to new ideas and ways of connecting with teachers, parents and children.

PARENTAL SUPPORT

In 1995 we noted that parents were very much involved in the life of the school and commented on a wide range of initiatives. We may have given the impression that was in some way easily won, but nothing could be further from the truth. The lives of parents and carers are clearly challenged by social and economic constraints and there is a high level of pupil mobility. In such circumstances, parental involvement is a continuous process – one of repeated re-engagement and a renewal of relationships. The parental project to which we referred last time has now taken root as 'Parent Partners', an approach which is central to the ethos of the school. This is immediately evident on entering the school. Three large notice-boards remind parents of the opportunities available to them through the parents' room, the toy library and the book shop, all of which they are encouraged to use. On these notice boards and through a termly newsletter they are given news and information in a variety of ways and in a range of community languages. The parents' room is used in partnership with the Manchester Adult Education Service to provide courses for parents and carers in English as a second or other language, in parenting – in conjunction with a neighbouring school – and a series of courses entitled 'Peaceful Children – Happy Families'.

When a child joins the school roll, parents are expected to sign a home–school agreement which sets out the reciprocal respon-sibilities of the school and of the parents and carers. This agreement encourages and supports rather than dictates. In the term before transition of children from the nursery to reception class, parents are encouraged to go into school to look at the baseline information for their child and to discuss individual learning targets for the transition period. They also discuss the part that they can play in supporting those targets alongside the work of the school. The total commitment to consultation with parents and their involvement in the life of the school has continued and deepened. Parents were fully consulted and involved in the drawing up of the home–school liaison agreement, in an audit of children's concerns about bullying and in a campaign for a dog-free zone in the park immediately adjoining the school – of which more shortly.

The fund-raising activities of parents of the school have continued unabated during a period in which the school eliminated its significant deficit. The 'Friends of Crowcroft Park' continue to raise money through a wide range of initiatives including coffee mornings, sponsored walks, spring fairs, and raffles. Parents' evenings continue to be well attended from the nursery right through to Year 6 with a high turnout in every case.

BEYOND THE FORMAL CURRICULUM

The range of extra-curricular activities has increased despite the difficult financial constraints. The wind and steel bands have grown with continuing support from the Manchester Music Service. I heard the choir rehearsing with their teacher, and the quality was outstanding. Since we last visited the school a computer club has started and an after-school games club has been developed. A football coach comes from a local professional club on Mondays to coach boys and girls, and all pupils in Years 5 and 6 have the opportunity of a weekend in the Lake District at the Manchester Outdoor Centre at Ghyll Head on the banks of Windermere. This rich experience for children – many of whom have had little experience outside of the city – used to take place for a full week and cover the full range of activities and curricular involvement. Unfortunately, budget constraints and the low income of many parents has meant that it is no longer possible to afford a full week and some are not even able to afford the weekend.

Crowcroft Park continues to encourage and allow the involvement of pupils in activities related to the needs of the community. My colleagues and I commented last time on an environmental project to brighten up an area at the back of a row of terrace houses adjacent to the school. Since then a group of parents complained about the amount of dog dirt in the park immediately adjacent to the school. As a result of this, the City Leisure Department suggested a working group of pupils should generate a range of ideas. This resulted in a design for a specially fenced area of park, with railings and seats and some landscaping established as a dog-free zone for the use of local residents. This is now an integral part of the local SRB urban initiative and a testimony to the continuing commitment of the school to the community which it serves.

SCHOOL POLICY – ASPECTS OF SCHOOL POLICY ON DEVELOPMENTAL PLANNING

The foundation of school improvement planning on collegiality continues to be a comprehensive and effective process. The quality of the planning has improved with respect to target-setting, identification of responsibility and accountability, and the short-, medium- and long-term planning is reinforced and reviewed at regular intervals. The OfSTED Inspection Report's key issues have been integrated into a school improvement plan which also takes account of Standards Fund and other external resources. This gives a real sense of a coherent strategy rather than a series of fragmented initiatives. This is reinforced by the process of school management. Five years ago we reported that the key component of the success of the school was the very clear and firm leadership of the headteacher. This is not simply a centralist form of leadership but a finely balanced mix of shared responsibility, individual accountability and autonomy, linked to well-understood leadership roles within the matrix of teams across the key stages.

STAFF DEVELOPMENT

In 1996 the school was awarded Investors in People status and was successfully reassessed and re-recognised in August 1999. The headteacher believes that the benefits to the school have been the development of a genuinely whole school-staff development perspective which is now more inclusive of part-time and non-teaching staff. Staff development is driven by the School Improvement Plan and national priorities, as well as by an audit of the school's needs and individual needs for continuing professional development. If the school was previously a learning community it is evident that it is now even more committed to a continuous process of individual and corporate learning.

TEACHING METHODS

The past five years have seen the introduction of the National Literacy Hour and the National Numeracy Hour and their associated national strategies as well as other revisions to the National Curriculum. The teachers' view is that the teaching methods across the school are now more directly whole-class and subject-focused. Despite some of the reservations of an essentially innovative and creative staff when these national approaches were first proposed, staff now recognise the benefits that have come with the prescriptions. They have also analysed actual outcomes and wider implications for the curriculum. They have had the courage to broaden and deepen their pedagogy in ways which extend their own repertoire and meet the particular needs of their pupils.

Shortly after our previous visit the school began the trial setting of pupils for core subjects but ceased that practice in order to get the literacy hour and the numeracy hour securely in place. They have spent a lot of time analysing the English, maths, science and PE curriculum and assessment policies alongside the implications of the literacy and numeracy hours on the wider curriculum. There was a corporate view that history, geography, arts and to an extent technology, were left highly vulnerable, and so blocks of time have been identified to ensure that they are protected. The Year 5 class has been introduced to French for one term in conjunction with the local high school which is a language specialist college. Fifteen multimedia PCs, three of which have been leased, now support the development of ICT (information communication technology) across the school through a specialist suite, and they complement the PCs available within each classroom. The suite is a new development for Crowcroft Park and, although enthusiastically used both in and out of class time, is challenging for teachers with classes of 32 pupils.

A lot of importance continues to be placed on the role of music as an extra-curricular subject through the wind band, the steel band and the choir. However, the school wishes that it could devote more time to music within the mainstream teaching time. In reality, the need to raise attainment in the core subjects from a baseline of low prior attainment means that the school has had to be both structured and inventive about the way it provides a broad curriculum. The head is still uncertain about some of the consequences. One teacher has piloted a whole week on design and technology with her class in order that they experience a continuous learning experience in that subject area. The school is still assessing whether or not the gains in the high quality of work achieved outweigh any implications of a long gap between this and the next major technology curriculum experience.

The headteacher and staff recognise that ICT has a crucial role to play in supporting teaching and learning. Therefore a great deal is being invested in the use of ICT within the school. A joint partnership, which includes the local college for a day a week, is enabling ten parents at a time to undertake the European Computer Driving Licence (ECDL). All staff have also signed up. Distance learning packages have been developed to support the project beyond the taught time. I believe that Crowcroft Park is the first school in Manchester to have all of its staff, teachers and nursery nurses spending four hours a week working towards the ECDL. The headteacher would like as many parents as possible to be able to develop ICT skills through such training, which is currently free for all unwaged parents and carers.

LEARNING SUPPORT

There are now more people directly involved in support of learning within the school. The Manchester Ethnic Minority Achievement Service provides 0.5 of a full-time nursery-nurse post and a 0.5 teacher who target intensive support to qualifying pupils. The Manchester Service for Inclusive Learning provides for half of the week a nursery nurse who has been targeting intensive support for pupils at stages 2 and 3 of the Code of Practice for Special Educational Needs. After only half a term this support has had quite dramatic results in terms of improvements for individual pupils with significant language difficulties. The support has included assessment of pupils, help with the writing of individual education plans, the development of work programmes and the setting of targets. Not only has this helped pupils, it has also influenced the way in which teaching staff approach assessment, moderation and target-setting.

The school also has two parents who have been trained to provide additional literacy support, between them for a total of three days a week. These parents have now completed a two-year part-time classroom assistant's course and are to be employed full-time by the school in September. This is yet another example of Crowcroft Park as a partnership learning community.

SPECIAL NEEDS

The school does not show as high a percentage of pupils with special educational needs as one might expect, partly because it makes every effort to provide significant support without having to stereotype pupils as requiring support at stages 2 and 3 of the Code of Practice. There are therefore considerably more pupils at stage 1 of the Code of Practice. The school's special educational needs co-ordinator carries out a rigorous analysis of need supported by the attached education psychologist who works primarily at stages 2 and 3 of the

Code of Practice, and of course on Statementing. The co-ordinator is also supported by a learning support assistant. A rigorous analysis of need is carried out and individual education plans are developed by the educational psychologist with the relevant classroom teacher, which focus as far as possible on in-class support. The primary thrust for special educational needs support is to reduce the number of pupils moving from stages 1 and 2 to stage 3 and beyond, through the early provision of intensive support. The two statemented pupils at the school receive additional support for half a week.

The school feels that the amount and quality of additional support provided has improved considerably since our last visit and there was evidence as I went around the classrooms that this was indeed the case. One group of Year 1 pupils with English as an additional language worked with the support teacher outside the classroom during the group work phase. She then came back into the class at the relevant point within the literacy hour so that their accelerated learning, particularly around difficult phonemes, could be applied within the context of the mainstream lesson. The use of mini-whiteboards – shades of 'return of the slate' – enabled the teacher to see quickly which pupils had managed to grasp particular phonemes and which were still struggling with them. This made assessment much easier and faster and teacher responsiveness much more effective.

COMMUNITY AND BUSINESS LINKS

Partly as a result of the Single Regeneration Budget, but mainly because the school has placed more emphasis on this work, there are more links with the business community. The headteacher is a director of the Progress Trust which links development for ethnic minority communities with urban regeneration. Links have been developed with Siemens in relation to ICT. Work with an artist in residence led to pupil involvement in the design and creation of murals for a subway under the main Stockport Road which passes by the back of the school. Pupils now have access to an after-school club on the school premises. Year 4 pupils are engaged in a link with a school in Italy through the Comenius European Fund. The school has developed a Commonwealth Games link with pen pals in two countries. The school continues to play a leading partnership role in the cluster of schools within its district of the city.

PREPARING FOR THE WORLD OF WORK

Motivating pupils for the world of work continues to be a difficult role for the school, given the high level of unemployment in the catchment area and the relative lack of sufficient role models within the community itself. The Year 6 class have carried out a survey of workers within the school, but this is one area which the school regards as a developmental need and so it will embark on a project with the Manchester Education Business Partnership in the next academic year.

EDUCATIONAL TECHNOLOGY AND OTHER INNOVATION

Apart from the computers which are networked into a single suite, there is at least one stand-alone computer in each class and several multimedia computers for design and development work within the school. Mini-whiteboards have also been bought for numeracy and literacy work. By developing the ICT skills of all of its staff and as many parents as possible, the school intends to be well placed to take advantage of the potential represented by the City Technology College developments within Manchester's Excellence in Cities programme and broadband connectivity.

SCHOOL POLICY TOWARDS TRUANCY AND BULLYING

On the whole, parents do not see bullying as an issue within the school and this is a reflection of the ethos and sense of community which the school has nurtured. Rather, they see it as something which their children might meet within the wider community. As a result, school policy has grown out of its parental involvement policy – in place five years ago – and which has been sustained as a living policy in practice. Every term there is a specific focus on bullying with an anti-bullying week held annually. This year a theatre group gave a performance of *Bullies' Paradise*.

There has been one permanent exclusion from the school during the past nine years and on that occasion it was a pupil with severe behavioural difficulties supported by a special needs Statement. Last year there were a small number of fixed-term exclusions of boys in Year 6 all of whom had first come to the school in their final years of primary education and took some time to adapt to the culture of the school. Given the high level of pupil mobility, with over 30 per cent moving in or out of the school within a given year, this is a testimony to the calm and consistent way in which the school's policy on behaviour and bullying is implemented.

The school successfully applied for help in setting up 'buddy' and peer mentoring through the LEA's Social Inclusion priority within its Education Development Plan. Now that the Excellence in Cities initiative, introduced to high schools in September 1999, is being rolled out to primary schools, this will move forward because the school has been identified as one of the first cohort of schools to be involved. It was selected because it ranked high on a needs-led basis but also because of its ability to work effectively with other schools.

WIDER SUPPORT SYSTEMS

As we noted last time, the school is a self-managing school, despite the considerable challenges which it faces. Thus, it has not been subject to any external intervention. Because many of its pupils start with a low prior attainment, it has attracted additional financial support from the LEA. The school has also received national grant-aid for its numeracy strategy and was in the last cohort of schools inducted into the literacy strategy through the LEA's programme of support. The Manchester LEA Adult Education Services Classroom Assistant Course for Parents has been opened up to other schools on the Crowcroft Park campus, and two of the parents who have gone through this are now employed within the school. Over the past four years it has had an artist in residence from one of the local colleges. This led to a group of 24 college students being paired with pupils working on exercises around artefacts, and to a series of designs for murals which have now been completed and attached to walls in the playground area.

ACCOUNTABILITY IN THE SCHOOL

In the past five years, the school has had to contend with a major budget deficit. This required a significant reduction in spending and the non-replacement of a teacher who had left the school. The LEA provided a three-year loan of £6000 per year as a small support for the school but it was necessary for the headteacher and governing body to set out clear spending parameters and involve everyone as part of the solution. This team effort resulted in the deficit having been eliminated by April 2000. The head emphasised the importance of the school bursar, whose attention to detail, understanding of the budget and close monitoring and support were vital. The impact of the long-standing deficit and the measures needed to eliminate it should not be underestimated, but the staff co-operated with wry humour. Top of the staff wish-list on the 1st of April was the plea 'Can we get the windows cleaned now?!'.

IMPACT OF PUBLIC REPORTING

Positive and honest reporting has always characterised the school over the last fifteen years and the OfSTED report was shared in the same manner as the headteacher's annual report. The headteacher's reports to the governing body are thorough, honest and comprehensive. They are prepared in a way which makes them genuinely accessible to all members of the governing body, to parents and to non-teaching staff, and the presentation of the school's performance data in relation to its targets is a starting point for analysing the implications for under-achieving groups of pupils and individual pupils and the teaching and learning approaches within the school.

SCHOOL SELF-REVIEW

Probably because this is an effectively managed school, the headteacher has welcomed the annual visit by the Senior School Improvement Officer from the LEA to discuss the school's target-setting process. The process through which the school goes is exceptionally thorough, honest and rigorous, using its own data from teacher assessment and optional and compulsory external tests, as well as the benchmark data provided by the national PANDA (Performance and Assessment) and the LEA's own benchmark tables.

The headteacher herself monitors literacy and numeracy in every class and provides individual feedback to teachers. This is in addition to regular review of curriculum planning and lesson planning. She has also attended the national and LEA training for school self-evaluation and has embedded best practice into the systems within the school. None of this is seen by the teachers as threatening, but as part of their continuous professional development. How far this is likely to be affected by PRP (performance-related pay) processes remains to be seen. Current indications are that this will not change the ongoing developmental approach within the school.

THE EFFECT OF THE INSPECTION SYSTEM

The school received a year's notice of its most recent OfSTED inspection. This was a long build-up and although the school and the headteacher prepared well, the staff nevertheless became very anxious, and they are still anxious about the next inspection because of the stress that was involved then. The OfSTED team were considered to have been professional in the way in which they carried out their job. However, the unanimous view was that inspection did not contribute significantly, 'if at all', to improvement within the school. My slight caveat to this is that the inspection did identify science as an area for improvement and the school has since raised standards considerably. But, as OfSTED frequently points out, cause and effect are not often easy to establish. Understandably, the headteacher is hoping for a short inspection next time round, in common with those schools who can demonstrate good 'added value' even though they have relatively low baseline attainment compared with the national picture.

The headteacher is concerned that in determining a full re-inspection, and in the judgements about under-performance, OfSTED does not give enough weight to 'added value': the progress pupils make, as opposed to raw scores. The school feels that if this continues, the credibility of the whole inspection process is called into question. The seed of hope lies in the plans to establish some form of added value analysis by 2002. The school is insistent that this would not deflect them from striving to raise standards faster and higher.

GOVERNORS

The governing body is wholly supportive of the leadership and management in the school and is supported by an ex-headteacher who clerks for the governing body. All of the governing body committees work well and play a supportive 'critical friend' role for the headteacher and the school. Governors attend training courses and events provided by the local education authority. It has become normal for teachers to be invited to make brief reports and presentations on areas of work for which they have been responsible to the governing body. This works exceptionally well and enables the teachers to feel valued and the governing body to develop a deeper understanding of issues and processes within the school.

OTHER SCHOOLS AND THE LEA

We reported last time that the headteacher was a respected member of the local cluster of schools. This role has developed much further with the development of Primary Local Area Networks of primary schools across the city and the representative Primary Liaison Group which meets on their behalf termly with the Chief Education Officer, Deputy Chief Education Officer and heads of key services. The head continues to help plan headteacher conferences involving external speakers and workshops provided by the Manchester School Improvement Service. She is also a member of the LEA's Asset Management Plan Steering Group, and the SEN Criteria Moderation Group. She has been influential in development of the Local Resource Management scheme within the LEA and continues to be involved in significant developments in the teaching of reading.

The LEA has asked her to act as an Associate School Improvement Headteacher for an interim period in another primary school which has been in Special Measures for some time. This is yet another indication of the external recognition of her skills in leadership and management and it shows that her school is sufficiently secure and self-managing to be able to continue its improvement without her constant presence.

In terms of the impact of central government policies, the headteacher stressed that she fully understood the importance of the emphasis on 'Education, Education, Education' but that there had been too much change too fast. She believed that the DfEE was beginning to listen but that the Secretary of State's recognition of the beleaguerment of primary schools has not yet been translated into any reduction in the bureaucratic burden; in fact, in her experience, it had worsened. She and the staff were appreciative of the significant additional funding coming through the Standards Fund with more flexibility to use it in ways which better match the aims of her school improvement plan.

KEY LEVERS FOR SCHOOL IMPROVEMENT

Two years after our first visit to Crowcroft Park the school received its first inspection. The OfSTED report confirmed our view that this was a good, efficient and effective school. It highlighted the progress made by pupils, the quality of teaching (100 per cent satisfactory or better with 50 per cent good and 13 per cent very good), the support of the governing body, and above all the excellent leadership and management of the headteacher and her senior management team.

At that time of the OfSTED inspection there was still no national comparative basis applied to the performance of 'similar schools'. The 1999 DfEE 'PANDA' analysis, however, gave the school straight 'A's for its performance in all of the core subjects – English, mathematics and science – in the SATs results for that year. In their own words, 'pupils' performance in all core subjects was well above average in comparison with similar schools'. The definition of similar schools in this context is based on free-school-meals national benchmarks using average National Curriculum points scores.

Whilst the percentage of pupils known to be eligible for free school meals has the highest correlation with pupils' attainment of any of the indicators there are other significant factors including, most significantly, the level of pupil transience. On average, over a third of the pupils who take the tests at the end of Key Stage Two have arrived in the school within that key stage and have tended to have low prior attainment on arrival. This often helps to explain the variability in performance from year to year and suggests that the value added by the school is significantly greater than a comparison of a cohort's Key Stage One and Key Stage Two results might suggest.

In the past five years there have been significant changes in the pupils' prior attainment at Crowcroft Park. While the level of free school meals has remained broadly constant, the percentage of pupils on stages A & B of the measurement of SELA – Stage of English Language Acquisition – has risen dramatically from 6.4 per cent of the pupil cohort to 21.1 per cent. This means that a significantly higher proportion of pupils from minority ethnic communities for whom English is an additional language, join the school with minimal prior attainment in English. There has also been a marked increase in the percentage of pupils scoring at the lowest levels against the baseline assessment on entry to the reception class.

Against this context the school has achieved an overall improvement in the results at the end of Key Stage Two, fluctuating with the prior attainment profile of each cohort. Compared with the 1996 results the level 4 SATs results for summer 2000 were 23 per cent higher in English, 28 per cent higher for mathematics and 42 per cent higher for science. For the first two years the Key Stage One results held up, but the impact of the falling baseline on entry saw a slight fall in the three-year average, though this has been reversed this year with a good set of results.

Crowcroft Park is therefore a classic example of a school which has been identified both by OfSTED inspection and by a statistical analysis of its standardised test results as a good and effective school, a school which performs very well when compared with schools facing similar challenges, a school where the notion of 'continuous improvement' takes account of the shifting pupil population and of constantly changing baselines. Only a value added approach can provide a fair and just assessment of the performance of such a school.

The evidence is that there has been steady improvement at Crowcroft Park against a fluctuating and falling baseline and, until recently, a serious budget deficit – not of the school's making. The factors behind this improvement remain those which we identified five years ago – they have simply been stepped up a gear in response to the increased challenge. The clear vision, direction and determination of the headteacher coupled with good support from the governing body provide the necessary leadership. Heather continues to 'walk the talk', modelling her expectations for teachers and staff alike as she moves around the school. There is another ingredient here which often characterises good leadership – opportunism. She has always been quick to recognise and seize opportunities, and where they don't appear to exist, to create them.

Management has always been strong at Crowcroft Park but it has been strengthened through the continuous development of the deputy head and the key stage co-ordinators, now extended to include a Foundation Stage co-ordinator.

The scrupulous appointment of teaching and non-teaching staff and their careful deployment against pupil needs and staff strengths has paid off handsomely in the standards across the school and in the quality of teaching and support recognised by the OfSTED inspection.

The pro-active approach to partnership with parents, community groups, local regeneration initiatives, neighbouring schools and the LEA has ensured a continuous renewal of ideas and resources for development and self-evaluation.

Collegiality was a strength five years ago and this is becoming even more evident now as the school develops its 'learning community' approach with the assistance of the National Grid for Learning and its inclusion in the first phase of the Manchester Excellence in Cities extension to primary schools.

Above all, the school has intensified its focus on the individual child through the loop of assessment, curricular targets and teaching, without losing its strong community ethos and reinforcement of respect for and service to others.

As we affirmed last time, there is no magic recipe at Crowcroft Park. A clear and unwavering vision, exceptional leadership and management, collegiality and shared sense of purpose, openness to partnership, a belief that all children can succeed, and that high-quality teaching can make that difference. These should be the aim of any school, however challenged. In common with many schools in Manchester the odds will continue to be stacked until underlying economic and social conditions, now being tackled, are improved.

Not surprisingly, those schools which fail to achieve this mix make the headlines, as do those which more effortlessly top the national tables. The many schools which are quietly succeeding to add significantly to the life chances of their pupils need to be recognised and praised. When you see the ingredients coming together in the way that they do in this school, it *is* magic!

4

FAIR FURLONG PRIMARY SCHOOL
City of Bristol
Agnes McMahon

INTRODUCTION

Re-visiting Fair Furlong school after a five-year period has been a powerful learning experience. A great deal has happened in the intervening years; the school has gone through some difficult times. Much has changed but there is also much that is familiar. Changes have taken place at national and local levels and in the school itself. Changes in education policy at national level are well documented and it is noteworthy that when the original case study was conducted, the school had not yet been inspected by OfSTED, SAT results at Key Stages One and Two were not published and the literacy and numeracy strategies had not yet been introduced. Much more data about school performance and pupil achievement is now available to teachers and the wider community. The major change at local level has been the dissolution of Avon LEA and its replacement by four unitary authorities. Fair Furlong school is now in the City of Bristol authority, and, as might be expected, the establishment of the unitary authority led to some changes in personnel and in the education policy framework. For example, the LEA adviser who now has responsibility for the school was not in this post five years ago.

Information about the developments in the school over the past five years was collected through interviews with three of the four

Table 4.1 Fair Furlong Primary School, City of Bristol

	1995–96	1999–2000
Headteacher	Mary Gray (apptd 1990)	Peter Overton (apptd 2000)
Number of pupils	358	345
% white pupils	98.9 (1996–97)	99.3 *English average: 86.0 (1)*
% pupils for whom English is an additional language	0	0
% pupils entitled to free school meals (FSM)	44.7	41.4 (1) *English average: 18.9 (1)*
% pupils with special educational needs, incl. those with Statements	36.3 *English average: 17.2*	41.1 (1) *English average: 20.8 (1)*
Pupil/teacher ratio, incl. head and nursery classes	21.4 *English average: 23.2*	25.3 (1) *English average: 23.3 (1)*
Support staff per teacher (2)	14.2	20.4 (1)
Key Stage Two: level 4+ in core subjects: total score (3)	65 *English average: 107.1*	79 (1) *English average: 215.8 (1)*

Key:
(1) 1998–99
(2) Full-time equivalent (f.t.e.) support staff hours per week, per f.t.e. teacher
(3) 300% = maximum score for Standard Assessment Tasks (SATs) maths, English and science combined

headteachers who have been in post during this time; with a senior member of staff in the LEA; with nine teachers, learning support assistants and school governors, seven of whom were in post when the original case study was produced and with a teacher who had worked at the school over the five-year period but who left in December 1999.

Since the first case study was conducted the school has experienced problems and has not been able to sustain the momentum for improved teaching and learning that was evident at that time, although it is now recognised to be on track again and making progress. Why did the school experience these setbacks? The outline of the story is quickly told: Mary Gray, the headteacher who was in post when the first case study was conducted, retired in the summer of 1996. The headteacher who took over the school was not successful in this context and resigned at the end of the 1999 spring term. An acting headteacher was appointed in the Easter holiday but he resigned after less than three weeks in post, at which point the LEA brought in an experienced headteacher from a neighbouring school to take over the leadership of the school. He was in post for two terms until the current headteacher, Peter Overton, took up his appointment in January 2000. This series of events led to a situation which was described by the OfSTED team who inspected the school in March 2000 as: 'a period of considerable instability caused by difficulties in the leadership and management' (OfSTED, 2000). Standards of pupil achievement declined during the period of instability, although they have now begun to rise again and SAT scores in summer 2000 were an improvement on the previous year. The OfSTED inspectors concluded that: 'although the school is now making steady improvement, it is not yet an effective school'. They recognised that the newly appointed headteacher had a clear view for the development of the school and was already making considerable improvements and stated that: 'the school now has a good capacity to improve' (OfSTED, 2000). Nevertheless, the school has been judged to have serious weaknesses in the quality of provision and much will have to be done to raise achievement.

How has this situation arisen, when five years ago the school seemed poised to make significant gains in teaching and learning? Many of the teachers and governors who were working in the school at that time are still in post, the community is reasonably stable and there have been no significant changes in the catchment area or in the type of children entering the school. There is no simple answer, rather a combination of factors appearing to have resulted in the school's losing momentum; issues about the pace of change and the management of change have been especially significant. Sustaining improvement and growth is a challenging task in any school; perhaps it is especially challenging in an area of social deprivation.

THE SCHOOL COMMUNITY

The area in which the school is situated remains one of social deprivation and many families still have to struggle with hardship and poverty. Withywood is in the 16 per cent most disadvantaged wards in England (1998 Index of Local Deprivation). A 1998 study conducted by the University of the West of England noted continuing poverty, ill health, educational underachievement, long-term unemployment, housing need, crime and drug misuse as problems in the area. Many of the difficulties that the community faced five years ago have not been overcome. The area remains removed from the city's growth areas and road access to the city centre and the motorways is poor, there are no large employers in the area and there is very little inward investment. Approximately 42 per cent of the families in the neighbourhood are in receipt of means-tested council tax benefits (Bristol City Council, Department of the Environment, Transport and Leisure, 1999). Shopping facilities remain poor. There are no banks or building societies in the area and no major supermarket; it is not easy to purchase fresh fruit and vegetables. Car ownership is low and there is heavy reliance on public transport. A significant number of families with dependent children are headed by a young single parent. Educational achievement in the area as a whole is low compared to the rest of the city: the two secondary schools have an average of 18.5 per cent of pupils achieving 5 GCSEs at grades A–C; the average percentage of pupils attending schools in the area and achieving level 4 at Key Stage Two is 40 per cent (Bristol City Council Education Service, 1999); 13.7 per cent of pupils leaving the two secondary schools do not go on to further education (Learning Partnership West, 1999); and only 1.9 per cent of residents in the area have higher education qualifications (1991, census data). The 1999 bid submitted by the City Council for Single Regeneration Funding for this area of Bristol argued that it reflected the problems of social exclusion:

- underemployment and low skill, particularly among youth;
- lack of employment opportunities, and access to facilities and training;
- particular issues of drug abuse and criminality;
- the attitude to ethnic minorities. (Black and mixed-race families form a relatively small, but growing proportion of the local population.)

However, there are signs that things are beginning to improve. One very obvious indicator is that several of the tower blocks of flats have been demolished and replaced by low-rise housing, and some of the existing housing stock is being refurbished. The Council's policy is not to house families with young children in the remaining tower blocks. Levels of unemployment in the area have reduced, although many people still travel to work in other parts of Bristol rather than finding jobs locally. A number of people suggested that the area is becoming more settled, families are choosing to stay in the locality, and there are some signs of a market building up in owner-occupied housing. A bid for funding for the area from the Department of Education and Employment's Sure Start scheme for the under-4s was successful and the project began in December 1999. The government's aim for the scheme is that it should work with parents and children to promote the physical, intellectual and social development of pre-school children, particularly those who are disadvantaged, to ensure they are ready to thrive when they get to school. The mission statement for the Bristol scheme, which includes Fair Furlong's catchment area, is: 'A confident community with confident parents giving children a sure start in life'. The project aims to link existing agencies working with children aged 0–4 and is putting initiatives in place to support families (e.g. extra health visitors, parentcraft classes, extra play centres, Book Start programme, co-ordination of childcare provision).

A 1999 bid submitted for funding for the Hartcliffe Withywood area from the Single Regeneration Budget Round 5 (SRB5) was also successful. The project has been granted £12.5 million over 7 years and has already started work on a number of initiatives to improve life in the neighbourhood (e.g. housing improvement programmes, community safety issues, health issues, play schemes). One aspect focuses upon education and the desire to build a learning community; the stated aim being 'to raise levels of achievement and aspiration amongst all children, young people and adults, create a community of lifelong learners and enable progression into employment and training'. The projects and initiatives started under the Sure Start Scheme and SRB5 are in their very early stages and it is too early to judge if their ambitious goals will be met. However, one very positive feature is that members of the local community were consulted and involved in preparing the bids and now share in the decision-making about what should be done. The stated aim of the SRB5 funding bid is to develop a strong local partnership which will reduce poverty and exclusion in the community (Hartcliffe and Withywood Community Partnership, 1999).

WHAT IS THE SCHOOL LIKE NOW?

Many features of the school are little changed since 1994. Fair Furlong is a large mixed primary school with a nursery class, taking children from ages 3 to 11. In July 2000 there were 345 pupils on roll including 41 in the nursery, a reduction on the 1994 figure of 382. This drop in numbers is partly due to a number of pupils being withdrawn from the school but also to a reduction in the number of school-age children in the community. The majority of the pupils are white (99 per cent) and there are no pupils for whom English is an additional language, a pattern that has not changed over the five years; 41 per cent of the pupils are entitled to free school meals, a reduction on the 1994 figure of 49 per cent. Eleven pupils have Statements (an increase on the number five years ago) and a total of 41 per cent of the pupils have been judged to have special educational needs (1998/99). The OfSTED report on the school noted that the number of pupils with special educational needs was above average, and that 'children start school with well below average skills in all the areas of learning, and that language and literacy skills are particularly poorly developed' (OfSTED, 2000: 13). The attendance rate at the school dropped over the past few years to a low of 88.5 per cent in 1998/99, though it is now improving again.

The school remains predominantly a female environment. With the exception of the male headteacher, all the staff who work in the school are women, a not uncommon pattern in primary schools. The general appearance of the school in the summer term of 2000 was very good. The headteacher in post five years ago had placed a high priority on making the building a good environment for teaching and learning and this appears to have been maintained. The corridors and classrooms are brightly painted with interesting displays of pupils' work, the classrooms seem well resourced, one classroom is now a dedicated information technology suite with fifteen computers for pupils' use. The hedge around the school boundary that was first planted by pupils, parents and teachers in the 1995/96 school year has now grown and most of it is thriving. The most obvious difference is that security measures around the school have been increased. The school had suffered from vandalism, broken windows and theft of equipment for many years and this became worse during the period of instability. In 1999, at the instigation of the acting headteacher, the LEA installed high steel railings around the front of the school and a fence was placed around the whole school perimeter. The school grounds back on to a large playing field belonging to the neighbouring secondary school. Pupils from the secondary school had used an open walkway alongside the primary school to reach their school and this could be a disruptive element in the primary playground, but this area has now all been securely fenced.

> I'm a bit of a railings man . . . I think that we should make a statement, this land belongs to the school and the children, keep out. I'm a community man, I want it used but monitored . . . otherwise the youth in the area abuse it.
>
> (Acting head)

This increased level of security has reduced the incidence of vandalism experienced by the school.

Visiting the school in the summer term of 2000 was an enjoyable experience. The pupils were friendly and well behaved as they moved around the school and in the playground. The atmosphere during class time was calm and purposeful. The OfSTED inspectors had noted that pupils' attitude to learning and their personal development and relationships were satisfactory throughout the school and that their behaviour was good (OfSTED, 2000). The parents were always very supportive of the school and this support has been maintained.

> We had a parents' evening last night and so many parents were so supportive and happy about the way their children were happy

to come to school and confident and had made progress – there was a much better turn out this year than last year.

(Class teacher)

Figure 4.1 Doing our best

WHAT PROBLEMS OCCURRED IN THE SCHOOL?

The headteacher who was appointed in 1996 was an experienced teacher and a successful headteacher. She had worked in a number of different schools and, prior to taking up her second headship in Fair Furlong, she had been head of a multi-ethnic school in a city in the south-east of England. A stranger to Bristol before her appointment, she had wanted to work in a larger school and a school that had challenge. She saw her priority task in Fair Furlong being to develop the curriculum: 'I gathered from the interview and from the previous head that I was there to develop the curriculum . . . standards were low and I was appointed to take that forward'.

Unfortunately, because of the difficulties that arose in the school, progress on curriculum development was slow. What caused these difficulties? There is no simple explanation – rather a combination of factors seemed to lead to the school going into a downward spiral. All the teachers, learning support assistants and governors who were interviewed in the summer term of 2000 had worked in the school before the appointment of the current head; six of them had been interviewed for the original case study. The two issues consistently cited as contributing to the difficulties in the school were: a decline in the standard of pupil behaviour and problems in communication which had led to a breakdown in relationships between the headteacher and the senior management team. The headteacher's account of the situation would support this analysis but opinions differ about where responsibility for this lay.

The management of pupil behaviour

One of the major problems in the school, reported by all those interviewed, was that over a two-year period there was a serious deterioration in pupil behaviour which contributed to a decline in teaching and learning. Five years ago the school had a clear behaviour policy in place which was based on assertive discipline.

Indeed, a similar policy had been adopted by all the schools in the local cluster. In Fair Furlong a key rule for everyone was: 'Everyone will act with courtesy and consideration to others at all times'. This was elaborated in seven supporting statements. The behaviour policy had been developed collaboratively by the staff and was linked to a system of rewards and sanctions which were clearly understood by pupils and staff and were applied consistently. Children who misbehaved had their names written on the board during the lesson and sanctions (e.g. some loss of play time) were applied. The headteacher appointed in 1996 changed this policy in her first year in the school. She was unfamiliar with assertive discipline and became increasingly uncomfortable with it.

> When I first went there . . . the first assembly I took, children were stood up in assembly, my abiding memory on the first day was this young person was stood up in assembly because she was talking and the humiliation that child felt . . . the assertive discipline policy was underpinned with the public humiliation of children and I felt deeply uncomfortable about that and it was something I couldn't work with.
>
> (Headteacher)

The head ended the practice of making children stand up if they misbehaved in assembly and, over the next twelve months, engaged in discussion with LEA personnel and the staff about how the behaviour management policy might be modified. In September 1997 staff were asked to stop putting children's names on the board with a cross beside them to indicate misbehaviour and to work with colleagues in their key stage team to develop alternative sanctions. Children were to be informed of this change in policy by their class teachers. The head wanted the children to take more ownership of their own behaviour and wanted staff to take more responsibility for the management of pupil behaviour in their classrooms rather than passing problems to another member of staff to handle, though she recognised that some teachers found this difficult. Several staff reported that the head wanted to move to a system which placed greater emphasis on self-discipline, negotiation and peer mediation, but their perception was that, although the school rules were unchanged, the sanctions had been removed. The changes were not fully supported by the staff, implementation faltered and pupil behaviour began to deteriorate.

> Well, the biggest change was that we had what was called an assertive discipline policy, with a lot of praise and a lot of positive reinforcement, but also strict boundaries and classroom rules and school rules. The children knew what the consequences were because it was written up and everyone was doing the same thing. It was smiley faces and sad faces – the change that was made was that the sad face was taken away because that was felt not good for the children but nothing else was put in its place . . . we were still giving positive reinforcement as much as we could but children didn't have the security of boundaries, they didn't know where the boundaries were and they were pushing all the time and going further and further and pushing staff . . . the sanctions were no longer clear to us, let alone the children and that's where it broke down and I think the children sensed that we weren't sure and it just went into a downward spiral and it was very difficult to get back at that time.
>
> (Class teacher)

> The new policy, it was a softly, softly, let's all be reasonable about this, policy, which might work if you started it with children in the nursery and grew it with them but you couldn't bring it in here, wham, with the children we have, because they are far too clever and play the game, and we lost every time. Even the good ones became awkward.
>
> (Learning support assistant)

> . . . in two or three years [assertive discipline] had reached a stage where it needed reviewing . . . in the short term it had a very good effect, you could change the behaviour of the children but at the end of the day various people had real concerns that the children didn't own their behaviour, so there was nothing about the children being independent and making choices and that was an issue.
>
> (Teacher who used to work in the school)

The LEA placed a special needs support teacher in the school for one day a week, but, despite this additional help, the standard of pupil behaviour continued to decline for the next couple of years and this led to other problems, not least with teaching and learning: 'the behaviour in the classroom was so bad that you couldn't get on with the teaching' (Class teacher).

Staff morale also declined: 'there was a lot of staff illness in the year before the head left, and people felt very low and depressed, and not feeling valued or achieving' (Class teacher).

Communication

Problems of communication between the head and the senior management team (SMT) appear to have developed during the first year. In 1996 the new headteacher inherited the existing senior management team whose members had worked closely with the outgoing head. She said that she became aware that her management style was very different. Whereas the previous head had very clear ideas about what she wanted to achieve and was ready to lead from the front, feeding in ideas for discussion, she aimed for a collegial approach in which 'people take areas of responsibility and some global responsibility for what is going on and it is a discussion in which I take a lead but people take responsibility within that'. In the event, after discussion with the LEA and the chair of governors, the head decided to restructure the SMT. One change was to include the special educational needs co-ordinator

(SENCO), who replaced one of the existing members. This caused a degree of bad feeling, and communication with the staff became more difficult. On another occasion, staff sought union advice on a particular staffing issue and a meeting was held with a national union representative. The head was present at this meeting and said that the experience had been 'amazingly damaging for everyone and for me'. As pupil behaviour continued to deteriorate the head decided to advertise a senior post and seek applications from the staff; this resulted in a member of staff, not at that point a member of the SMT, being appointed as behaviour manager. This teacher supported the head's approach to behaviour management which they tried to implement without the full backing of the staff. Whereas this decision had been a good one for the head – 'I felt I had some support – up till then I felt really isolated' – the communication problems with other members of staff continued. Over the next year, relationships with senior staff continued to decline and fewer SMT meetings were held, although staff meetings were maintained. It appears that the management group effectively became the head, deputy and behaviour manager. The downward spiral in the school was difficult to reverse: because the management of pupil behaviour became a key issue for all the staff, less attention was paid to curriculum innovation and developing teaching and learning strategies; as communication between the head and some of her staff deteriorated, there was less discussion about school policy and less staff ownership of changes that were introduced.

> The SMT virtually broke down because we couldn't get across to her what we felt was happening, we didn't feel she was listening to us.
>
> (Member of SMT)

> There was a lack of people pulling together, things not being seen through, a lot of negative feeling and people reacted in a way that wasn't good for the children.
>
> (Class teacher)

> . . . she had very clear ideas about how she wanted things done and she had a habit of scrapping something and putting something else in place almost immediately without discussion or scrapping something and then never quite getting round to replacing it.
>
> (Class teacher)

At a midpoint in the headship, the SMT members raised their concerns about the management of the school with the chair of governors, who in turn contacted the LEA. The LEA came into the school to review the situation, supported the strategies that the headteacher was putting in place and agreed academic targets with her for school improvement. However, when these were reviewed a year later it was judged that insufficient progress had been made, and the head resigned at the end of the 1999 spring term. She said that she had realised that the school was in 'negative collusion' and felt that she could not take it any further.

GETTING BACK ON TRACK

The school faced the prospect of going into the 1999 summer term without a headteacher, but the governors, on the recommendation of the LEA, appointed an experienced, retired head from outside the authority as acting headteacher. He began the term but resigned within three weeks. This contributed to a further drop in staff confidence and morale. However, the LEA provided immediate support for the governing body by bringing in the headteacher of a neighbouring primary school on the estate as acting headteacher, and he remained in this post until the current head took over in January 2000. He, the acting head, was – and is – a well-respected head, well known in the community, with eight years' experience of headship in his school and a previous headship in the neighbourhood. He retained the headship of his own school, and the role that he agreed with the LEA and the governors of both schools was 'to go into Fair Furlong to support their staff in sorting out their difficulties'. He began to work immediately with the staff. He closed the school on the Monday after he had been appointed and had a whole-day meeting with staff, listening to their accounts of what the problems were and encouraging them to commit to changing the ethos. This seems to have had a cathartic effect:

> He was very good, let us say what we felt, get it off our chests and then said right, that's it, now let's move forward.
>
> (Class teacher)

> At the end of the INSET day he said – is there anyone here who doesn't think that this school can be turned around?
>
> (Class teacher)

This was a very difficult time for the Fair Furlong staff:

> We felt vulnerable, felt we were total failures, all of us.
>
> (Class teacher)

The acting head brought two members of his own staff with him to the first meeting at Fair Furlong and made it clear that he would not be the only one providing support to the teachers.

> I felt I needed a member of staff, for me one of the problems with the 'super-head' label is just that, the idea that they come in like a knight on a charger to sort things out, and very often from what I can tell they do it on their own . . . I wasn't prepared to do that.
>
> (Acting head)

His immediate priority was to support the teachers in managing pupil behaviour, and he used a number of strategies to do this. One was to provide additional support in ICT. Fair Furlong has a dedicated computer suite, although the ICT curriculum was not being fully implemented in the school at that time. The head brought in a member of his own staff as an ICT co-ordinator to work in the school for a number of hours each day. She was to take half a class at a time to work on an integrated learning system so each teacher had an opportunity to do good work with the remaining half of the class. A firm believer in the importance of ICT – 'in areas like this I think computers are going to be one of the ways of breaking this glass ceiling that we are all hammering at' – he also used the computer room as part of his strategy for managing behaviour.

> A computer room was a wonderful place where you could have control in a relaxed manner that the children respond to – and they are also doing educational work as well. As I patrolled the school, taking children out, they would go into that room sit down at a desk and be perfectly quiet; other children were working and they had no way of responding to an audience or anything else.
>
> (Acting head)

A second major strategy was that he put himself in the forefront of pupil management. He said that the behaviour of Fair Furlong children was always excellent at assemblies. He took the assembly every morning, using this as a means of establishing his own credibility with the children. He then spent the teaching time patrolling the corridors, going into classrooms to assist teachers when required, removing pupils who were being disruptive. He aimed to support individual teachers in the way he felt they needed to be supported rather than attempt to review the whole school policy on behaviour management. He also encouraged the teachers to reinstate the lunchtime and after-school clubs and activities which had not been running for some time. He held detentions at lunchtime:

> . . . to get the rogues off the playground. Pupil behaviour . . . it's the key thing. If you haven't got control of your school in an area like this you don't get anything. You don't get any achievement,

or very little – everything is affected, including staff morale. I have never met a professional body of teachers so de-skilled.

(Acting head)

He felt that it was crucially important to gain the support of the parents in managing pupil behaviour; so he held a meeting with them on the first day, sent a newsletter home to make it clear that he was not prepared to tolerate bad behaviour and called parents into school if a child broke the good behaviour policy. 'In the first week I saw loads of parents.'

Within a few weeks the standard of behaviour began to improve in the school, and teachers regained confidence as they realised that he would provide back-up support.

He put rules back in and sanctions back in and we could see a difference within half a term, the children's behaviour improved tremendously.

(Class teacher)

Nevertheless, the time and energy that the staff had to devote to behaviour management meant that little work was done on developing the curriculum, assessment systems and general policy development. Much remained to be tackled.

There were some staff changes in the summer term and a number of new staff were appointed for September 1999. The current headteacher took up his post in January 2000 and eight weeks later the school had a full OfSTED inspection. Although the inspectors judged the school to have serious weaknesses, they recognised that it was poised once again to make significant improvements, and early evidence of this is already becoming apparent.

WHAT CAN BE LEARNED FROM THIS EXPERIENCE?

Many people suffered because of the difficulties that Fair Furlong experienced: the children, the parents, the headteacher and the staff.

No one wanted such a state of affairs to occur, children were unhappy and staff were stressed and demoralised. Why did it happen? The answers are complex and perhaps everyone who experienced it will have a different explanation.

> I don't understand why everything fell apart when Mary went – I don't understand why with a change of head everything deteriorated so quickly because almost all the same people were here except her. I can't understand why we didn't get together and say, this isn't going to happen in our school – we are going to do this. But nobody did and it fell apart. . . . I hope that people have learned that every single person has got their role and they've got to do it, regardless of what's going on around them.
> (Learning support assistant)

This case study can only present a partial window on events. Nevertheless, even this brief study prompts a number of questions about what are appropriate forms of leadership in urban schools, about how to handle transition from one headteacher to another, about the management of change and about how schools are supported.

Leadership

In the English education system the role of the headteacher is paramount and the headteacher is widely regarded, not least by government, as the key ingredient in an effective school. One potential problem with this view is that too much can be laid at the head's door and insufficient attention paid to the need for everyone to participate in the leadership of the school. The need for the head to be a team builder is often emphasised, but less consideration may be given to the notion of shared leadership (MacBeath, 1998) where the school leader works to maximise the leadership qualities of others. One of the goals of the current head at Fair Furlong is to establish an ethos in the school where the children and staff all accept some responsibility for maintaining and improving the school community. Several of the staff who were interviewed clearly supported this view of shared leadership. They suggested that the school needed a leader who would work with them, who would back them up, especially in matters of pupil management, but they recognised that each member of staff also needed to 'do their bit'.

> Schools like this need a kind of leadership that, when that leader leaves, the school doesn't fall apart . . . leadership where the skills to lead the school are passed to other members of staff. For behaviour issues you need someone strong at the top who will go head-on with children and will take them on, because we do have some very challenging children who will go head to head with you. You need someone at the top who will back you and say, that's not acceptable and it will be dealt with, and will deal with it appropriately, but you also need someone who will allow us to manage our subject areas and develop our own professional skills because a lot of the behaviour issues are related to professional practice − children misbehave if you deliver lessons which are at the wrong level. You need someone at the top who will help us develop those professional skills.
>
> (Class teacher)

Several people also argued that, in schools such as Fair Furlong, what was needed was a 'hands-on' form of leadership − 'someone with extra special communication skills' (Class teacher) − who was able to build strong relationships with children and parents as well as the staff; someone who would spend time in the classrooms with the children and the teachers, help with pupil management at break times and be at the school gate to chat to the parents.

> Both of them [current head and acting head] are the same. They've had those children in the palm of their hands when they

walk into assembly. The children respect them, they adore them and they are frightened of upsetting them and that sort of very outgoing personality is important in a school like this. That was where the previous head didn't succeed, she was more quiet and calm and not very giving of herself.

(Class teacher)

Changing headteachers

The question of how the transition from one headteacher to another should be handled is not one that has received much attention. A typical pattern is that the incoming head will visit the school on one or two occasions, probably meet the staff and the current headteacher and have access to the paperwork. There is normally little opportunity to do more, not least because they are probably themselves working in another school. This was certainly the case with the head who was appointed to Fair Furlong in 1996. She made two short visits to the school before her appointment, had only a brief meeting with the previous head and wasn't given the keys of the school until her contract started on 1 September. Only when a new school is being established do heads seem to be given a few months to learn about and prepare for the job. There appears to be a widely held assumption that the new headteacher will come in with their own ideas and vision of what needs to be done (which may have been discussed with the governors at interview) and will make a fresh start in the school, rather than work to understand, consolidate and build upon what is already in place.

In Weindling and Earley's (1987) study of secondary head-teachers, one of the main problems cited by new heads was 'difficulties caused by the style and practice of the previous head'. By implication this was because it contrasted with what they want to do (Weindling, 1999). Yet the transition stage can be crucial. Mary Gray, the head who was in post in Fair Furlong when the original case study was conducted had achieved a great deal. She had put systems in place in the school which were leading to improvements in teaching and learning; she was respected and well liked by staff, children, parents and the wider community; she played an active role in the cluster group for local headteachers; and in very many ways she was a hard act to follow. It cannot be easy taking over a school from a head recognised to be very successful.

> She [the incoming head] wanted to stamp her own personality on the school. She tried to change too many things too quickly, though this wasn't obvious at the time.
>
> (Class teacher)

Mary Gray had taken the school forward a long way, but she recognised that much remained to be done. Her successor was judged to have the skills necessary to make the next leap forward, focusing on the curriculum and standards of teaching and learning, but her management style and ways of working with staff were different. How does a school community, especially the staff, learn to adapt to different leadership styles? How can two different management styles be made to gel? Should more time be allowed for the transition process? Should provision be made for incoming heads to spend preparatory time in the school observing systems, talking to people and gaining a fuller understanding of the way the school is working before taking up the appointment?

Supporting headteachers

Fair Furlong school is situated in a disadvantaged urban area. Life is difficult for many families and the children bring problems with them into school. In such schools, teachers and headteachers have to work especially hard to make the school effective. They have to work together inside the school but they also need access to other forms of support. Successive government policies over the last ten years have led to a diminution of the LEA role in relation to schools.

Schools have more responsibility for self-management and can buy in professional help, but are less likely to have an LEA adviser coming into the school on a regular basis to monitor and support their work, not least because there may be fewer advisers in post. In the case of Fair Furlong, the LEA did provide support and acted quickly to bring in an acting headteacher in the 1999 summer term. Their effective intervention was noted in the OfSTED report (OfSTED, 2000).

Headteachers may also look to colleagues in neighbouring schools for support. Fair Furlong has not been the only school in the neighbourhood to experience difficulties and one positive outcome has been to strengthen the cluster of local schools. There are twelve schools in the cluster and the headteachers meet on a fortnightly basis. Could they have been more supportive when Fair Furlong was experiencing difficulties? In the event they were unaware of any problems. The headteacher commented:

> They are a group of very professional people and I have a high regard for them. They were very well established and perhaps if I had felt comfortable in going to them and saying what was happening, I am sure they would have been supportive. Because I was new to the area, because they had worked together, they were unaware this was happening . . . it's a difficult thing to share . . . it's a very personal thing.
>
> (Headteacher 1996–99)

The headteachers and governors recognise that they are facing the same issues in the same area and have now committed themselves to working on problems in a collaborative fashion. They have drawn up a joint school development plan for the cluster with additional specific targets for individual schools, they have planned in-service training for subject co-ordinators from all the schools for the next year. Plans are under way for a bid for funding to become a mini-Education Action Zone. The current headteacher in Fair Furlong is an active member of the cluster group and sees it as a key means of providing support for school development.

Teachers' professional development

Good teaching is central to pupil achievement. All teachers have had to develop new skills and expertise in response to the multiple innovations in curriculum and assessment; teachers in challenging schools need to be especially skilled. Excellent teaching and classroom management can stimulate and engage children, but, when classes become disruptive, teachers experience stress, their morale drops and this is likely to have a negative effect on their practice. In February 2000, the OfSTED inspectors judged that the quality of teaching was satisfactory overall and some was very good or excellent. Examples of good teaching were seen from all teachers. In the last year there have been staff changes at Fair Furlong and a number of young teachers with good subject knowledge and skills and fresh ideas have been appointed and this is reported to have had a positive impact on the school as a whole. The current head is actively working to promote continuing professional development for the staff, supporting their attendance at in-service courses, working with them in the classrooms and encouraging discussion about how to improve teaching and learning. His prime focus is on school improvement and how best to achieve this.

There is an underlying question about how best to promote continuing professional development for teachers. In recent years most teachers have experienced only short (e.g. half-day) training courses related to specific innovations rather than more sustained educational opportunities (e.g. long courses, periods of secondment) which might have a more positive effect on their practice in the longer term (McMahon, 1999). A number of the teachers at Fair Furlong are very experienced and have taught in the school for many years. The challenge that they and many other teachers face is how to keep their practice fresh and innovative and be themselves responsive to change. Over the five-year period the school did have a number of strategies in place which help to develop professional experience (e.g. taking responsibility for teaching a different age group, classroom observation with feedback, mentoring schemes, INSET courses) but this may not be sufficient. After many years in the classroom teachers may gain much more benefit from periods of secondment, business placements, study visits, etc., and the government appears to recognise this (DfEE, 2000).

Management of pupil behaviour

Every school has to resolve the question about what are the most appropriate ways of managing pupil behaviour but the challenge this poses will be greater in some schools than in others. The difficulties in Fair Furlong arose in part because staff held different views about how the children's behaviour should be managed. A central school-wide system for behaviour management clearly can work very well but a view was also expressed that it may be de-skilling for individual teachers who simply apply the system rather than engage with the underlying issues.

The governors

The governors of Fair Furlong School are committed and loyal and several have worked for the school for many years; many of them come from the local community. Should they have been more aware of the problems that the school was experiencing and have inter-vened more quickly? Perhaps. The OfSTED inspectors (OfSTED, 2000) reported that the governors had not ensured that identified weaknesses had been addressed but recognised that this was due in part to difficulties in communication with the head and noted that they are now making significant improvements. However, it can be argued that the responsibility placed on governors for the management of schools is too great. This is certainly the view of the

National Primary Heads Association which stated that: 'the expectations placed on governors, unpaid and often in full-time employment, were totally unrealistic and needed to be reassessed' (Education and Employment Committee, 1998, para. 51).

CONCLUDING NOTE

School improvement is not easy. The history of Fair Furlong over the past few years illustrates how hard it can be to sustain improvement and how quickly a school ethos can change. There are lessons to be learned from this experience, certainly for the staff of this school and possibly for others who might find themselves facing similar difficulties. A key underlying message is that the transition from one head to another is in itself a major innovation for a school and it needs to be carefully planned, managed and supported.

REFERENCES

Department for Education and Employment (2000) *Professional Development: Support for Teaching and Learning*, DfEE 0008/2000, London: DfEE.

Education and Employment Committee (1998) *Ninth Report: The Role of Headteachers Volume 1*, London: HMSO.

Hartcliffe and Withywood Community Partnership (1999) *Working Together for Change: Funding Bid for Single Regeneration Budget Round 5*, Bristol City Council.

MacBeath, J. (1998) (ed) *Effective School Leadership: Responding to Change*, London: Paul Chapman.

McMahon, A. (1999) Promoting continuing professional development for teachers: an achievable target for school leaders? In: T. Bush, L. Bell, R. Bolam, R. Glatter and P. Ribbins (eds) *Educational Management: Redefining Theory, Policy and Practice*, London: Paul Chapman.

OfSTED (2000) *Inspection Report: Fair Furlong Primary School*, London: OfSTED.

Weindling, D. (1999) Stages of headship. In: T. Bush, L. Bell, R. Bolam, R. Glatter and P. Ribbins (eds) *Educational Management: Redefining Theory, Policy and Practice*, London: Paul Chapman.

Weindling, D. and Earley, P. (1987) *Secondary Headship: The First Years*, Windsor: NFER-Nelson.

5

LOCHGELLY NORTH SPECIAL SCHOOL
Lochgelly, Fife
John MacBeath and Donald Gray

A SPECIAL KIND OF DIFFERENCE

It is now five years since we last visited Lochgelly North School in Fife. It was recommended to us by Her Majesty's Inspectorate who had described it at that time as 'a very special school'. It sought and gained success against the odds, not simply of economic deprivation but of personal disabilities which denied opportunities for mainstream education or an independent way of life. Its definition of success was not in terms of national standards or predetermined attainment targets but the enrichment it could bring to the lives of the 18 individuals who made up its pupil body.

We wrote then that a school is an organism which is created and re-created by the people who inhabit it and give it its identity at a particular time. Times change. Communities grow and decline. Teachers and pupils come and go. Nothing stays the same. Lochgelly North has changed in many ways in the last few years, in response to changes in the outside world and internally as relationships have been redefined and renewed.

The major change in the political landscape has been the election of a Labour government and the subsequent devolution of power to a Scottish Parliament. With it came a further restructuring of

Table 5.1 Lochgelly North Special School, Fife,

	1996–97	1999–2000
Type and status	Special School for pupils with sensory, severe and complex learning difficulties	Special School for pupils with sensory, severe and complex learning difficulties
Pupil roll	22	28
Headteacher	Maureen Lorimer (apptd 1992)	Helen Farmer (apptd 1996)
Pupil/teacher ratio (incl. head)	4.6	4.3
Support staff ratio hours (1)	67.0	76.2

Key:
(1)   Full-time equivalent (f.t.e.) support staff hours per week, per f.t.e. teacher

authorities' roles and responsibilities as a new tier was added to central and local decision making. Both the new Labour government and the new Scottish Parliament enjoyed a year or more of honeymoon, new optimism and suspended disbelief.

Education was threefold at the heart of government policy. The economy was enjoying a new vitality. In the five years between 1994 and 1999 unemployment in Scotland dropped from 9.2 per cent to 5.4 per cent. In Lochgelly North it fell from 13.4 per cent to 7.7 per cent. The extent to which this represented greater prosperity is, however, debatable, and the optimism that things would be different has been gradually eroded. By the summer term of 2000 when we re-visited the school the Blair government was at its lowest ebb and the Scottish Parliament was under siege from the press.

New Labour did bring with it a whole raft of changes. While its effects were most strongly felt 'south of the border', the indirect effects were also experienced in Scotland. Although different in many significant respects, Scotland has followed the main principles of an agenda which put the raising of standards at its centre and the setting of targets as a strategy to realise that aim.

Scotland has no OfSTED, no National Curriculum, no national assessment, no literacy or numeracy hours, no EAZs, Beacon schools, Advanced Skills Teachers, Teaching Awards, Fresh Start Schools or City Academies. Education authorities have continued to play a more directive and protective role than their English counterparts with local management of schools taking a less competitive market form. A director of a Scottish authority describes its significance in these terms:

> Pupil numbers, although strongly influencing the size of the school's budget are not regarded as overwhelmingly the main determinant as happened in England and Wales. Thus, it remains possible to allocate additional resources to schools serving deprived areas. . . . The teacher staffing component is usually based upon average salaries rather than actual costs thus avoiding the difficulty faced by many English schools of having to dispense with more experienced staff as they move up the salary scale.
>
> (Bloomer, K. 1999: 165)

Scottish schools have been less subject to a rapid series of structural and curricular changes but schools have felt the impact of a new Scottish Executive with a determination not to be left behind nationally or internationally. So schools have been set achievement targets, to be negotiated with their authorities. These have had a direct impact on the 'delivery' of the 5–14 curriculum which is now a fact of life for special schools as well. At the upper end of secondary a new qualifications structure – 'Higher Still' – has emerged after half a decade of central insistence and local resistance, but again incorporates special schools by offering special access modules. Very much like their English counterparts, Scottish teachers and heads complain of too much change too quickly and speak of a lowering morale among the teaching force who feel teaching time has been sacrificed to monitoring, accounting and recording. New policies on early intervention, however welcome, have had an adverse impact on the school, making it harder to recruit staff with the necessary skills for working with younger children.

THE SCHOOL

All of this provides an important backdrop to what is happening in one small special school in a corner of the Kingdom of Fife. In 1995 we described the school in these terms:

> The school sits on the edge of the town, its north-facing classroom windows looking across fertile valley and farmland to the kingdom of Fife. The southern aspect is less picturesque – a 1960s council housing scheme. The only tourist to see this part of the town, or indeed the town itself, would be one who had lost their way *en route* to a more celebrated destination.

Little has changed in external appearance of either community or school, but that belies what is happening inside Lochgelly North. The school has not only grown in size but in new directions, mostly in response to the changed world of the third Millennium. Since 1995 the school roll has increased from 18 to 28 pupils and began the new session in August 2000 with 31. To accommodate the growth in numbers the school has added two classrooms. Pupils range in age from 6 to 18 and across a wide spectrum of need and ability. At the lower range there is a marked increase in children on the autistic spectrum. There are now nine, only one of whom is able to speak. This growing skew towards more severe learning disabilities is because the local primary school has improved its own provision for special needs, while, further up the age range, the ability of the school, the child or the family to cope with main-stream life and curriculum becomes increasingly strained. So, at the upper end of the school are many young people on the borderline, capable of at least partial integration and potentially capable of independent living.

There are now six full-time teachers and one half-time teacher, all women. They are complemented by a full-time equivalent of 11.6 support staff, giving a full-time equivalent staffing complement of nineteen. Twelve new staff have been added since 1995 to accommodate rising numbers. Six of the teaching staff have been there since our first visit. Helen Farmer, previously a member of teaching staff in the school, took over as headteacher in 1997.

Our reappraisal of Lochgelly North followed the same path as our original study – visits to the school to observe and participate in classes, interviews with a sample of five parents and a sample of five teachers and educational assistants, and the headteacher; plus questionnaires to all parents and all staff.

A GOOD SCHOOL

> This is a good school. We are extremely happy with what we have received here. Mark is happy here and for us that means everything. We are confident they will drive him as far as he can go.
>
> (Parent)

Parents described Lochgelly North as a 'good school'. This is perhaps not surprising given the common tendency for parents to describe their child's school in this way. Parents of children with special needs, however, are not easily satisfied and many Lochgelly parents (and others from further afield) had looked around and tried other schools before settling for this special school.

> It was the fifth school we visited out of six and we thought 'Well, this is going to have to be something special', and as soon as we walked in the door we knew that this was the place.
>
> (Parent)

The 'something special' was frequently put down to the 'feel' of the school, the impact it made on the visitor, its transparent concern for young people manifested in the way people spoke to one another, the patience and perseverance of staff confronted day-to-day and moment-to-moment with challenging and often disturbing behaviour. The words most commonly used by parents to describe the school's ethos were 'caring', 'warm', 'friendly'.

> We were looking for a supportive environment rather than a cloistered environment and we cannot praise the school high enough.
>
> (Parent)

First impressions are significant. They are the manifest ethos, the face which the school presents to the outside world, the outer expression of an inner, more deeply hidden, culture. Probing more deeply into the culture of the school revealed different facets of an organisation more complex and more multi-layered than its surface presentation. It revealed:

- a commitment to the learning and growth of each individual child;
- a growing flexibility in placement of individual children through close and continuous monitoring of behaviour and progress;
- a shared recognition of the importance of parental partnership, but tensions and frustration at the inability to involve all parents;
- a mixed response among staff to external change and pressures of central government policy;
- a determination to keep a focus on the school's traditional philosophy and values in the face of perceived difficulties, distractions and changing priorities.

A FOCUS ON LEARNING

The central feature of Lochgelly North, consistent over the five years, is its commitment to learning and individual growth. The headteacher puts it in these terms:

> Success is every pupil reaching his full potential. In the mainstream setting that means passing exams but in here it means they become as independent as possible by any means whatever. We work in any way that will achieve that. It is totally child-centred and the energies and aspirations that staff have for the kids, and the energy we put into it, is tremendous.

The school's success in achieving this aim is attested to by parents who spoke not dutifully but with enthusiasm about what the school had done for their children. A parent, and chairman of the school board, describes the school as having exceeded his expectations, taking his son beyond what he thought possible.

> Mark is much further on than we ever thought he could be. His communication is much better. He has been driven on. That is a big plus. He is much happier here.

Another parent describes how she sees this as being achieved:

> The best thing that they will find the child's ability and be able to stretch it that bit more or and make it very relevant to everyday life. There is a great deal of consolidation of skills. Things are not taught in the abstract. They're taught the relevance to everyday living. They make Alan do things that I would not have attempted at home and he wouldn't do and certainly his social integration has come on tremendously – asking questions, or listening to others, being aware of other people as well, which autistic children aren't necessarily good at – considering other people's feelings and the consequences of their actions.

Widener

Harvard University Library
Messenger Service

Harvard University Library
Messenger Service

From

Date
Stamp

Deliver to

Other parents also spoke about the importance of the contextualised nature of lessons. Speaking about her daughter's progress one parent said:

> She had previously great difficulty in remembering things and had to have constant reminding and reinforcement. Now she is able to do and remember more because of the practical nature of the activity she is undertaking.

Figure 5.1 Water play is a whole-body sensory experience!

While this commitment to individual learning is unchanged since 1995, there has been a change in the approach to teaching, reflecting advances in knowledge and methodologies. Symbolic communication and picture exchange have, says the head, created a new buzz among staff and an empowerment of children. Handing, receiving and exchanging cards has raised the level of activity and initiative-taking in the classroom. Children are now more likely to initiate communication rather than just responding to questions, to be pro-active rather than simply reactive. Parents are encouraged to use this technique at home and some of the parents we interviewed spoke of the breakthrough this had achieved.

The contributions of the three therapists, occupational therapist and two physiotherapists, have, in Helen Farmer's view, had a massive impact on curriculum development. They work 'on an educationally integrated basis', as she describes it, rather than the Health Board's standard approach of working with parents and child only in the home context. 'All the therapies are fully integrated into classroom practice and so it's not the therapist does this and the classroom teacher does that.' They work with the child and the teacher in the classroom. They become involved in staff development, have specific curriculum consultation time, contribute to the school development plan, attend parents' evenings, do home visits, linking in-school and out-of-school activity. They have moved from the periphery to the centre of the school's activity. It is a model of inter-professional collaboration which has encouraged the school to apply, along with its partner schools, for status as a 'new community school'. This brings an extended definition to the 'community school', extended in the sense of articulated, family-centred provision of services, but also extended in the sense of geographical community with boundaries reaching the neighbouring towns and villages.

Visiting teachers of art, music and drama also work closely with Lochgelly North staff. They have at times found it difficult, but with the support of teachers have been able to acquire new skills and share their skills with school staff. 'They are', says the head, 'observant, perceptive, intuitive, innovative – just everything – and we are very fortunate to have them.'

TARGET-SETTING AND CURRICULUM CHANGE

Five years ago target-setting was a common feature of the school but as it became a government priority the nature of target-setting changed. In line with government policy the school is expected to reach the magic 80 per cent figure – 80 per cent of pupils reaching the targets set in literacy, numeracy and personal/social education. This is, in the view of some staff, unattainable or simply 'daft'. The orthodoxy of SMART targets, while endorsed in principle by the headteacher, has diverted energy into formulation 'and tight specification of' detailed behaviours. This has immensely increased staff skills in target-writing but contributed little to the achievement of those targets. There are also concerns about maintaining the breadth of experience in the drama, art, music and sensory stimulation which are such essential sources of learning and pleasure for children with special needs.

The 5–14 curriculum is, unlike its English/Welsh counterpart, not a National Curriculum in the sense of requiring certain content and methodology but a framework of learning objectives and key developmental stages. The introduction of 5–14 has created tensions between a pupil-centred approach and a curriculum-centred approach and however much teachers have worked hard to reconcile these, there is a residual frustration at the extra burden it imposes.

Increasing pressure is real and perhaps unavoidable as new guidelines are introduced for at-risk registers, continuous filling of forms to record incidents (teacher–pupil, pupil–pupil) and informing parents. There is constant vigilance and 'watching your back', in a world where a school's and a teacher's reputation can hang on the perilous thread of one accusation or insinuation. The perception of imposed changed is cumulative.

Helen Farmer is a pragmatic as well as a principle-centred head. She has worked hard to blend the school's own traditional commitment to individual target-setting with new policy directions. She is a self-confessed autocrat when it comes to holding to the vision while accommodating change and *Realpolitik*. So, the 5–14 curriculum is married to individualised programmes. Pupils are encouraged, wherever feasible, to be involved in setting their own targets. Long-term targets are set for each child and discussed with parents, leading to short-term targets and individual education plans. Long-term targets are assessed every year and the short-term targets every term. However much it has introduced new pressures, the 5–14 curriculum is, for Helen Farmer, highly significant: 'It has put us on the continuum of provision. We're part of the link. It has given us a credibility that we didn't have before and this is good for the kids.' Lochgelly North, previously pursuing its own curriculum in its own way, has, in the head's view, gained greater credibility and flexibility of provision by using, and being seen to use, the same curriculum framework as everyone else.

THE POWER OF PLACE

Targets take many different forms. For Andrea, success was measured in her progress from 'bum shuffle and a roll' to crawling, then walking with some aid, until the celebrated breakthrough of walking down the school corridors without support or help. The ultimate target is not walking unaided in school but in the world 'out there' to which skills have to be applied, but not always with ease. For Donald, a target is to transfer his in-school behaviour to other contexts. The contextual contrasts are illustrated by researcher notes and the headteacher's description:

> Donald, hair cut short and a ring in his left ear stood up from his seat and walked over to us. He said 'Hello. I'm Donald. How are you doing?', and held out his hand. I shook his hand and said,

'Hello, fine, how are you?'. Donald replied that he was fine and returned to his seat.

And from the headteacher:

> On his first day at college he was rude to people on the bus and was rude and arrogant to people in college . . . Within the school he is a model child but as soon as he gets outside these walls his behaviour changes.

Helping children to make the transition from school to community contexts, from dependence to independence, is one of the central aims of the school, although for some this will always be a bridge too far. For those who can, travelling from Lochgelly to Dunfermline with support is a first step to independent travel. With raised self-confidence they are able to make the trip to Lauder College – the further education college – totally independently. Residential experience away from the protective clutch of parents, independent trip to the shops, work placements, are all part of the effort to break, or at least stretch, the umbilical attachment to school or home. Two students in the past year have worked one day a week in the local baker's while another student has worked in the Somerfield supermarket.

This recognition of the context of learning – the power of place – is of critical relevance in a school like Lochgelly North. The difficulty in transferring things learned in one context to another – classroom to classroom, school to home – is, as we know, difficult enough to achieve in a mainstream school context. For children with special needs this is an even greater challenge.

HOME AND SCHOOL

As one parent pointed out to us, the transferability of skills from the school to the home cannot simply be taken for granted. His description of his son as doing much more in school than he would at home might be explained by the specific context – the behaviour setting – of the school and its day-to-day norms. It may be related to the peer environment. It might be explained by the expectations of teachers as compared to those of parents. Indeed, all of these influences may be at work. The challenge it offers is to find ways of building the bridge between classroom and home contexts, between school behaviour and behaviour in the community.

Mechanisms for creating a bridge include the home–school diary which records each day what progress the child has made. The diary is complemented by video recordings of children's behaviour in school, not only providing parents with evidence of progress but modelling what they can do at home. Video recordings can travel in the opposite direction too, allowing teachers and education assistants to see what accomplishments or problems occur in the home context. Parents are also invited to observe their child in class, with support from staff on how those classroom skills may be extended to the home situation.

Success is ultimately measured less by what is achieved in school than by what happens in home and the community. One mother, citing an example of success, talks about her daughter now having the confidence and security to sleep in her own bed. Doing the dishes, running the messages, handling money confidently, doing the baking, are ways in which improvement in the quality of life can be measured.

Alan's mother describes how they worked on the concept of time at home. They had two clocks on the wall at home, the ordinary clock and a cardboard one on which they practised moving the big hand to denote passage of time, later extending this to a minute timer so that Alan eventually became conscious of what a minute, five minutes and ten minutes meant.

It is, as teachers constantly stressed, important that parents are able to see how the most effective learning is contextualised and that it can also transcend specific contexts. Learning needs to be related to everyday practical tasks and events and, when this principle is grasped, parents can help at home, teaching things to their children in a very concrete manner: talking about quantity, time and relationships of one thing to another.

A bigger challenge, for many of the parents, it to accept that their children can fend for themselves in what are seen as risk-laden situations. The school has worked hard at gently leading parents away from over protectiveness and the dependency relationship which it can all too easily reinforce. This is achieved in part through a flow of information from the school, but more importantly by allaying parental concerns by taking them along to Lauder College or visiting their children on their first residential experience. By making the first residential stay in a centre outside Edinburgh, a relatively short drive from Lochgelly, Helen Farmer can pick up concerned parents and take them for a reassuring day visit to the centre. With this first-hand reassurance parents find it easier to let go.

THE INTEGRATION QUESTION

The integration of children with special needs into mainstream schools has been a policy priority of the last decade and more. It is seen as good not only for children with special needs themselves but also for those who need to be exposed to, and live positively with, difference and disability. In Lochgelly North integration has been a running theme for a long time and the future of the school has never been completely secure. Yet, numbers continue to rise and children continue to come from mainstream schools, many with special educational needs departments, because the school has either not been able to meet the children's needs or has been unable to cope with challenging behaviour.

Many children, in the early months and years at Lochgelly North, were 'defiant', 'aggressive', 'violent', intimidating', 'running teachers ragged'. This presented an extra pressure for staff who saw it as their own, as well as the child's responsibility, to improve behaviour.

> Staff get very upset if they feel that someone is looking at them and if you have got a kid who is effing and blinding and barging their way down the corridor and you feel that people are looking at you and thinking – well she's not managing that very well – it's very destructive. Everyone has to know that everyone has a strategy and that has been discussed and approved by me.
>
> (Headteacher)

The solution lies in strategy and teamwork, a recognition that this is not an individual but a shared responsibility, that there is a systematic approach to changing behaviour, skills and values. There were many examples given of children who had blossomed since leaving mainstream schools or departments of special education. One parent described how her daughter had begun to feel a progressive widening of the gap between herself and her peers as she progressed through the primary school. Although they were keen for her to remain in the mainstream as she moved to secondary, it soon became apparent that her confidence was ebbing away. 'Her outgoing personality had gone because she felt so bad about herself.' Her confidence in herself was being eroded by her conspicuous inability to keep pace with her peers. She would hide herself behind a book simply to 'keep up appearances', but the strain of maintaining the pretence was sapping her morale. The move to Lochgelly North had seen a progressive growth in her confidence, ascribed by her mother to more relaxed and smaller classes, more one-to-one attention, being with other children more like herself, getting praise and recognition from teachers, receiving certificates, sometimes simply for working well.

As her mother describes it, she is a very good swimmer, has won four medals at the gala and has been picked for special coaching and could go on to be one of the top swimmers for Scotland at the Paralympics. Describing the deep change in her daughter's attitude to learning she says, 'Whereas she always used to say, "I can't, I can't", and she wouldn't try, now she tries'.

The ability to persevere, to cope with failure, to take risks is seen by researchers as one of the most significant of learning-to-learn skills. It represents a paradigm shift from the helpless to the mastery response and is underpinned by a sense of self, self as competent rather than incompetent, independent rather than dependent. This is 'the gift' of Lochgelly North, as one parent describes it. None-theless, the goal of integration continues to be pursued. The school is persisting with ways of integrating pupils into the mainstream, on however partial and temporary a basis. Senior pupils who were judged able to cope with mainstream schooling spend some time in Lochgelly High School, primarily in practical subjects.

> And then they go off to Lauder College and Lauder College is a huge place. It is very scary, even for big grown-up people let alone for kids with learning difficulties so it's a very gradual process – a first visit to the cafeteria with support and gradually built up over a period, sometimes as long as two years until they get to the stage where we can say 'right off to the college'. That has been successful for all pupils we have sent on.
>
> (Headteacher)

In the near future pupils will leave school with something to show for their achievements, for example, Higher Still certificates which are internally assessed and moderated courses especially designed for young people with special needs. These include Home Economics, Language and Communication, Understanding Environment, Expressive Arts, Personal and Social Education.

AN EFFECTIVE SCHOOL?

There was a high level of consensus that Lochgelly North is a 'good' school; but is that the same as an effective school? While measurement of the 'good' tends to rely on value-judgement, often subjective, intuitive and impressionistic, the term 'effective' tends to rely on measures of added-value, attainment over and above expectation, benchmarks, comparative performance against norms and national standards. Whether or not these are the right or adequate criteria to apply to mainstream schools is a matter of considerable debate, but in the context of this special school, this community and these children such measures are unavailable, of questionable use and generally inappropriate. How then are we to judge Lochgelly North's 'effectiveness', or indeed 'improvement'? How can we judge how well this school is succeeding against the odds – economic, social and personal?

We might evaluate the school's effectiveness in terms of its own aims as described in its development plan. These number 10 main aims, with 23 more detailed aims under those 10 headings. The following is a representative sample of these aims across the 10 areas:

- to provide breadth and balance, and ensure continuity and progression by developing individualised programmes which take account of the curriculum as specified in '5–14' and in the elaborated curriculum support for learning and Higher Still;
- to ensure that each pupil reaches their maximum level of personal achievement;
- to develop skills and knowledge, promoting learning experiences which are stimulating and enjoyable and which offer success to pupils;
- to develop self-esteem and confidence by providing opportunities which strengthen a sense of identity and personality: promoting a sense of responsibility in pupils for their reactions; fostering an environment in which pupils and staff respect and care for reach other; encouraging pupils to express their own feelings and recognise and respect the feelings of others;
- to recognise learning as a continuous process taking place within the context of home, school and community;
- to increase pupils' awareness and sense of personal identity as

members of the school, their own family and extended family, their local community and the wider community;

- to provide appropriate and effective learning and teaching resources;
- to foster effective teamwork;
- to value staff and promote the development of skills by providing opportunities to share expertise and learning with colleagues and other professionals;
- to review the quality of planning by using *How Good Is our School?* (SOEID, 1996) and the manual of 'Support for Learning' (SEED, 1999) as tools for evaluation.

Alternatively, or additionally, we may evaluate the school against the National Commission's 10 criteria for an effective school:

1. strong, positive leadership of the headteacher and senior staff;
2. a good atmosphere of spirit, shared aims and values and a good physical environment;
3. high and consistent expectations of all pupils;
4. a clear and continuing focus on teaching and learning;
5. well-developed procedures for assessing how children are progressing;
6. responsibility for learning shared by pupils themselves;
7. participation by pupils in the life of the school;
8. rewards and incentives to encourage pupils to succeed;
9. parental involvement in children's education and supporting the aims of the school;
10. extra-curricular activities.

There is a close correspondence between these two sets of criteria. While the school aims say nothing of leadership it may be taken as implicit in the realisation of the school's aims. Extra-curricular activities are not specifically mentioned in the school's aims but they do perhaps go further by considering the seamless nature of learning across school, home and community contexts. On the other hand, the National Commission criteria do not include staff development, teamwork or self-evaluation.

How then does the school perform against these combined and demanding set of 'indicators'? In the following responses from questionnaires we have used percentages, even though numbers are small (18 teachers, 12 parents) in order to make comparison easier.

Leadership

Leadership is seen positively by both parent and teacher groups, with a small body of dissent among teachers. This is not, however, simply synonymous with the person of the head, as responses to the second question show. As the tables indicate, most staff, in the view of parents and teachers, exercise leadership roles:

There is strong positive leadership in the school

	Strongly agree	Agree	Disagree	Strongly disagree
Staff	33	61	6	o
Parents	50	50	o	o

Staff have leadership roles

	True of all	True of most	True of a few	True of none
Staff	11	67	22	o
Parents	33	58	8	o

Atmosphere

There is a significant body of testimony to the positive atmosphere of the school. Parents and staff agree (with one dissenting member of staff). The fact that parents are more unreservedly positive is probably because they do not have to live with the daily tensions and pressures that arise in what can at times be a fraught working environment, exacerbated by external demands and pressures.

There is a good atmosphere in the school

	Strongly agree	Agree	Disagree	Strongly disagree
Staff	33	61	6	0
Parents	92	8	0	0

High expectations

Again there is ample testimony to the high expectations of staff and broad agreement among staff and parents as to the applicability of this to all children. The small body of dissent is a reference to the word 'all' and a residual feeling that there are a few children of whom more could have been expected. The dissent on this item appeared to be explained in two ways – one, by differing perceptions of 'teaching' and, two, by 'bureaucracy' which had detracted from the school's singleness of pedagogic purpose.

There are high expectations of all pupils

	Strongly agree	Agree	Disagree	Strongly disagree
Staff	39	50	11	0
Parents	33	58	8	0

The main focus in this school is on learning and teaching

	Strongly agree	Agree	Disagree	Strongly disagree
Staff	35	35	18	0
Parents	50	40	10	0

Meeting individual needs

There is little dispute that Lochgelly North puts the needs of individual children first, in both policy and practice. Whether this is true of all staff is less agreed, referring on one hand to the fact that staff do not deal with all children in the school and, on the other, that some staff are not as fully aware as are their colleagues of the needs that lie, sometimes deep, beneath the presenting behaviour.

Staff know the needs of each individual child

	True of all	True of most	True of a few	True of none
Staff	61	33	6	0
Parents	67	33	0	0

Pupils make good progress in learning

	True of all	True of most	True of a few	True of none
Staff	28	61	11	0
Parents	57	43	0	0

There is a strong body of consensus as to one of the school's main aims of encouraging independence.

Pupils are encouraged to be as independent as possible

	Strongly agree	Agree	Disagree	Strongly disagree
Staff	77	23	0	0
Parents	77	23	0	0

The views of pupils are not always easy to elicit or listen to, and the lack of verbal skills of a significant minority make this an ambitious goal. Encouraging children to express their own views and feelings is, however, a shared concern of all staff.

Staff listen to the views of pupils

	True of all	True of most	True of a few	True of none
Staff	33	61	6	0
Parents	58	42	0	0

Praise and encouragement

Praise and encouragement of success is deeply embedded in the school's culture and is a moment-to-moment feature of its life. On this issue there is strong consensus and it is the only issue on which staff are more positive than the parents. Taken together with the negatively phrased item 'staff don't encourage pupils enough' it provides a fairly strong weight of evidence.

Staff praise children when they have done well

	True of all	True of most	True of a few	True of none
Staff	89	11	0	0
Parents	83	17	0	0

Staff don't encourage pupils enough

	Strongly agree	Agree	Disagree	Strongly disagree
Staff	0	6	39	56
Parents	0	0	12	88

Parental involvement

Parental involvement, as has been seen from the testimony of parents and staff, is strong, and consistent efforts are made to keep parents in touch with their children's life in school.

Parents are kept in touch regularly with how their children are getting on

	Strongly agree	Agree	Disagree	Strongly disagree
Staff	50	50	0	0
Parents	67	33	0	0

However, the other side of the coin – support from parents for the school – receives a much more ambiguous response. What 'full support' means is, of course, a matter of differing interpretation, and may be very active or entirely passive. Helen Farmer is insistent that staff do not rush to judgement on parents, some of whom have to deal with virtually unrelieved stress and anxiety. In her view only one parent is reluctant to make contact with the school, unable to face up to the child who is her lot.

Parents give the school their full support

	True of all	True of most	True of a few	True of none
Staff	6	61	33	0
Parents	25	58	17	0

Extra-curricular activities

As in 1995, this is the item which receives the least positive response from parents and, although staff feel that some progress has been made, there is a general feeling that more could still be done.

There isn't enough in the way of extra-curricular activities

	Strongly agree	Agree	Disagree	Strongly disagree
Staff	17	67	6	6
Parents	33	50	17	0

Working with the community

An eleventh and highly important indicator of the school's success is its challenge to and support from the local community. In our 1995 study we commented on the importance given by the head at that time, Maureen Lorimer, to challenging suspicious, hostile or anxious attitudes to the disabled. The evidence from one source at least suggests that the school has been successful in that respect. A newcomer to the community remarked spontaneously how much more accepting than others Lochgelly people seemed to be of the disabled children and young people in their midst. Helen Farmer sees this as a welcome affirmation of efforts made on both sides – school and community – to support young people with disabilities. Successful fund-raising, five and half thousand pounds for a new sensory room for example, has been not just about money but goodwill. Concerts, fêtes, Saturday afternoon entertainment in the local social club, bringing local residents into the school, have all played their part in making Lochgelly North students a visible and welcome presence in the local community.

HAS THE SCHOOL IMPROVED?

This is a complex assessment and depends on the implicit criteria which different people hold. Comparing responses on two question-naire items provides a similar picture across both years, although with a small dissenting minority. From discussion with staff and parents these would appear to reflect the larger body of staff, the changed profile of the pupil intake, the changed political context and external pressures, notably in respect of target-setting and extra paperwork.

I am in favour of everything the school is trying to do

	Strongly agree	Agree	Disagree	Strongly disagree
Parents, 1995	79	21	O	O
Parents, 2000	75	25	O	O
Teachers, 1995	38	62	O	O
Teachers, 2000	11	78	11	O

Staff don't work well together

	Strongly agree	Agree	Disagree	Strongly disagree
Parents, 1995	o	o	36	64
Parents, 2000	o	o	35	65
Teachers, 1995	o	o	46	54
Teachers, 2000	o	11	61	28

We also asked the question more directly: is Lochgelly North now better than it was? What the following table shows is that a substantial number of parents and teachers are unsure of how to make such a judgement, while those who do hold an opinion are divided. Nonetheless there is a very clear majority of parents and teachers who believe that the school has indeed improved.

The school is better than it was

	Strongly agree	Agree	Disagree	Strongly disagree	Undecided
Staff	o	50	28	o	22
Parents	25	33	17	o	25

A judgement from us, as external visitors, is difficult to reach on the basis of limited visits and conversations but it is apparent to us that the school has moved on in its thinking and its practice. The odds are in many ways greater than they were in 1995. People seem to be working longer and harder, meeting a much wider range of expectations, but still achieving a quality of care and education in no way diminished from that five years previously. The school has better instructional and evaluative tools at its disposal and that is clearly to the benefit of the pupils.

In our experience, it is an unusual school, or indeed an unusual organisation in any sphere, in which there is consensus and harmony. Indeed, it may be argued that dissent is healthy for the growth of any organisation and that how the organisation meets and deals with dissent is a key indicator of its capacity for change. This is the challenge for Lochgelly North as a learning community – to listen to and learn from differing viewpoints. Honest, open and critical self-evaluation will be the key to the school's future success in meeting and beating the odds.

There was a one consistent theme which characterised both our first and second visits to Lochgelly North. It is expressed as 'she's a totally different child'. That phrase, repeatedly used by parents and teachers, spoke volumes about the ability of school to make a difference – or at least for one small school to make a special kind of difference.

REFERENCES

Bloomer, K. (1999) The Local Governance of Education: An Operational Perspective in Bryce, T. G. K. and Humes, W. M. (eds.) Scottish Education. Edinburgh: Edinburgh University Press.

SEED (1999) A Manual of Good Practice in Special Educational Needs, Scottish Executive Education Department, Edinburgh: HMSO.

SOEID (1996) *How Good Is our School?*, Audit Unit, HM Inspectors of Schools, Scottish Office for Education and Industry Department, Edinburgh: HMSO.

6

BURNTWOOD SECONDARY GIRLS' SCHOOL

Wandsworth, London

Kathryn Riley, Jim Docking, Ellalinda Rustique-Forrester and David Rowles

A story of young women of tomorrow

The school has made me become independent and it has made me more like a woman. I stand my ground and [I'm] not afraid to say what I think if someone challenges me . . . I know it's the school because when I first started, I was very quiet and shy. I can see a very clear change from my Year 6. I am more clear about my life – it has helped me with my mind, and I am a better person inside.

(Year 9 student)

The overall vision for the school, articulated by the head and fully endorsed by the staff, is to value achievement in every sense and to create the women of tomorrow. This message is sold hard to the pupils from the outset and is readily acceptable to the vast majority. From the first minute they are here, we encourage them to aim high and to value achievement.

(Member of the senior management team)

INTRODUCTION

The notion of schools *succeeding against the odds* is a powerful and attractive one. It engages the imagination. It challenges traditional deficit approaches to educational reform – what Seymour Sarason has described as the tendency to focus on the supposed villains of the piece – 'inadequate teachers, irresponsible parents, irrelevant or inadequate curricula, unmotivated students . . . an improvement-defeating bureaucracy' (Sarason, 1990: 12). It is a recognition that some schools facing formidable challenges have, nevertheless, created educational environments which are stimulating and rewarding, for teachers and students alike. Attractive though this concept is we have to guard against setting up an alternative – but equally limited notion of schooling – the super-heroic.

Super-heroic schools are characterised by valiant headteacher leadership. Teachers scale an educational Kilimanjaro – without oxygen. Previously disenchanted communities hail the renaissance. Politicians queue up to have their photograph taken. Teachers in neighbouring schools cast a jaundiced eye, either because they don't believe the hype, or because, if they do, this belief increases their own sense of inadequacy. The super-heroic school, led by the super-hero or -heroine who seemingly (overnight and single-handed) turns round a 'failing' school is a construct which is appealing to TV producers and politicians alike, but has little grounding in reality. Work we have carried out previously on school leadership and organisational change has led us to a very different set of views about leadership, change and school improvement (Riley and Louis, 2000) – something we will explore later in the chapter.

When we were asked to review the progress of Burntwood School in Wandsworth, a multiracial girls' school with over 1600 students, over the five intervening years since the original case study had been undertaken, we had a sense of trepidation – similar to that which many teachers experience when the inspector calls. The original case study team (Howard Davies, Peter Mortimore and Sarah Portway)

Table 6.1 Burntwood School for Girls, London Borough of Wandsworth

	1995–96	1999–2000
Type and status	Grant-maintained 11–18 (Girls)	Foundation 11–18 (Girls)
Pupil roll	1503	1620
Headteacher	Brigid Beattie (apptd 1986)	Brigid Beattie, CBE
% white pupils	37.7	35.9 *English average: 88.5 (1)*
% pupils with English as an additional language	39.9	57.4
% pupils eligible for free school meals (FSM)	34.6	24.6 *English average: 16.9 (1)*
% pupils with special educational needs, incl. Statements	35.9	26.2 *English average: 22.0 (1)*
Pupil/teacher ratio (incl. head)	16.2 *English average: 16.6*	16.5 *English average: 17.1*
Support staff ratio hours (2)	7.1	7.8
% pupils obtaining GCSE (A*–C grades) 5+ subjects	49 *English average: 44.5*	54 (1) *English average: 47.9 (1)*
Average GCSE point score per pupil	Not applicable	42.1 (1) *English average: 38.1 (1)*
% year 11 students with no GCSE passes	0 *English average: 7.8*	1 (1) *English average: 6.0 (1)*
Post-16 participation in full-time education or training (%)	96.3 *English average: 70.4*	99.1 (1) *English average: 70.1(1)*

Table 6.1 continued

OfSTED grade (PANDA) re: GCSE/GNVQ score per pupil in similar FSM school group	Not applicable	A* (1) (3)
OfSTED grade (PANDA) re: GCSE/GNVQ score per pupil in similar school group re: prior attainment at Key Stage Three	Not applicable	A (1) (3)

Key:

(1) 1998–99
(2) Full-time equivalent (f.t.e.) support staff hours per week, per f.t.e. teacher
(3) OfSTED PANDA rubric:
   A* PANDA pupils' results were **very high** in comparison with the average for similar schools
A PANDA pupils' results were **well above** the average for similar schools

had concluded that, broadly speaking, Burntwood was a 'good school' (Mortimore *et al.*, 1996). But could we capture the complexities of the story? Could we get beyond a saints-or-sinners analysis? What would we say to the principal if the news was bad?

We began by posing a number of key questions for ourselves as a research team and we have used these to frame our chapter. Our questions included the following:

- What were the findings from the 1995 case study, and what was the evidential basis for those findings?
- Had the composition of the school population changed?
- On the basis of a range of indicators was the school still a 'good school'?
- If so, why was this the case; if not, why not?
- What were the 'surface' and 'subterranean features' which appeared to characterise how the school was led, managed and organised, and what messages about teaching and learning were embedded in those features?
- What could be learned from the Burntwood study?

To answer these questions we looked at the evidence (from the original case study and from OfSTED), pupils' examination performance, and the perceptions of pupils, teachers and parents. The previous research team had drawn on comparative data from a national questionnaire administered by the National Foundation for Educational Research (NFER). We decided to build on this data by re-administering an updated questionnaire and introducing a parallel questionnaire for parents and teachers. To complete our groundwork, we interviewed staff and students,[1] and the female members of the team became students for the day – a particularly enjoyable and rewarding experience.

We wanted to produce a case study which was more than a stiff Victorian photograph – 'family' members dressed in their Sunday best – but instead was a portraiture which captured teachers and pupils in their workaday clothes. We were strongly supported in our endeavours by the school itself. Staff and pupils went out of their way to let us see, and be a part of, the school at work and at play. Staff were eager to use any insights gained from our analysis to help them reflect on their practices. Pupils wanted to know what we thought, and were keen to encourage us to come and teach at the school. We are not going to spoil our story by summarising our findings at this early stage. We want to encourage you to read the Burntwood story. It is a compelling one.

IS THE SCHOOL STILL A GOOD SCHOOL?

The previous case-study evidence about the school (summarised from Mortimore *et al.*, 1996, in Box A) was very positive. The OfSTED report in 1997 supported these claims:

> Burntwood is a very good school. It significantly adds value to the students' achievements and development. Expectations are high: there is a strong commitment to achievement which is generally shared by teachers and students and is reflected in

positive attitudes to learning. The principal and both the teaching and non-teaching staff have been successful in creating a harmonious and supportive community characterised by good relationships and well-motivated students.

(OfSTED, 1997: para. 1)

Box A

BURNTWOOD SCHOOL

The previous story (1995)

- An oversubscribed entry
- GCSE results above the national average
- Very low absence rates
- Higher than average participation in further education
- Strong positive leadership by head and senior staff, with a higher degree of delegation combined with support for post-holders and participatory decision-making
- A clear and consistent focus on learning
- High expectations set, with a focus on quality and frequent monitoring
- School grounds well kept
- Constructive, warm relationships
- A collective, 'whole-school' feeling, despite dispersed buildings
- A range of extra-curricular activities
- A commitment of staff, students and governors to a set of clear aims, principles and values
- Efficient management and good communications
- Parental and community involvement

Figure 6.1 Year 8 school journey to the Lake District

HAS PUPIL PERFORMANCE CHANGED?

Since 1994/95, the school has increased the numbers on roll by over 10 per cent from 1467 to 1620, with admissions in Year 7 exceeding the official standard number by up to 5 per cent during the last five years. Much has also been achieved by retaining more pupils and by increasing significantly the numbers in the sixth form (from 128 to 223). Indeed, 99 per cent of students either stay on at 16+ or continue their education at another school or college. The student/staff ratio of 16.5 (excluding the principal) has remained fairly constant over the five years.

The school continues to be a community of many ethnic heritages, with 37 per cent white students (cf. 89 per cent nationally, for England), 28 per cent black (cf. 3.1 per cent nationally), 27 per cent Asian (cf. 3.9 per cent nationally) and 8 per cent of another ethnic background (cf. 1.8 per cent nationally – DfEE, 1999a). (Inevitably, the school has undergone some changes over the five year period and some of these are shown in Box B.) The percentage of students for whom English is an additional language has increased from two in five to well over half (57 per cent). This compares with just 7.3 per cent for England in secondary schools and 17.7 per cent in all inner London schools (DfEE, 1999b). Although the numbers eligible for free school meals has fallen (from 33 per cent to 25 per cent), as they have for England as a whole, the proportion is still well above the English average of about 17 per cent, though below that of the borough as a whole (about 30 per cent) (DfEE, 2000a). The percentage of students with special educational needs (including those with Statements) has also fallen from 39 per cent to 26 per cent, though this is higher than the English average of 20 per cent for secondary schools (DfEE, 1999c), and the number of children with statements of SEN has doubled from 10 to 20.

Box B

BURNTWOOD SCHOOL

Major changes 1994–9

The past five years were described by one staff member as a 'period of many changes, both inside and outside the school':

✔ In 1994, a partial (30 per cent) selection admissions policy was introduced in response to the local educational context in Wandsworth schools and to provide a comprehensive balance of intake.[2]

✔ Staff turnover is approximately 10 per cent per annum. The school principal has been in post for 14 years.

✔ The school is now a foundation school, having previously been grant-maintained.

✔ In 1999, the school earned Beacon status, and it is also part of the national 'Excellence in the Cities' initiative, as are all Wandsworth schools.

✔ In 1994 the school's management structure was divided into two key stages, with the creation of an upper school (Years 10 and 11) and a lower school (Years 7–9). Pupils have different form tutors in each key stage.

✔ With the impact of the national literacy and numeracy strategies, new programmes of support were developed for low-achieving pupils in 1999. The school has also made a series of changes to the timetable and curriculum to integrate these programmes, which include academic monitoring and counselling. These programmes build on previous work in the school.

✔ Policies for behaviour and discipline have been re-examined and re-written. A new set of pupil and staff expectations is now reflected in the school's code of conduct called *Burntwood's Expectations Policy* and in *The 5 P's for Positive Classroom Behaviour.*

Performance in public examinations has improved at a faster rate than the English national average and demonstrates a substantial value-added component to the students' achievements. In 1995, 47 per cent of students achieved five or more A*–C grades. By 1997, this had climbed to 58 per cent, and in 1999 was 54 per cent – more than three points above the national average for girls in comprehensive schools and nine points above the borough average for girls (DfEE, 2000c: Tables 1, 2). In 2000, with the first partially selective intake, the figure was 57 per cent (no national comparisons available at the time of writing). As is the case nationally (DfEE, 1999d), there were marked differences in performance according to ethnic background, with Indian and other Asian students achieving a higher proportion of grades A*–C than White students, who in turn performed better than Black students.

At A/AS-level, the average point score in 1999 was 16.5, which contrasts with the score of just 8.6 in 1994 when, as noted by Mortimore *et al.* (1996), the school was struggling to retain its most able candidates. A fairer index might be the more recently available combined A/AS and advanced GNVQ average point score, which in 1999 was 16.5 – in line with the English national figure for females in comprehensive schools (16.6) and above the figure for females in the borough as a whole (15.2) (DfEE, 2000c: Table 12). In 2000, the score leapt to 20.0 (national comparisons not yet available).

Rates of truancy are below local and national averages, and exclusion rates are about the same. The percentage of unauthorised absences in 1998/99 was 0.6, which represents an improvement over the previous five years and is below the borough average of 1.2 per cent and the England and Wales average of 1.1 per cent (DfEE, 2000d). The number of permanent exclusions remains low – just one during 1999/2000 (0.06 per cent of the school roll, about the same as the English national average for girls (0.05 per cent) (DfEE, 2000e).

WHAT DO PUPILS, PARENTS AND TEACHERS THINK ABOUT THE SCHOOL?

In exploring whether Burntwood was still a good school, we recognised that examination performance was only one measure of what makes a school 'good'. Indeed, notions of what constitutes a 'good' school are bound in culture and context, and interpretations and perceptions can change over time (Riley, 1998a). As stakeholders may hold differing views about what a 'good' school is, we were particularly keen to examine whether key stakeholders at Burntwood (pupils, parents and teachers) held similar views about the school's merits and weaknesses. Our view was that the triangulation of these views would give us critical insights into the life of the school, and the expectations and experiences of the school community. The previous research team had drawn on comparative data from a national questionnaire administered by the NFER to Year 9 students (Keys and Fernandes, 1993). We decided to build on this data by administering an updated questionnaire and introducing a parallel questionnaire for parents and teachers.

The items in the original pupil questionnaire, called 'What do students think about school?', were designed to elicit students' attitudes to school and learning, their perceptions of teachers and lessons, their self-reported behaviour, and their perceptions of parental interest and home support. There was also space for students' free comment about their school experiences. The NFER were able to compare the findings for Burntwood with those of female students from the national sample. The conclusions were mixed for Burntwood. For example, Burntwood girls were:

More likely than those in the national sample to believe in the value of school and education . . .	. . . but slightly less likely to express positive attitudes towards their school.

| More likely to say that teachers praised them for good work . . . | . . . but less inclined to agree that they liked all or most of their teachers. |
| More likely to say they behaved well in school . . . | . . . but also more likely to say they received punishments and that the discipline was too strict. |

With permission from the NFER, we re-administered the questionnaire to the Year 9 pupils (1999/2000). Although we could not compare the girls' responses with those of a recent national survey, the findings would enable us to see if attitudes to schooling had shifted or remained fairly stable. We also wanted to ask students to record their ethnic heritage for cross-tabulation purposes. All students (except fourteen who were out of school on the day the questionnaire was administered) responded. Additionally (again with the NFER's permission), we devised two further question-naires, one for the teachers of Year 9 and the other for the parents. The items were worded to enable us to compare the extent to which teachers, parents and students shared the same perceptions of school. For example, in the students' measure, the girls were invited (using a five-point scale) to indicate the strength of their agreement with a series of statements such as 'I am very happy when I am at school', 'School is a waste of time for me' and 'People think this is a good school'. For our teachers' questionnaire, the equivalent statements were 'Year 9 students are very happy when at school', etc., while the statements in the parents' questionnaire were 'My Year 9 child is very happy when at school', etc. Three in five of the staff and two in five of the parents responded.

Three striking findings emerged from our analysis.

Pupils' views had changed little

The first finding was that in 56 out of the 64 items, responses among the current Year 9 students did not differ significantly in statistical terms from those of their predecessors in 1995 – indeed, in many cases the percentages for the choice answers were remarkably similar. This means that, in the main, the students of 2000 were neither more positive nor more negative about school work and life than the equivalent group five years ago. The exceptions to this stability of perceptions were interesting.

The girls were *less* likely to agree that:	But they were *more* likely to say that:
• their school was clean and tidy; • teachers made them work as hard as they were able; • they read for fun outside school; • they talked to their form tutor about their work.	• they were never or seldom punished; • they expected to stay on into the sixth form at Burntwood (as distinct from going elsewhere); • they expected to go on to university.

The proportions of students saying they intended to continue education at their own school beyond Year 11 (almost half, compared with a quarter in 1995) and to read for a degree (two-thirds, compared with about half in 1995) suggest increasing confidence in the school staff and in their own ability to succeed academically. The more positive attitudes to continuing education at Burntwood, and the drop in the frequency of reported punishments, are also interesting, since the 1995 students had been less inclined than the national sample to say they intended to stay on into Year 12 at their own school and less likely to report few incidents of punishment.

Parents, pupils and teachers shared many common perceptions

Secondly, for a number of items, perceptions among all three respondent groups (parents, students and teachers) were congruent – particularly with regard to the value of school and work, the purposes of school, the public's perception of the school, levels of bullying, the value of homework, and what parents think about the value of education. For instance, teachers and parents were spot on in their estimates that nine out of ten students or more would agree that:

- 'school work is worth doing';
- 'schools should help students to be independent and stand on their own two feet';
- they have never or hardly ever been bullied during the current year;
- homework is important for doing well at school;
- their parents think it important for them to do well at school.

Further, almost all teachers and parents, and nine out of ten students, agreed that 'people think Burntwood is a good school'. Indeed, in their free comments, two out of five parents chose to express enthusiasm about the school and its staff. Typical comments were: 'We are very happy with the care and consideration that Burntwood School has shown in its dealings with our daughter', 'Impressed by teachers' dedication and commitment' and 'The school is open and receptive to parental concerns and suggestions'.

However, we also found some differences. Teachers (and sometimes, but not always, parents too) were more likely than students to return positive responses on items concerned with students' liking of school and finding lessons interesting, the cleanliness of the buildings, whether most teachers mark students' work and can keep order, whether the school has sensible rules and the appropriate number, whether teachers get it 'about right' in the way they maintain discipline, and whether students are usually well-behaved. Teachers also *underestimated* parents' interest in how their daughters were doing at school (93 per cent of parents said they were 'always' or 'nearly always' interested, but the staff estimate was 70 per cent), whether they made it clear how well their daughters should behave in school (98 per cent v. 63 per cent), whether they made sure homework was done (83 per cent v. 49 per cent), and whether they attended parents' evenings (91 per cent v. 74 per cent). Interestingly, students' perceptions of their parents' attitudes about these matters were remarkably accurate.

On some issues, parents' perceptions were more positive than their daughters'. In particular, parents were more likely to believe that their Year 9 children read for fun outside school (71 per cent v. 55 per cent) and would stay on into the sixth form at Burntwood (63 per cent v 46 per cent), and they were somewhat more likely to assume that their children were never or seldom punished (92 per cent v. 84 per cent). On the basis of students' self-reports, parents also overestimated – but teachers underestimated – the amount of time the girls spend watching TV or videos (61 per cent of students said they watched for up to 3 hours a day, whereas teachers estimated the percentage would be 44 per cent and parents 75 per cent).

There were few differences related to ethnic heritage

The third main finding was that, with certain exceptions, ethnic heritage was not a factor that accounted for differences in responses to those issues on which student opinion as a whole was divided. For example, ethnicity made no difference to what students said about their happiness at school, its cleanliness, whether lessons were interesting, whether lessons were 'a waste of time', the value of school work, whether 'teachers try hard to make me work as hard as I am able', the girls' liking for working on their own, perceptions of teachers' ability to keep order, the way discipline was maintained, the number of school rules, levels of teacher praise, levels of bullying, the frequency of talking to the form tutor about work, participation in lunchtime and after-school activities, reading for fun outside school, and expectations for going to university.

However, there were some significant differences. Black students were least likely to say they liked their teachers; Asian and 'Other' students were more likely to agree that the school's rules were sensible; Black and 'Other' students were more inclined to think that schools should help students use their leisure time; Asian students appeared to spend the most time on homework and were also the most likely to anticipate staying on into the school's sixth form; and White and Asian students watched less TV than Black and 'Other' students.

On the basis of the evidence about pupil performance on national examinations and from our analysis of the questionnaire data we concluded that, in the terms defined some five years ago, the school was still a 'good school' and that performance had improved. In reaching this conclusion we struggled with the question: Given the changes in the composition of the school, are the challenges facing Burntwood easier than in the past? In 1994, the school first selected 30 per cent of its students – but in response to a local environment in which secondary selection is the norm, and as a policy decision aimed at trying to retain a comprehensive intake. It has fewer students eligible for free school meals than in the past – but this is a trend consistent with national patterns. It has fewer students with special educational needs – but more pupils with Statements. What can be said about pupil performance is that there has been a steady upward trend over the last five years, ahead of the new admissions arrangements. The impact of the 'selective' cohort appears to have generated some additional improvement.

Our overall conclusion was that not only was the school still a good school, but that many aspects of the educational experience offered to the young women of Burntwood appeared to have been enriched. We were particularly struck by the common understandings which parents, teachers and pupils share and which appear, in our view, to underpin the success of the school.

HOW IS THE SCHOOL LED, MANAGED AND ORGANISED?

Having concluded that the school remains a 'good' one, we decided to use our interviews with teachers and pupils to try to understand more about the ingredients of its success. What were the *surface* and *subterranean* features which appeared to characterise how the school was led, managed and organised? What messages about teaching and learning were embedded in those features? We defined *surface* features as the policies, structures and articulated goals of the school and *subterranean* as the ways in which the surface features are played out within the school on a daily basis, supporting or impeding the daily practices of teachers and the processes of teaching and learning. We came to see the issue of leadership as creating the bridge between the two.

The surface features

Evidence from our interviews points to a complex set of structures and policies which staff see as being flexible and open to regular adjustment, and are sustained by the management team. Behavioural or pastoral policy stress rewards, as much as sanctions. There is an established Student Council, run for pupils by pupils and supported by a staff facilitator, which provides an excellent vehicle for giving sixth-formers responsibilities. The school's structures are supported by a strong governing body, members of which, according to one interviewee, are 'proud of what they are governing and very passionate about it – that comes through at governing body meetings' (Member of SMT).

The school management strives to reduce the administrative burdens on staff to allow them to devote more time and energy to teaching. Members of the SMT see their collective task as acting as the 'eyes and ears' of the school, and, although the school has the hierarchical structures typical of large secondary schools, staff feel that they have ready access to SMT members, including the principal herself. In order to provide a fresh challenge and experience, the allotted roles and responsibilities of members of the SMT are changed on a regular basis, 'We all get to do everything – you find out if you are creative or not' (Member of SMT).

Policies are formed through a process of continuous discussion and incorporate the views of all staff, including newly qualified teachers (NQTs) and support staff. Policies are not set in tablets of stone but, according to staff, are 'looked at again and again' to ensure that 'they work for staff and pupils'. (A number of examples were cited here, including a policy on developing the able child.) New policies are drawn up to address identified needs and, over the next three years, the school plans to concentrate on:

- enhancing pupil understanding about the ways in which target-setting can help them improve their performance;
- consolidating understanding about the new school behaviour policy; and
- developing both staff and pupil competence in ICT.

Although over recent years various policies have been introduced in response to national directives (e.g. on curriculum or pastoral matters) Burntwood staff pride themselves on *interpreting* national policies – rather than being governed by them – whilst remaining wholly faithful to the school's ethos and beliefs. An annual review of the school's vision is undertaken and this sets the challenges and pace for the ensuing school year. Success at both individual and whole-school levels is applauded, but the possibility of error is accepted, 'You have to make mistakes – you learn from them' (Teacher).

A clear set of understandings govern staff–pupil relationships. Pupils sign up to fulfil their commitments and expect a similar commitment from their teachers. This mutual understanding of expectations rests on three principal tenets: a profound commitment to equal opportunities ('not just a piece of paper – something in reality' – Member of SMT); a determination to celebrate the multi-ethnic richness of the school population; and an aspiration to create high levels of academic achievement for all pupils, 'whether that be 4 or 12 GCSEs' (Teacher). Achievement is not restricted solely to academic performance in prestigious areas, and all subjects of the curriculum are valued, as are the benefits which can be gained from extra-curricular activities.

The subterranean features

Having looked at the polices and practices of the school, we then turned our attention to the less obvious and 'subterranean' aspects that lie beneath the surface. We explored how the school functions on a daily basis, first in terms of teaching and learning, and secondly, in terms of the relationships amongst and between teachers and students. We considered those elements to be 'subterranean' because they lay beneath the surface of the school, reflecting the pedagogical values and the overall ethos of the school and sustaining the momentum for change and improvement.

The ethos of teaching and learning

What has emerged from our exploration of teaching and learning is not a picture of uniformity in practices: indeed, there is a rich diversity of pedagogical styles and approaches across departments. What teachers have in common is a clear and consistent focus on encouraging pupils to become independent and critical thinkers. It is this overarching ethos and philosophy which characterises how teachers and pupils interact with each other.

Theme 1 – Teaching is not uniform, but consistent in its focus on pupils' needs

Through our shadowing of pupils and observation of classes, we saw numerous examples of different styles of teaching. Some teachers were more formal in their teaching styles than their colleagues. Some were less tolerant of chatter in how they managed their classrooms, whilst others seemed to tolerate more noise. Such variance might be considered by some as inconsistency in the teaching and learning environment within a school. However, the differences we observed did not appear to translate into a confusing set of expectations for pupils, but a rich set of experiences, valued by them.

According to Amsel, one of the pupils we shadowed, 'Every one of my teachers has a different style, but I still feel that I learn from each of them . . . because they are all good in their own way'. Amsel explained this in terms of the differences she perceived in the instructional styles of her maths and English teachers. In maths, she explained, the teacher was 'more stern' and 'didn't like chatter' and lessons were very orderly and rigid. But, even though you felt more 'nervous' in his classes, she said, 'I know that he cares about whether we are learning, like, he will come over when everyone else is working quietly and show me something in my book that I didn't do correctly [on my homework] and explain why'. In contrast, Amsel described her English teacher as having a more informal style. 'He likes it when we all start talking at once about a subject, because he says that it means "we are all engaged".' This made him 'a different kind of effective teacher'.

Amongst Burntwood's teaching staff, there is a clear recognition that departments have different styles and approaches to teaching and learning. The pedagogical differences are appreciated. Our interviews with two NQTs confirmed the differences perceived by Amsel about the teaching styles of her maths and English teachers:

Maths NQT: Maths has a reputation – partly because there is a core textbook and it seems to be very ordered and organised and step by step and for long periods they work silently. This seems to be more traditional really.

English NQT: English is different, we are assessing speaking and listening, every year, as well as reading and writing. We don't have a core textbook, we use different books for different things, it is quite a big resource department. We use all sorts of media like newspapers and magazines. [The pupils] are doing quite hands-on work. The lessons are [noisier] and there is group work and interaction and the sharing of ideas, and you need [pupils] to mix.

Such pedagogical differences are welcomed by the senior management of Burntwood and seen as reflecting the diversity of expertise amongst teachers.

What is unique [about Burntwood] is that there is a consistency about the quality, and a consistency about the regularity about the importance of the delivery of information to the students . . . It is not a question of doing things one way; the bottom line is, if you can prove that the way you do this is of benefit to the students and it fits in with the general area – fine! . . . There are differences, for example, in the English and the Maths classroom. [Teachers use] different methodologies . . . to disseminate information – but the students really enjoy both styles.

(Senior teacher)

Theme 2 – Learning is about encouraging pupils to be active thinkers

The intellectual environment at Burntwood encourages students to be independent thinkers. Teachers encourage students to apply their thinking in order to make choices. One example of this was the PSHE curriculum for Year 7 pupils, where we observed tutor groups being given a range of exercises in different kinds of thinking. During this formal activity, teachers asked pupils 'to work together to interpret different kinds of symbols'. Students were asked to 'think about how this applies in real life' and 'to come up with your own forms of symbols'. Another example was a lesson in which pupils were asked to create a newsletter for Year 6 pupils, and to include in their newsletter what 'they felt was important to them in considering whether or not to attend Burntwood'. We also observed a whole-school assembly in which the headteacher announced an essay contest. Students had to write, in ten sentences or less, what it meant to be a Londoner. The principal described the task as 'not so much a contest in writing, but an exercise in thinking'. She explained, 'I want to know what you think, girls. . . . But you must be able to say it, in writing, succinctly and carefully.'

In asking what it meant to be a Burntwood 'woman of tomorrow', teacher responses included: 'being critical and active thinkers', 'not being accepting', 'being articulate', and 'understanding why they think the way they do'. None of the teachers we interviewed conceptualised their goals for pupils in terms of exam or assessment targets. Teacher expectations were expressed in terms of the kinds of thinking pupils needed to apply to their learning – now and in the future.

Staff and student relationships

Theme 1 Roles and lines of communication are clear and the different voices listened to

Research on school and teacher effectiveness suggests that effective schools are supported by clear organisational structures. What is interesting about Burntwood is the way in which those structures guide and shape how the staff and students interact with each other.

The comments of one teacher we interviewed are typical. She explained that 'the structure of the school and the set-up of all the systems in place [gives] very clear guidance as to what to do and when'. She contrasted Burntwood with her experience in other schools: 'You never feel alone. In some schools you feel that you are going in different directions. Here', she added, 'you know what you are working for'. The two NQTs we interviewed felt that having clear structures enabled more effective teaching to take place. One commented, 'I think [the structures] make a difference as to how kids arrive at a lesson . . . You don't want to worry about behaviour and sanctions issues really, you want to teach to the best of your ability and you want to put your efforts in here.'

The structures at Burntwood provide opportunities for teachers to participate in the decision-making of the school. As another NQT explained, 'We all help to plan [the curriculum]. Time is made for us to contribute ideas; we are introduced to the whole thing by Brigid. We go off into groups and things will be taken into account.' According to another teacher, the equal voice that teachers have is 'the sort of thing you get from the children as well . . . they know that if they work hard then what they have done will be recognised . . . [the school] revolves around recognition of what you are doing'.

Theme 2 – Individual strengths are appreciated and recognised

Regardless of a teacher's role or seniority, or a pupil's background or ability, within Burntwood there is a whole-school ethos – sustained by the principal and her leadership team – which recognises individual strengths and values diversity. Trust infuses relationships and communication. Pupils describe their teachers as 'not racist' and 'seeing in everyone the good that is there'. 'Even if you gave yourself a bad reputation', one Year 9 pupil explained, 'the teachers don't give up on you, but they say we have tried.'

SHARED LEADERSHIP IN PRACTICE

All of the evidence obtained indicates that the school benefits from outstanding leadership from the principal. Teachers at all levels of the school expressed their confidence in the leadership of the school. When asked what was special about Burntwood, most interviewees simply replied, 'Brigid'. When asked to enlarge, they stressed that she had a real vision for the school but also kept her finger very much on the pulse. Lest you think we are extolling a charismatic leadership-from-the-top model, this is not the case:

> [Brigid's] style is essentially collegiate, even though she is not afraid of making difficult choices and can be 'the iron fist in the velvet glove'. Even if she does make an individual decision staff are gratified that they are always given the reason why certain things will happen. It is not a case of being a charismatic leader or somebody who makes sudden decisions – it's always based on needs and what we want to achieve.
>
> (Middle manager)

According to one NQT, the principal 'delegates really well and takes advantage of people's strengths – properly'. 'She doesn't manage people – she leads them', a senior management team member told us; she is 'someone who delegates . . . and I think we recognise the trust that she places in you and the responsibility that she trusts you to take on'. Students, particularly the sixth-formers, relish the leadership challenges which she gives them. The principal herself describes leadership as 'a shared responsibility'.

The principal's leadership is visible and she attempts to be around the school as much as possible, despite being, as she described it to us, 'bogged down with paperwork'. According to her staff, as she circulates around the school, she makes a particular point of talking to new staff and to pupils, 'who feel quite honoured by this'. Through these discussions she is able to convey her pride in the school and her passionate commitment to raising achievement, thereby reinforcing the ethos of the school.

By her own account, the principal strives to achieve a balance between an internal presence in the school and an external involvement. She maintains a broad perspective on education by nurturing outside contacts, undertaking a number of roles with local educational groups and higher education, and inviting people to visit the school and to contribute to debate and discussion – 'I am a great believer in having researchers in school', she told us.

Middle managers are recognised as a vital and dynamic element of the school's operation. They are encouraged to make a genuine input into policy-making, even if the SMT are the ultimate decision-makers. They are regularly given a 'front-of-house role', whereby they are expected to make presentations or receive visitors – 'we are representing the school at all times' is how middle managers see their role. The head clearly recognises the key role of middle managers in ensuring that teaching standards are maintained, as do the managers themselves. 'In practice, it is the middle management who make things happen' (middle manager). She is also aware of the pressures on them, but, as one middle manager told us, 'Make no mistake about it, Brigid will stand up against middle managers like us – she will come out fighting if she thinks we are being unreasonable – and if she says it, you know it is true'. However, the principal is also keen to hear staff views and, in almost every instance, debates and discussions are carried out in a rational manner and arguments are referred back to the school's underpinning equal opportunities policy – 'there is a logic that flows from that – it will end up what is best for the pupil' (Member of SMT).

One fundamental aspect of the principal's leadership is seen as her ability to make good staffing appointments and to put people who subscribe to the school's ethos into key roles. Her criteria for selecting staff are 'intelligence and commitment to the school's ideals'. Expectations are high and all new staff are given a clear indication, either by the principal or by other members of the SMT, of what they should achieve. Considerable emphasis is given to such aspects of their work as setting appropriate standards, timekeeping, marking and returning work and, above all, lesson presentation – 'If you walked round this building you would be hard-pressed to find a lesson that wasn't a lesson' (Member of SMT).

Respect and encouragement from senior management appear to contribute to the high staff morale. The head constantly refers to successes achieved in the course of any given year and although staff are expected to work hard, they feel that they are valued. The principal expects staff to be interested in wider educational issues and to be, in her terms, 'educationally literate'. At the beginning of each academic year, she delivers a 'state of the nation' address which touches upon national, local and school issues and pulls the threads together. Such an approach leads to staff being more focused and better equipped to participate in consultation. From the outset, NQTs are encouraged to undertake a whole-school role in an area that goes beyond their subject expertise.

Inevitably, teachers and pupils have some concerns about, for example, the lack of ethnic diversity within the teaching staff. Whilst teachers welcome the robust departmental culture which characterises the school, they also regret the lack of a strong staffroom tradition and the opportunities which this creates for the more informal exchange of ideas across departments. As one teacher remarked ruefully, 'We are sometimes introduced to a new member of staff at the beginning of the year, and then never see them again'. The issue of 'succession' when the current principal stands down is also in teachers' minds, although there is a shared view that whenever that happens 'the fundamental ethos of the school' will remain untouched.

WHAT CAN BE LEARNED FROM THE BURNTWOOD EXPERIENCE?

There is much to take from the experience of Burntwood school. There are issues to do with gender. The young women of Burntwood thrive in a culture which reinforces their sense of themselves as young women. At recreation they have fun, enjoying the talents and exuberance of their peers. The intellectual challenge within the school and the broad definition of achievement help reinforce the view that success is not a minority occupation reserved for the academic high-flyers.

There are issues to do with structure and a recognition that good schools are not made overnight. Well thought-out and executed management systems and policy arrangements are critical in a school as large and complex as Burntwood. They help set the boundaries and expectations about what can be achieved and how. How has Burntwood maintained such high expectations and a coherent set of policies, practices and structures when some schools have buckled under the pressure of a changing system? Much is to do with the underlying set of beliefs embedded in the practices and relationships.

Core Belief 1 – Everyone is valued

> You feel valued . . . and that comes from the headteacher and gets reinforced by the senior management team. The fact that people have different ways of communicating and showing [that belief] does not change the fact that everyone knows they are appreciated and has a role within the school.
>
> (Teacher)

> If you need to talk, [the teachers] are there . . . and they will help you.
>
> (Pupil)

On the surface, Burntwood's organisational and management structure closely resembles that of other schools. It is led from the top, operates through departments, and there are clear demarcations between the roles of pupils and teachers. What distinguishes Burntwood is that both teachers and pupils feel valued members of the school. This sense of appreciation was perceived by senior managers and teachers alike as coming from the principal. She is seen as a crucial force in nurturing and reinforcing the belief that every individual is part of the Burntwood community, and she treats everyone accordingly. Trust is the key. The principal trusts her staff and gives them responsibilities. They in turn trust their students and give them responsibilities. The caring and nurturing attitudes of teachers reinforce students' feelings of being valued as individuals. Pupils describe themselves as 'feeling respected as women' and 'being well looked-after'. Teachers 'make you feel good', 'reassure you', 'give you advice'.

Core Belief 2 – Everyone can succeed

> Teachers and students work incredibly hard here, and I think the work rate here is phenomenal. It seems to me [that there is] a different measure of effort here. In schools in which I have taught previously, teachers have worked hard but there seems [a kind of] urgency here.
>
> (Member of SMT)

> [At Burntwood] you are free to make the choices for the future and it is clear. It is like the slogan! The best education today for the women of tomorrow! It is very like that here – you learn you have choices here.
>
> (Pupil)

In addition to feeling valued, teachers and pupils have strong feelings of optimism, often expressed in terms of 'high expectations', which are reinforced by a central belief that everyone is expected to work hard and to achieve. There is a sense of urgency which stems, according to a senior management team member, from 'a desire to do the best job possible . . . Something that is instilled into students.' The students we interviewed told us that 'by working hard', 'you can succeed in life'.

Core Belief 3 – Everyone is entitled to an equal opportunity to succeed

> [The school aims to] develop pupils' skills to the highest level. . . . All things funnel into that, both academically and socially . . . There is a recognition that the students are a part of a major multicultural institution and . . . need to have choices. Brigid talks to us about pathways . . . and that is important for students in where they want to go.
>
> (Member of SMT)

> [My learning support] is not embarrassing . . . because everyone wants you to do well. I'm getting extra help because my form tutor and my teachers thought I could use it. And they wanted me to do better in my lessons. And it is definitely helping!
>
> (Pupil)

The common belief that teachers and pupils feel valued is enhanced by the opportunities and choices offered to them. Success depends not only on individuals' being offered different pathways, multiple opportunities, but on being given support to maximise those opportunities.

The significant increase, over the last five years, in the level and types of academic support directed towards pupils of low ability has enabled them to make choices. For low-achieving students in particular, being given the opportunity to succeed is about not being labelled by their teachers, despite previous mistakes. 'If you get yourself a bad reputation because of your behaviour', a pupil told us, 'the teachers don't give up on you.'

There are choices and opportunities for staff, as well as pupils, for what one teacher described to us as 'leadership and growth . . . The principal looks carefully at what people might be ready for and so it is not just sink or swim . . . she is honest and [willing to] admit that something is not working, but [then wants] you to become part of the solution.'

And finally at Burntwood, strongly connected to these core beliefs, there are issues to do with leadership. School leadership is conventionally conceived, as editors of an international book on leadership have described it, as 'a role-based function assigned to, or acquired by, one person in an organisation, who uses his or her power to influence the actions of others' (Riley and Louis, 2000: 213). They offer an expanded view of leadership which has four key elements, all four of which are evident at Burntwood.

The first is to do with the 'mobility and fragility of leadership, the shifting sands, the need to manage conflict as well as competing expectations' (ibid.: 214). Effective school leaders need to be adept at responding to the complex and fluid inner life of the school, as well as to the demanding and ever-changing external context (Riley and MacBeath 1998; Riley 1998b). At Burntwood the school's capacity to 're-invent itself' (as the principal described it to us) in response to a changing internal and external environment has enabled it to maintain momentum. What could have been experienced by staff as turbulence has been received as exciting professional challenges.

The second component of this expanded view of leadership is a recognition of the *diverse and values-driven* nature of leadership. Effective leaders recognise that leadership is beyond the heroic undertakings of one individual in a school – the headteacher or school principal – and seek to provide opportunities for teachers to study, to learn and to share in a leadership approach which is rooted in values.

The third component is to do with the notion of leadership as an *organic* activity, dependent on *interrelations and connections*. The school is not an isolated institution but is connected to a wider educational community, both locally and nationally.

The fourth and final element of this conceptualisation of leadership is to do with the strong connections which are made between *leading and learning*. Successful school leaders model professional values and aspirations, have clear goals about student learning, and support teachers in meeting professional challenges (Riley and Louis, 2000: 215).

What stands out about Burntwood is the way that support and motivation go hand in hand. Pupils and teachers exude confidence and self-worth. The school is successful because success is defined in broader terms than raising achievement. It is defined in terms of the school's desire to provide every pupil with the opportunity to succeed, in whatever choice they make – for 'the best way for them'.

NOTES

1 We interviewed 15 members of the school staff: the headteacher, 4 senior managers, 3 middle managers, 4 main-grade professional teachers, 2 newly qualified teachers (NQTs) and 1 learning support staff member. We talked with 5 pupils (shadowed 1 Year 7 and 1 Year 9 student and interviewed 2 Year 9 students and 1 Year 10 student).

   Brigid Beattie, Headteacher of Burntwood School 1986–2001, died suddenly in March 2001. This account of her work bears testimony to the real difference she made to hundreds of teachers and pupils.

2 There are ten state secondary schools in Wandsworth. Three are non-selective, three operate a banding policy (i.e. endeavouring to recruit across the ability range) and four (including Burntwood) are partially selective.

ACKNOWLEDGEMENT

The authors would like to thank the Burntwood school community for their open and supportive responses to our many inquiries.

REFERENCES

DfEE (1999a) *Statistical First Release 15/1999.*
DfEE (1999b) *Statistical Bulletin 3/1999.*
DfEE (1999c) *Statistical Bulletin 12/99.*
DfEE (1999d) *Statistical Bulletin 4/1999.*
DfEE (2000a) Annual Schools' Census Data (Form 7), 1999/2000.
DfEE (2000b) *Statistical First Release 18/2000.*
DfEE (2000c) *Statistical Bulletin 4/2000.*

DfEE (2000d) *Statistics of Education: Pupil Absence and Truancy from School in England 1998/99*, London: Stationery Office.

DfEE (2000e) *Statistical First Release 20/2000*.

Keys, W. and Fernandes, C. (1993) *What Do Students Think about School?* Slough: National Foundation for Educational Research.

Mortimore, P., Davies, H. and Portway, S. (1996) Burntwood Secondary Girls' School, Wandsworth, in National Commission on Education, *Success against the Odds*, London: Routledge.

Office for Standards in Education (1997) Burntwood School for Girls Inspection Report, March.

Riley, K. A. (1998a) *Whose School Is it Anyway?* London: Falmer Press.

Riley, K. A. (1998b) Creating the leadership climate, *International Journal of Leadership in Education*, 2, 137–53.

Riley, K. A. and MacBeath, J. (1998) Effective leaders and effective schools, in J. MacBeath (ed.) *Effective School Leadership: Responding to Change*, London: Paul Chapman.

Riley, K. A. and Louis, K. S. (2000) *Leadership for Change and School Reform: International Perspectives*, London: Falmer Press.

Sarason, S. (1990) *The Predictable Failure of Educational Reform*, San Francisco and Oxford: Jossey-Bass Publishers.

7

HAYWOOD HIGH SCHOOL
Stoke-on-Trent

Valerie Hannon

In *Success against the Odds* (1996), Michael Barber and his colleagues summed up their chapter on Haywood High School with the following words:

> Haywood High School is certainly an improving school, and has travelled a long way from the gloomy place it found itself to be in the late 1980s. This improvement can be seen in its results, its staying-on rates, attitudes within the school and community attitudes to the school. The school hopes that the investment of thought, commitment, energy and insight that it has made will also bear fruit in terms of those stubborn, hard statistics of examination achievement. It is hard to be certain, but the evidence indicates, in our view, that the process of improvement will indeed continue in the next few years.

Were they right?

The recent history of the school may for convenience be divided into three phases. In the decade leading up to 1989, low numbers and other problems led to an amalgamation which in itself was traumatic and left the school at a low ebb. The reputation of the school had fallen dramatically, in part as a result of poor pupil behaviour and truancy connected to low staff morale. Instead of its standard number of 180, the school managed to recruit only 100 students, and the year group entered the school with very poor levels of literacy and minimal parental support. In 1989 a new headteacher, Yvonne Jeffries, was appointed. She led a school improvement strategy with tangible and remarkable results, and it was this strategy, over 1989–95, upon which the previous *Success against the Odds* chapter reported. At that time, when asked to reflect upon the school's achievements in terms of exam success, and whether the results would be better in 1995, the head replied: 'They have to be'. The third phase, 1995–2000, has seen the completion of Yvonne Jeffries' tenure of leadership of the school with her retirement. It is an appropriate moment to reflect upon the questions central to this volume. Has improvement been sustained? If so, how has this been achieved over this length of time, and can the school now be said to be a successful school?

THE EVIDENCE: OUTCOMES

In the case of Haywood High, evidence of continued improvement is easy to find. To begin with 'headline' performance data which appear in league tables – and, in turn, influence perceptions of the school – the figures show a steady improvement in performance since 1995. Then, 28 per cent of students achieved 5 or more grades A*–C at GCSE, and 84 per cent achieved 5 or more grades A*–G. In 1999, the respective proportions were 36 per cent and 92 per cent. In 1999, the improvement has been steady with the exception of a 'blip' in 1997, which is discussed below. The proportion achieving 5 or more grades A*–G actually exceeded the overall national average for that year (88.5 per cent). On this measure, the school is now successful in absolute as well as relative terms. Comparison of the 5 A*–C measure with the national average (47.9 per cent) shows that the school is still trailing in absolute terms: however, and crucially, the *rates* of improvement on both measures are higher than those achieved nationally. Average points scores per

Table 7.1 Haywood High School, City of Stoke-on-Trent

	1995–96	1999–2000
Type and status	County School 11–16 (Mixed)	County School 11–16 (Mixed)
Pupil roll	881	996
Headteacher	Yvonne Jeffries (apptd 1989)	(a) Yvonne Jeffries, CBE (b) David Dickinson (apptd spring term 2000)
% white pupils	87.7	87.9 *English average: 88.5(1)*
% pupils with English as an additional language	11.4	9.1
% pupils eligible for free school meals (FSM)	27.0	29.3 *English average: 16.9 (1)*
% pupils with special educational needs, incl. Statements	5.1	16.9 *English average: 22.0 (1)*
Pupil/teacher ratio (incl. head)	17.6 *English average: 16.6*	18.0 *English average: 17.1*
Support staff ratio hours (2)	7.8	10.3
% pupils obtaining GCSE (A*–C grades) 5+ subjects	29.0 *English average: 44.6*	36.0 (1) *English average: 47.9 (1)*
Average GCSE point score per pupil	Not applicable	32.7 (1) *English average: 38.1 (1)*
% year 11 students with no GCSE passes	1 *English average: 7.8*	4 (1) *English average: 6.9 (1)*
Post-16 participation in full-time education or training (%)	59.4 *English average: 70.4*	66.3 (1) *English average: 70.1 (1)*

Table 7.1 continued

OfSTED grade (PANDA) re: GCSE/ GNVQ score per pupil in similar FSM school group	Not applicable	B (1) (3)
OfSTED grade (PANDA) re: GCSE/GNVQ score per pupil in similar school group re: prior attainment at Key Stage Three	Not applicable	D (1) (3)

Key:
(1) 1998–99
(2) Full-time equivalent (f.t.e.) support staff hours per week, per f.t.e. teacher
(3) OfSTED PANDA rubric:
    D PANDA pupils' results were **below** the average for similar schools
    B PANDA pupils' results were **above** the average for similar schools

pupil improved from 1998 to 1999 from 31 to 32.7 – roughly the same rate as the national improvement (from 37 to 38.1)

Of more significance, of course, are statistical comparisons which take into account context and value-added elements over time. The OfSTED PANDA benchmark data (which compares the performance outcomes of schools with similar levels of eligibility for free school meals) rates Haywood High School as above average in relation to the proportions of students achieving 5+ A*–C and 1+ A*–G (or GNVQ equivalent); and the school is rated as well above the average for similar schools in relation to the proportion of students achieving 5+ A*–G grades.

Value-added indicators are more difficult to interpret. In this case 'value-added' indicators mean evidence which compares the school's performance in increasing the rate of pupils' achievement scores between Key Stage Three (KS3) and GCSE against that of schools with similar levels of prior performance. The OfSTED PANDA report for 1999 suggests that, in relation to schools with similar levels of performance at KS3, Haywood High School's performance is above-average regarding the 5+ A*–G indicator, average respecting the 1+ A*–G indicator, and below-average regarding the 5+ A*–C indicator.

Arguably, the 'YELLIS' system gives a more accurate assessment of the value added by a school. 'YELLIS' is the Year 11 Information System run for some years now by Durham University under the direction of Professor Carol Fitz-Gibbon. It uses pupil-level data, comparing GCSE achievement in each syllabus with the scores on a previously administered baseline test. This is put in the context of the achievement of similar pupils in other schools. This analysis over 3 years indicates that, other than a setback in 1997 (again, discussed below), using the most accurate methods available, with fair comparisons pupil by pupil, Haywood High School is doing well. The 1999 profile shows positive value-added results across all subject areas save two, some of them particularly good. This is described as 'an impressive achievement'.

These rates of improvement, and everything which leads to their achievement, have begun the happy spiral upward of success. The drift away has ended. The school has continued to grow since the 1995 case study when there were 830 pupils: by September 2000 there were 1030. The school has become much more attractive locally, admitting above its standard number of 180 in the last two years, and this year facing 34 appeals over the limit for entry to the school. Participation rates in education post-16 have also risen. From 21.9 per cent in 1989, the rate had risen to 59.4 per cent in 1995 and to 66.3 per cent in 1999. Again, there have been some 'blips': the rate of improvement between 1989 and 1995 had outstripped that of Stoke, Staffordshire and the national average; recently it has slowed.

The school came under the scrutiny of OfSTED in 1997. The inspection team concluded that:

Haywood High School is a very good school, with a record of sustained improvement . . . There is a strong emphasis on raising the pupils' achievements and improving standards. The school provides its pupils with a good education in a supportive, orderly and safe environment. It is strongly supported by staff and pupils and is highly regarded in the local community.

. . . Sound academic standards are achieved and they exceed what could be expected from the overall attainment of pupils on entry to the school.

. . . Standards of behaviour and pupils' punctuality for lessons are very good.

. . . Pupils receive a good education. The quality of teaching is at least sound in all subjects, and it is good in a number of them . . . Overall, the curriculum shows breadth and balance in both key stages and courses are effectively planned . . . A wide range of extra-curricular activities provides pupils with opportunities to extend their curricular experiences and broaden their social development.

. . . The partnership between the school and parents is making a very positive contribution to the quality of pupils' education. Information for parents is good . . . Generally, parents are very supportive of the school.

. . . The school is very efficient . . . and very well managed.

(Haywood High School OfSTED Inspection Report,
21–25 April 1997)

HOW STACKED ARE 'THE ODDS'?

How difficult is the challenge facing this school? There is no doubt that Haywood High School serves a relatively disadvantaged area. The surroundings of the school have changed little since Michael Barber's team visited in 1995. Situated in Burslem, it still serves the same large deprived housing estates; there are still the second-hand shops and the run-down feel to the neighbourhood. There has been

Figure 7.1 Independent learning at its best: pupils working alongside an artist in residence

no dramatic upturn in the economic fortunes of this part of the Potteries; indeed the view was expressed that it had been experiencing a mini-recession, with property prices falling. This view is not altogether upheld by the data on unemployment rates, which show, in March 2000, a fall to about a half of their 1996 level (8.3 per cent). More broadly however, Stoke-on-Trent is the 48th most deprived local authority area (out of 354) in the UK. The OfSTED Inspection team found that

> there is a significant degree of social deprivation and the proportion of pupils from disadvantaged backgrounds is higher than the national average. The number of pupils eligible for free school meals is above average, whereas the percentage of pupils from advantaged backgrounds is well below the national average.

> . . . police have identified a significant amount of criminal
> and anti-social behaviour in the school's immediate neighbour-
> hood.

Today, the proportion of students eligible for free school meals is 29.3 per cent, in contrast to the England and Wales average of 16.9 per cent. High though this is, it does not place the school in the most challenged category. Thus, for example, in its June 2000 report *Improving City Schools*, OfSTED used as its criterion for inclusion in its sample of significantly disadvantaged urban schools those with free school meals (FSM) eligibility of over 35 per cent; and the secondary schools it visited for the purpose of that report had FSM eligibility averaging 57 per cent. With regard to other factors which add to the challenges faced by a school, Haywood has 12.1 per cent of its pupils from ethnic minority groups (the same as the OfSTED sample), broadly comparable to the English figure of 11.5 per cent. The proportion of pupils with English as an additional language is 9.1 per cent (7.8 per cent for England). Levels of special educational needs are about average. It was not reported that the school faced particularly outstanding difficulties of highly challenging behaviour from new entrants, or high levels of pupil mobility.

To say all this is not to detract from the challenges the school does face and has met. In such circumstances to have sustained progress and improvement to such a degree over 11 years is a remarkable feat, and one worthy of investigation and reflection.

THE TOOLS FOR THE JOB?

If we are to understand and, hopefully, apply more broadly the lessons from Haywood High School's sustained success, we need to have a grasp of its starting position in terms of the resources available to it to do the job. Are the financial and other resources which Haywood's problems attract significant, and to what use have they been put? This becomes a particularly interesting question in light of OfSTED's finding (in *Improving City Schools*) that the well-known variation in funding from school to school increases with greater levels of disadvantage.

It is important to remember too that, in addition to the particular problems of disadvantage, the range of initiatives, requirements and expectations have markedly increased with the election of the new government in 1997. More paperwork, but, also, more opportunities to bid for extra cash.

In 1995 the school was facing cuts and had little in the way of reserves. The story of Haywood frequently throws up examples of optimistic opportunism, or 'embracing the obstacle'. This is one such example. The head used this otherwise unwelcome and potentially damaging requirement to change the profile of the staffing. In particular, it enabled some staff, whose classroom practice was not showing signs of improvement or who, for other reasons, were not able to make a vigorous contribution to the development of the school, to take early retirement or depart voluntarily. She no longer expected to hear the rhetorical question 'What can you expect from the Burslem child?' uttered in the staffroom.

The overall financial position of the school has undoubtedly improved, due in part to the virtuous cycle of success (increased rolls generating a stronger resource base), in part to improved funding from the local authority, and in part to opportunistic exploitation of the availability of other income streams. The basic funding per pupil (that is, the total delegated budget divided by the number of students on roll) in 1999/2000 was £2096. This is low when compared with the overall picture nationally and is very much at the lower end of the spectrum when compared with the OfSTED sample of (admittedly more disadvantaged) schools. What is clear, however, is that the school has been adept in utilising additional sources. These include the Two Towns Project (a school improvement initiative financed by the Paul Hamlyn Foundation, Staffordshire County Council and the local Training and Enterprise

Council); more recently, the Cobridge Single Regeneration Budget (SRB); and, imminently, the Excellence in Cities programme. Moreover, echoing OfSTED's finding, it is clear that what resources have been available have been managed with skill, so that all funding has been very well used. Interestingly, one variation on the OfSTED findings is that increasing the proportion of funding spent on employing teachers has not been Haywood's highest priority. Although the overall number of teachers has increased to 53 (from the 1995 level of 46), the proportion of the budget spent on teachers has decreased, from 77.2 per cent in 1997/98 to 74.7 per cent in 1999/2000. However, the school places a premium on staff development and has resourced it accordingly.

In capital terms, the last phase of the new building work which was incomplete in 1995 is now in place, and the overall environment is well-kept and reasonably attractive, though by no means outstanding. In particular, the school lacks important facilities such as a sports hall. Whilst just adequate, the school's resources in information and learning technology are not extensive. The school is hoping that this position will be transformed through a series of new funding streams: Capital Challenge, the Private Finance Initiative and the Excellence in Cities programme (by which it will become a City Learning Centre – described below in 'The Future').

We have, then, a picture which shows that the financial fortunes of the school have improved but have not been radically transformed. It has certainly enjoyed a greater level of stability and predictability than formerly. What has been central has been an emphasis on good management of the resources available; and, as the story below shows, leadership which puts people first.

HAYWOOD'S STORY OF SUSTAINED IMPROVEMENT

Success against the Odds in 1996 described how the school had overcome reorganisation trauma and potential meltdown. Reading it now, one has the sense of foundations being laid: the beginning of a journey of self-belief. There is a sense too of the fragility of things ('Would the results be better?', 'They have to be.'). The sections above have sought to provide the necessary hard evidence of continued improvement, and document some of the characteristics of this, now unequivocally, successful school. But they cannot capture the sense of confidence which now pervades the school and the conversations with all those who work within it or who know it well. There has been, not only consolidation, but a sense of unstoppable momentum generated which, even to a hardened observer, is striking and humbling.

The previous volume postulated ten 'features of success' (presented again in Appendix A), and the circumstances of each school were evaluated against that template. In reassessing them in the case of Haywood, there is little doubt that whilst all the ten continue to have relevance, the overwhelming importance of the first – the quality of the leadership of the head and the senior staff – simply cannot be overemphasised. All roads of enquiry eventually led back to this central feature. The capacity to focus on the other features, to select and implement key policies, depended fundamentally on this quality. In view of this it is important to record the characteristics of the leadership encountered at Haywood High.

Leadership at Haywood: determined optimism about people – shrewdness of judgement

It should first be remarked that whilst leadership at Haywood has been a shared and collective affair, this has only been possible, paradoxically, because of the extraordinary qualities of Yvonne Jeffries, the head who has led the school for eleven years. She was awarded a CBE early in 2000, when she also retired, only because retirement age rules required it and through no sense of exhaustion on her part. Indeed, Yvonne is now active within the LEA helping to restore the fortunes of other schools. In relation to her management qualities ('style' seems too ephemeral a word to capture characteristics of which people had such a vivid sense), *Success against the Odds* (1996) listed three of note: a rare awareness of, and focus upon, people; her ability to delegate; the ability and readiness to take responsibility for tough decisions.

Five years on, the harvest of the combination of these gifts is there to see. One outcome is a relatively large Leadership Group which is highly pro-active, energetic, and empowered. The new head-teacher recounted how impressed he was by the cohesiveness and stability of the group. So committed to the school do individuals tend to be that one member, having left the school, subsequently chose to return to it. Moreover, it was striking how far Yvonne Jeffries' attitudes towards people had been internalised by the members of the Leadership Group. Her optimism about and belief in people turned out to be contagious. One put it succinctly:

All her geese are swans.

Her recognition of the potential of people transferred to Leadership Group members – not least because they had experienced it in relation to themselves. Another remarked:

You're not going to get the best out of people unless they feel special – staff and students too. You've got to value, value, value staff.

When asked why he had stayed with the school for so long – in what was clearly an exhausting and challenging environment, one Leadership Group member replied:

It's always felt like exciting times. There's such momentum now – it's a dynamic thing. You feel as if you are making an impression and you can't let go. I feel such a pride in the school. I've never felt stuck in one role – because there's always opportunities if you work hard.

The use of 'we' characterised the discourse of the Leadership Group:

> We know we've got the support of the staff even though there are a lot of initiatives on the go – it's because they know they will have the opportunities for professional development – *and* personal development.

And, in relation to perceptions of the students:

> We now know that there's a lot more to come from these children. And that all originates from Yvonne. We never have moaning sessions. The team is so strong – it always pulls you along.

Delegation and empowerment extended beyond the Leadership Group:

> It has all been exhausting – but it's been the way it was done. I do get tired out and sometimes feel cynicism. But we all feel a part. If you want to change something, you can get involved – right now there's a number of working parties on the go – and it becomes a policy.
>
> (Long-serving teacher)

In view of the range and demands of the initiatives that the school has under way, what is of particular interest is how momentum, energy and commitment seem not only to have been sustained over this period, but actually to have increased. Yvonne Jeffries' approach was shrewd, discriminating *and* passionately idealistic:

> The key issue was to develop self esteem in the staff and the pupils; and to be very very discriminating in choosing initiatives. I always tried to be alert, looking around. I looked at a lot of stuff on motivation [the school eventually adopted the Pacific Institute

'Investing in Excellence' approach]. If people could feel the school was really improving, then they could see everything as an opportunity. And then – well, I was always energised by what was going on in school.

To sustain herself, Yvonne took advantage of the opportunities for networking and development offered by Keele University; she benefited from one-day drop-ins to the Stoke-on-Trent Community Partnership; but there were no lengthy secondments or job-swaps.

If colleagues, staff and students rated Yvonne Jeffries highly five years ago, then that esteem has grown immeasurably in the subsequent period – because she showed resilience and stayed with the school for the long haul. One of the issues which must concern all who are concerned with policy in this area is what the cost might be to those who are prepared to commit themselves to the leadership of schools. Yvonne Jeffries did not dwell on this, other than to say, 'Let's just say I paid with my private life'.

A good atmosphere generated by shared aims and values and an attractive physical environment

The atmosphere – or ethos, or culture – has been one of the main beneficiaries of the leadership style of the school. Because it has been so person-centred, the resulting atmosphere is unusually welcoming and friendly – a feature remarked upon by all respondents in this study. It immediately struck the newly appointed headteacher when he attended for interview. The atmosphere influences other staff when they look around the school prior to interview. In two focus groups held with students it was top of the list of both when asked what they liked most about the school. They commented further on the calm, 'respectful' attitude of the staff. The 'morning briefing' for staff has continued to be an important feature, providing opportunities for sharing information, successes, encouragement – and a laugh.

The school has benefited simultaneously from continuity of staff – especially the senior team – remaining in post, alongside intensive staff development. Staff mobility has been relatively low, but not stagnant. That has enabled judicious selection of newly qualified teachers (often drawn from the cream of the crop placed in the school on the Keele PGCE course) to inject freshness and new ideas. When long-serving staff were asked why they had stayed at Haywood, their replies touched on the same issues: the friendliness, the openness, the valuing. A further outcome is that much developmental work, as well as many extra-curricular activities for students, has been unpaid. Like all other school staffs, Haywood High teachers sometimes feel that enough is enough:

> Everybody works really hard! I don't know how they keep it up really. I think it's because they feel appreciated. I feel really supported by my head of department. It's nice to get a pat on the back, and I feel there's a respect for my skills.
>
> (New teacher)

In summary, therefore, the physical environment at Haywood High, although pleasant, with interesting displays, carpeted, clean and tidy, is not spectacular. The social, interpersonal environment, however, is just that, and its value is probably inestimable.

Emphasis on staff development

This characteristic, which was not singled out in the previous volume, is one which seems to have emerged in Haywood High School as a key focus. Staff at all levels repeatedly referred to its importance to the school. Moreover, the reported *substance* of the developmental opportunities or activities appeared to relate very closely to the postulated features in *Success against the Odds* (1996) – especially high expectations of students, their motivation, rewards and incentives. Good-quality in-service training seemed to be an accompanying feature of new developments: for example, the academic tutoring programme and the revised approach to target-setting. Extensive use seems to have been made of the opportunities provided by Keele University in terms of lectures, its 'Masterclasses' and other programmes. Staff development was not confined to formal or external courses. A relatively new teacher described how her skills had been developed by being observed by a senior colleague and by receiving reinforcement as well as positive proposals. The deliberate emphasis on staff development has paid enormous dividends, directly to students in terms of improved teaching as well as to the staff who know that their skills are being enhanced, and that they are in turn valued for it.

Focusing on teaching and learning

The other key initiatives which would seem to have been central to the school's improvement over the past five years could be categorised in a number of ways; but fundamentally they all relate to the school's approach to teaching and learning. Amongst many which could be listed are:

- The introduction of an academic tutoring system. Introduced at the end of Y10 and continuing until the end of Y11, this is intended to support students on issues such as coping with coursework, strategies for revision, or personal concerns. It promotes student self-evaluation.
- A whole-school target-setting initiative. The school took two days out to enable more in-depth discussions with parents and students than are possible in conventional parent evenings, to determine individual learning targets.
- The introduction of mentoring schemes involving external mentors.
- Involvement in the Port Vale Football Club 'Playing for Success' scheme, which targets 80 primary and secondary pupils a night

to utilise the study centre established by the initiative, to focus primarily on literacy, numeracy and ICT skills. This scheme (part of a national programme) is a partnership between the school, the club, the LEA and the DfEE.

- A 'Learning Enhancement Programme' under which core skills are taught intensively, by cross-curriculum delivery, to students identified through testing.
- Involvement in the 'Cognitive Acceleration in Science' (CASE) initiative.
- Engagement in 'Aiming High', a creative arts and school improvement project involving all Y9s – a local business initiative.

'Initiative overload' has been avoided – but only through the creation of the conditions described earlier in the case study. Judicious selection, backed by sound staff development in a generous, supportive atmosphere has meant that staff have embraced development.

> You're either going forward or you're going backwards. There's now a culture where staff see that there really do exist opportunities for their own development: but we always come back to – what's the impact on the children? We're always looking for ways to impact.
>
> (Leadership Group member)

Moreover, the school has continued to engage in and encourage networking, despite the demise of the Two Towns Project (which was undoubtedly instrumental in giving the school a vital initial impetus). Subsequently, the school has been anxious to avoid becoming isolated. Keele University has been significant to it in avoiding this, as was the local Community Partnership. For the future, the school is looking to the LEA's Six Towns Project, and to the Excellence in Cities programme to provide it with the networking opportunities it feels it needs.

Other 'features of success'

Focus on the above characteristics of Haywood High School – which seem to me to be pre-eminent in having contributed to sustained improvement – should not be taken to imply that the other 'features of success' postulated in *Success against the Odds* (1996) have been irrelevant or neglected. It is possible to discern advances on all of these fronts. Work on assessing how students are progressing, for example, had been taken forward by means of developing the 'day book' (or student planner) system, which was also being used as a vehicle for more regular and pro-active communication with parents. Similarly, work was being done through the medium of a number of schemes to increase students' understanding of grading systems so that they were able more capably to self-assess. It has already been remarked how the system of rewards and incentives had been the subject of a staff working party which had overhauled it with the aim of making it more inclusive. The school was seeking to systematise its approach to self-evaluation, with a more standardised cycle of planning and review: it felt that a stronger framework would help it to formalise and keep better track of the progress of initiatives.

THE IMPACT OF EXTERNAL POLICIES AND CHANGE

Like all schools Haywood High has had to adapt to a fast-changing national and local policy framework. At local level, it became a part of the newly created unitary authority of Stoke-on-Trent in the local government reorganisation of 1997, having previously been a part of the large and well-regarded Staffordshire County Council. The school was phlegmatic about the change:

> We missed the size, and the County meetings, those opportunities for networking. There's less diversity. There are few

subject specialist inspectors now, which is a bit of a problem —
but there are advisory teachers. It's more intimate now.

(Leadership Group member)

The transfer was pretty seamless. It didn't really make a lot of
impact.

(Former headteacher)

Having been initially 'deeply dispirited' by the introduction
of published league tables, the school came to regard them 'as a
kind of necessary evil'; some respondents believed that they had
contributed to raising achievement, especially when concepts of
benchmarking were more widely understood.

The single policy which attracted the greatest opprobrium within
the school was the OfSTED inspection process — and this is so,
notwithstanding the fact that it took place three years ago and that
the resulting report was excellent.

It set us back a year, no question. It drained me and it drained
the staff. Everybody was tired and exhausted. At the end, I just
felt I had to go away and mourn privately.

(Former headteacher)

The 'set-back' was no mere psychological phenomenon. The year
of the inspection, 1997, is the one year when, as the analysis in the
previous section on 'outcomes' demonstrates, examination results
did not continue on their steady upward trajectory, but fell back,
before picking up again in 1998. Displaying its characteristic
opportunistic optimism, the school, of course, looked for the
positive points and tried to move forward:

It did demoralise — so much work just to get ready for it! But we
said: Let's see what we can get from it. We tried to use it like a
spur.

(Leadership Group member)

Interestingly, no one made reference to the Inspection Report's 'Key Issues for Action' as significant in developing the improvement strategy. There is little evidence to be found here to support OfSTED's claim, made in *Improving City Schools*, that amongst the features which enable schools to sustain improvement against the odds is 'the rigour with which they are scrutinised'.

THE FUTURE

The story of Haywood High School shows, amongst other things, how success builds success. One of the key disadvantages of schools in challenging circumstances is the difficulty in attracting leaders of high calibre. The school looks to its future under the new leadership of an experienced and successful headteacher who was drawn to work at the school – notwithstanding its disadvantages – by an appreciation of what had been achieved and how this might be built upon. Though he had experience in the inner cities, his immediate past headship had been in the well-heeled environment of Winchester.

> One of the parents said to me: what on earth have you moved here from there for? But I'd read the account in *Success against the Odds*; I liked the idea of working with a new LEA – they seemed very go-ahead. And I was so impressed by the atmosphere here.
> (New headteacher)

With the new head, the Leadership Group are now energetically devising new lines of development. They have responded relatively positively to the government's introduction of thresholds and performance pay, whilst feeling that it has been done on too tight a timescale, with insufficient time for the depth of preparation which the school prefers and which has marked its work. The system is judged to be an improvement on the previous system of appraisal and to sit well with the school's own system of performance management. In turn, it is felt it will provide an additional spur to improving the school's use of data, which many mentioned as an upcoming focus for development.

There was no shortage of ideas for the kinds of directions in which the school might move in the coming years. More intensive focus on teaching and learning was anticipated, especially utilising understandings of multiple intelligences, differing learning styles, and the contribution new information and learning technology could make. The school was excited by the scope engagement in the Excellence in Cities programme as a City Learning Centre would provide; it was chosen for this by a partnership of headteachers and the LEA. This will lead to Haywood becoming a community school, and sharing initiatives on innovation in teaching and learning. Moreover, the school was becoming yet further aspirational in respect of outcomes: it is looking to achieve 65 per cent of its students staying on in education post-16 (from 57 per cent in 1999) and is broadening its curriculum accordingly and forging closer links with post-16 providers to achieve it.

The overpowering impression conveyed by Haywood High is one of unstoppable momentum. It would seem that through inspired leadership the right foundations can be laid – especially in terms of the development of a critical mass of skilled and committed people. These, in turn, transmit those qualities to others. Thus, it is possible that the fragility of continuing improvement, the susceptibility to exhaustion and set-back, is overcome. This is not to negate the importance of systems and structures: they are vital as the secure scaffolding to support the building work. But they are not what motivate professional people to stay the distance despite the difficulties:

> It's not always roses. Sometimes I've thought: if there's one more initiative, I'm out the door! But when I see how the children have changed. The self-esteem. It's just – pushing forward.
>
> (Long-serving teacher)

8

HAZELWOOD COLLEGE
Belfast
Tony Gallagher

INTRODUCTION

Hazelwood College is religiously integrated, co-educational and comprehensive. All three characteristics mean that it is unlike most schools in Northern Ireland. Northern Ireland retains a selective system of grammar and secondary schools, although the future of this system is to be reviewed by the Northern Ireland Assembly. Following the 1989 Education Reform Order there has been a marked increase in the number of religiously integrated schools, but they still account for less than five per cent of the total enrolment of pupils. Among post-primary schools, the integrated sector accounts for 13 schools out of a total of 165 secondary and 73 grammar schools.

When the original fieldwork for *Success against the Odds* was being carried out, the initial cease-fires by Republican and Loyalist paramilitary groups had been declared and the first faltering steps towards peace talks appeared to be on the verge of starting.

At that time we concluded that Hazelwood was a successful school and that the ten criteria identified by the National Commission on Education could be found within the school. However, the fieldwork suggested that there were a number of distinctive aspects of the school that appeared to be particularly

Table 8.1 Hazelwood College, City of Belfast

	1995–96	1999–2000
Type and status	Grant-maintained 11–18 (Mixed*)	Grant-maintained 11–18 (Mixed*)
Pupil roll	639	685
Headteacher	Tom Rowley	Noreen Campbell (apptd 1996)
% white pupils	N/A	99.6 *N.I. average: 98.0*
% pupils with English as an additional language	0	0.4 *N.I. average: 0.3*
% pupils eligible for free school meals (FSM)	31.1 *N.I. average: 25.0*	34.0 *N.I. average: 23.2*
% pupils with special educational needs, incl. Statements	N/A	24.8
Pupil/teacher ratio (incl. head)	N/A	14.3 *N.I. average: 14.6 (1)*
Support staff ratio hours (2)	N/A	10.5
% pupils obtaining GCSE (A*–C grades) 5+ subjects	26.0 *N.I. average: 28.0*	33.0 (1) *N.I. average: 33.0 (1)*
Average GCSE point score per pupil	Not applicable	Not applicable
% year 11 students with no GCSE passes	2.0 *N.I. average: 7.0*	6.0 (1) *N.I. average: 6.0 (1)*
Post-16 participation in full-time education or training (%)	65.4 *N.I. average: 80.0*	57.0 (1) *N.I. average: 82.0 (1)*

Table 8.1 continued

OfSTED grade (PANDA) re: GCSE/GNVQ score per pupil in similar FSM school group	See (3)

Key:
*   Also 'Integrated', non-denominational
N/A: Not available
(1) 1998–99
(2) Full-time equivalent (f.t.e.) support staff hours per week, per f.t.e. teacher
(3) School's GCSE/GNVQ score was between upper quartile and 95 percentile in its FSM group of similar schools. *Source*: Benchmark data, DENI School Performance Tables (1998)

important in its development and success. These included the following features:

- The school manifested a clear sense of ethos and purpose that had developed in part because the school offered a distinctive mission, based on a child-centred and inclusive set of principles, not the least of which was its specific commitment to religious integration.
- Within this ethos was a commitment to academic excellence and high achievement, while at the same time recognising the differing needs and aspirations of their pupils, and the different forms that success could take.
- We found evidence of a strong and positive relationship between staff and pupils, and it was clear that the staff were deeply committed to the school.
- The school operated effective monitoring arrangements for pupils which (a) were designed to identify and deal with potential problems at an early stage, and (b) were based on rewards for appropriate behaviour rather than punishment for inappropriate behaviour.

- The school also demonstrated a particular commitment to ritual, as a way of building a sense of community, and was particularly welcoming of visitors.

The period of the fieldwork also identified a number of particular challenges being faced by the school. The first of these arose from the fact that the school had only come into existence in 1985 and that that was followed by rapid growth, and the fieldwork came not long after enrolment stability had been achieved. As the school had grown, new systems and procedures were being developed. Throughout that evolution, one area that had arguably received less attention was arrangements for staff development.

The second challenge arose from the very poor quality of school accommodation. Indeed, while the original report was being prepared, the Department of Education announced that funds for a new school had been approved.

The third challenge came just as the original report was being finalised and the then principal, Tom Rowley, entered into dispute with his board of governors. When *Success against the Odds* was published in 1996 this dispute had not yet been resolved.

CHANGES IN NORTHERN IRELAND

Above, we prefigured some of the dramatic changes that have occurred in Northern Ireland since 1995. As is now known, the original impetus of the peace process was dissipated, the IRA cease-fire was to collapse, albeit temporarily, and the street conflict over disputed parades was to become a ubiquitous feature of the summer months. It was not until the election of the new Labour government in 1997 that renewed impetus went into peace talks, leading eventually to the establishment of a devolved Assembly with legislative powers and an Executive comprising ministers drawn from the Ulster Unionist Party, the Democratic Unionist Party, the Social Democratic and Labour Party, and Sinn Fein.

The responsibilities of the old Department of Education in Northern Ireland (DENI) were spread over three new government departments: the Department of Education, the Department of Further and Higher Education, Training and Employment (DFHETE) and the Department of Culture, Leisure and Arts (DCAL). The Department of Education's responsibilities largely focused on schools, while responsibility for post-compulsory education in all but grammar schools moved to DFHETE. In a decision which provoked some protest, the first Minister of Education was Martin McGuinness, a long-standing leader of Sinn Fein who, in the 1970s, had negotiated with the British government on behalf of the IRA.

The devolved Assembly and Executive have themselves proved to have a fragile existence. The first period of devolution ended in suspension as a result of disputes over arms decommissioning. The suspension was revoked in 2000 and, at the time of writing, the Executive continues to operate. The effect, however, is that the timetable for devolution in Northern Ireland is running behind that of Scotland and Wales. In consequence the impact of locally elected politicians on education policy remains, as yet, somewhat muted. The Executive is only now preparing its first programme for government under which spending priorities can be determined across Departments.

For this reason, the most significant changes in education policy in Northern Ireland have followed decisions made by Labour ministers with responsibility for education under the direct rule arrangements. Under the previous Conservative government various raising-standards initiatives had been focused on a relatively small number of low-achieving schools. New Labour introduced the School Improvement Programme (SIP) which explicitly focused on all schools. Contained within SIP was the familiar concentration on literacy and numeracy, and a continuing commitment to accountability systems allied with new support systems to encourage improvement strategies. A special School Support Programme (SSP) was introduced to focus on low-achieving schools. More recently, six schools that appear not to have responded to these support measures have been permitted to derogate from the statutory Northern Ireland Curriculum.[1] The option of closing and reopening schools under Fresh Start conditions is not so easily available in Northern Ireland since less than half the schools are owned by the local authorities.

The other significant development was a review of the selective system (Gallagher and Smith, 2000; Department of Education, 2000) followed by the establishment of a Review Group for Post Primary Education. The Review Group has been asked to bring forward recommendations for the future organisation of second-level education by May 2001. A range of other issues has been on the policy agenda over the past three or four years, but many appear to have been in a state of suspended animation due to the ups and downs of the peace process. Some major decisions have been put off over this period and only now are being faced by the devolved Assembly and Executive.

POSITION OF THE SCHOOL

What has been the position of Hazelwood College as these events have swirled around it and throughout the wider society in Northern Ireland? In this section of the paper we review some of the statistical evidence on the progress of the school over the latter part of the 1990s. We will then go on to discuss the significance of these data in the light of broader changes that have impacted on the school.

As part of the preparation for this series of follow-up reports on all the *Success against the Odds* schools, a common framework of data was collected. These data are in the School Statistical Profiles, available on the RoutledgeFalmer website. However, the framework for these data was set by the parameters of the English school systems. The system in Northern Ireland differs in two important

Figure 8.1 Electronic music-making

regards.[2] Pupils in Northern Ireland start primary school a year earlier than their peers in England and spend seven years there before transferring at age 11 years to either grammar or secondary schools. Thus, in Northern Ireland the first year of post-primary education is termed Year 8. Second, due to the selective arrangements, aggregate data on post-primary schools as a whole tend not to provide an appropriate baseline for comparisons across schools. This is so because of the markedly different academic entry and outcome profile of grammar schools in comparison with secondary schools. Although Hazelwood operates on comprehensive principles – for example, the school remains committed to mixed-ability classes with setting only in a minority of subjects in the senior school – it is cast by the system as a secondary school. For this reason we have used secondary schools in Northern Ireland as the comparator for the present discussion and excluded data from grammar schools.

The four charts presented here provide a picture of the academic position of the school over the latter part of the 1990s. Figures 8.2 and 8.3 provide information on input factors. Figure 8.2 shows the proportion of pupils entering Hazelwood with 11+ transfer grades[3] along with the comparable proportion for all secondary schools. Figure 8.3 shows the proportion of pupils in Hazelwood and all secondary schools who are entitled to free school meals. The School Statistical Profiles on the RoutledgeFalmer website contain the figure for 1999/2000 and the school's figure for the actual uptake of free school meals. Figures 8.3 and 8.5 provide information on output data. Figure 8.4 shows the proportion of Year 12[4] pupils who achieved five or more GCSEs at grades A*–C from 1992/93 to 1998/99 for Hazelwood and for all secondary schools. Figure 8.5 shows similar data for 1997/98 and 1998/99 disaggregated by gender.[5]

From Figure 8.2 we can see that the attainment profile of pupils entering Hazelwood was broadly comparable to the profile for all secondary schools in Northern Ireland throughout the 1990s. If anything, up to 1997 the proportion of 'graded' pupils entering

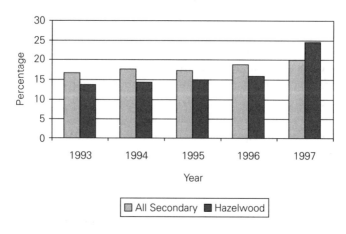

Figure 8.2 Entry profile: percentage of pupils with 11+ grades A to C2

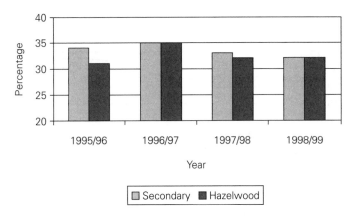

Figure 8.3 Percentage of pupils entitled to free school meals (FSM)

Hazelwood was a little less than for other secondary schools. The data for pupils who did not enter the Transfer Tests confirms this picture. On average, between 1993 and 1997, 46 per cent of pupils entering secondary schools had not entered the tests, as compared with a figure of 42 per cent for Hazelwood. Figure 8.3 also shows that the level of social disadvantage in Hazelwood, as measured by the proportion of pupils entitled to free school meals was comparable to the average level in all secondary schools. In the original report on Hazelwood these input characteristics were important as some of those critical of integrated education claim that they are middle-class alternatives to grammar schools. In our original report we dismissed this claim on the basis of available input data. The newly available data further confirms this position.

Figures 8.4 and 8.5 provide a picture of the academic outputs from Hazelwood. When the original paper was prepared, GCSE data for 1992/93 and 1993/94 were available. From Figure 8.4 we can see that the very high attainment level achieved by Hazelwood in 1992/93 was not sustained over the following years. In fact, simply on the basis of the overall GCSE level the data suggest that Hazelwood's position was comparable to the average level of

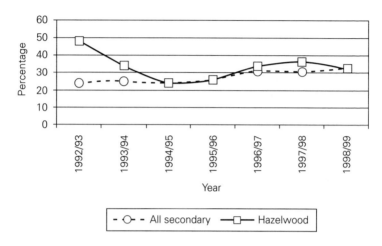

Figure 8.4 Percentage of Year 12 pupils achieving five or more GCSEs at grades A*–C

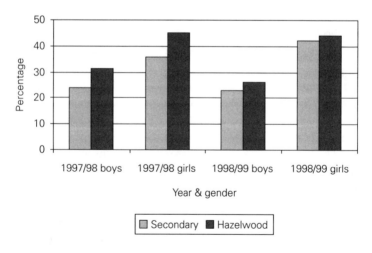

Figure 8.5 Percentage of pupils achieving five or more GCSEs at grades A*–C by gender

secondary schools.[6] Figure 8.5 offers a slight caveat to the overall pattern by presenting data for 1997/98 and 1998/99 disaggregated by gender. This figure suggests that the attainment profile for Hazelwood was a little above the average for secondary schools in both years, although perhaps only slightly so in 1998/99. It should be noted also that Hazelwood has fewer girls in its enrolment in comparison with other co-educational secondary schools[7] and has achieved a balanced gender intake only in 2000.

Perhaps it should also be noted that Hazelwood has achieved a level of attainment which is consistently higher than the average level for the secondary schools within the Belfast Education and Library Board (BELB) (see Table 8.2). It should be noted, however, that whereas the FSM level for Hazelwood in 1998/99 was 32 per cent, the average for BELB secondary schools was 49 per cent.

The other way we can examine this issue is by trying to combine aggregate input and output information. Data were available on the intake profile of secondary schools in 1994/95 (Year 8) and their GCSE profile in 1998/99 (Year 12). Although there will have been some change in the pupil cohort across this period, it allows for an estimate of value added at a school level. Analysis of these data indicated a model where the GCSE outcome (proportion of pupils achieving 5+ GCSEs at grades A*–C) is predicted by a combination of the proportion of pupils entitled to free school meals (negative factor), the proportion of girls in the school and the proportion

Table 8.2 Attainment of Year 12 pupils: Hazelwood College and the average for all secondary schools in the Belfast Education and Library Board

% Year 12 with 5 or more GCSEs at grades A*–C	1992/93	1995/96	1998/99
Hazelwood College	48	26	33
Average of BELB secondary schools	16	18	23

of Year 8 pupils in 1994/95 with 11+ grades A or B.[8] The resultant model explained 33 per cent of the variance between secondary schools. The predicted outcome for Hazelwood is close to the achieved outcome – the actual outcome is only 0.2 standard deviation above the predicted outcome. When the same exercise is repeated for the proportion of Year 12 pupils achieving 5+ GCSEs at grades A*–G the resulting model explains less of the variance (27 per cent) but Hazelwood's actual outcome is now 0.85 standard deviation above the predicted outcome. A similar analysis for the previous year's GCSE data yielded a very similar result.

Overall, then, the consideration of attainment data for Hazelwood suggests that while it has retained an above-average position in comparison with other secondary schools, it has not perhaps sustained the high level of success that was evident when the original report for *Success against the Odds* was carried out. In the next part of this paper we explore some of the changes that have occurred in the school and the impact of wider changes in Northern Ireland.

CHANGES IN CIRCUMSTANCES

In the opening sections of this paper we have highlighted some of the challenges that were facing Hazelwood in 1995 and discussed some broader social changes that have occurred in Northern Ireland since that time. The first challenge concerned the dispute between the then principal and the board of governors which eventually resulted in the principal's leaving the school. As noted above, this issue had emerged just as the initial *Success against the Odds* report was being finalised. During this period one of the vice-principals, Noreen Campbell, served as acting principal. When the principal's post was advertised she applied for and was offered the post. Noreen, who was one of the founding teachers of the school, continues to serve as principal. However, since Tom Rowley had been the school's first principal the manner of his leaving inevitably caused some instability.

The next challenge facing the school in 1995 arose, ironically, due to its success in gaining approval for a new school building. Work on the new building began in 1997 and was only finally completed in early 2000. The capital spending in the School Statistical Profile on the RoutledgeFalmer website reflects the cost of the new school. Where once the school operated in fairly dilapidated buildings and many classes were provided in 'temporary' mobile classrooms, the new building highlights a remarkable transformation in the appearance of the school and has been used to provide new opportunities for development. However, the principal indicated that the period during which the new school was being built was marked by much disruption.

The school is based on a compact site. During the building phase most of the old buildings were demolished and practically all teaching was reallocated to a new set of mobile classrooms that took up most of the play area available to pupils. In addition, a major portion of the site was given over to the construction contractor. Thus, for a period the space available on the site narrowed considerably and much noise and dirt was inevitably created by the major reconstruction programme. Not only did this cause some disruption to normal school activity, but it also meant that the school was not able to offer an entirely pleasant vista to prospective parents and pupils, for all the promise that the new school would eventually entail.

An additional problem created by the building programme was that, in a self-governing school, the principal effectively had to take on the role of project manager since the limited space and tight schedule of the contractors required close supervision of the work. Obviously, this limited the time available for other school tasks.

A third factor that was on the horizon in 1995 was the para-military cease-fires and the nascent peace process. We noted above the way this had developed, and it might be expected that an integrated school such as Hazelwood would benefit from any new atmosphere of reconciliation that might emerge from peace. On one level the school has seen a tangible benefit in that there has been an increase in the number of Protestant pupils who apply to and attend the school – a factor that is important in maintaining a religious balance in the student body. Integrated schools, like grammar schools, tend to draw their pupils from quite wide catchments in comparison with 'typical' secondary schools. Hazelwood is no exception. In fact, one of the developments of recent years is that a significant number of pupils apply to the school from Protestant West Belfast,[9] an area of significant social deprivation where traditionally academic achievement has been low.[10] In part this new process may have been encouraged by the fact that a prominent Loyalist politician from that part of the city chose to send his child to Hazelwood.

In other respects, however, Hazelwood has been embroiled in the controversies and tensions that have arisen from the peace process. Following the appointment of Martin McGuinness as Minister of Education, pupils from a number of Protestant secondary schools walked out of school in protest.[11] Some of these walk-out protests occurred in schools in North Belfast and, on a number of occasions, pupils involved in the protests marched towards the gates of Hazelwood and attempted to encourage Protestant pupils from the school to join the protest. This was exacerbated by attempts by one pupil within the school to generate support for a walk-out. In the event, however, there was no walk-out by Hazelwood pupils. Rather, in keeping with the spirit of dialogue that was so evident in 1994/95, the school encouraged discussion and listening among pupils and staff on the differing perspectives involved in the protests.

The incident is indicative, however, of broader social tensions in the area surrounding the school. One of the disappointing consequences of peace in Northern Ireland has been the emergence of street-level sectarianism. The clearest manifestation of this has been evidenced through the disputes over parades, but numerous petrol-bomb attacks have been made on schools, churches and Orange

Halls over recent years. In North Belfast, an area pock-marked by sectarian interfaces, some of these sectarian tensions have been particularly evident. The environment created by these tensions has been palpable in Hazelwood, but thus far the integrated and open style which we commented on so favourably in the original report on the school has held firm and appears to have allowed the school to deal with these tensions and pressures.[12]

If the challenges discussed above were evident in 1995, a number of additional ones have emerged in the years since. In large part these challenges relate to the dynamics of competition with other schools. In common with other parts of the UK, Northern Ireland operates procedures for open enrolment and parental choice. However, a significant difference is created by the selective system where grammar schools are popular due to their high academic achievement. One consequence of open enrolment has been that a higher proportion of pupils go to grammar schools in comparison with the past.[13] In addition, the accountability systems have enhanced school improvement strategies in some schools. Where these have been seen to be successful then pupil preferences have shifted direction. Although Hazelwood appears to be have largely been immune from the most negative consequences of this situation, there is no doubt that open enrolment in a selective system creates a less stable environment for secondary schools generally.[14]

However, there is some evidence that Hazelwood has been more directly affected because of competition from other integrated schools. Up to the start of the 1990s there were only two integrated post-primary schools, Hazelwood and Lagan College. Partly in consequence of the 1989 Education Reform Order the number of integrated post-primary schools has grown quite markedly during the 1990s. However, as new schools have opened up so they have recruited staff from the more established schools. As an illustration of this, after a new integrated college opened in South Belfast one of the vice-principals in Hazelwood was appointed to the post of principal and he was followed by seven of the Hazelwood staff over the next few years. This has resulted in a level of staff turnover that was previously unknown in Hazelwood. This is, of course, a mixed blessing. On the one hand the school has lost some highly experienced and dedicated staff, while on the other hand the growth of the integrated sector has provided career routes for teachers and the injection of new staff into Hazelwood has been beneficial.

A number of issues were being addressed by the school at the time of the original *Success against the Odds* report. One of these concerned measures to place the management system of the school on a firmer basis. To the extent that there had been a problem it was largely related to the rapid period of enrolment growth from the school's foundation in 1985. At present the senior management system is well-established and, in the view of the principal, is working effectively. One interesting feature of senior management in the school is that it is almost entirely composed of women.

Another issue in 1995 concerned an identified weakness in the area of staff development. This issue too has been addressed. All staff maintain their own professional portfolio and systems operate to identify and prioritise staff development needs. One area where specific staff development activity was implemented was in ICT. Although the Department of Education has an ongoing initiative to enhance the use of ICT by teachers, Hazelwood took the opportunity provided by a new building to incorporate an intranet system and trained all teachers to use it. The downside is that the agreed capital funds for the new school did not include the intranet. The school has with some degree of success sought funds from a number of external agencies to pay for the intranet.

The school also sought to take advantage of the new building by incorporating innovative design features to allow for the flexible use of space. The rationale for this was to provide a learning environment that looked forward rather than one that was rooted in assumptions of the past. Unfortunately, the building regulations governing new schools are not sufficiently flexible to include such innovative aspects and only limited developments of this kind were actually possible, as further additional funds would have been required.

The development of the intranet and the attempt to make creative use of space in a new school building are, however, good examples of the continuing vitality and imagination in Hazelwood. This sense of purpose and innovation was clearly evident in the original *Success against the Odds* report, and it is good to see that this spirit has been maintained, even if the wider education system is not always in a position to promote such thinking.

A further example of the forward-looking approach of the school can be seen in the role adopted by the board of governors. In the original report the board of governors was described as very directly involved in school life. This remains the case. However, over recent years a significant number of new members have joined the board. Taking advantage of this opportunity, the board decided to initiate a 'vision process'. The purpose of this was to engage in widespread consultation and discussion with staff, parents and pupils in order to explore the extent to which the school's original mission remained relevant, and where people thought the school was going or ought to go. In addition, the governors addressed a particular focus on the pressures faced by teachers due to the demands of key stage assessment and monitoring to explore whether this had impacted on their approach to teaching and learning. As a contribution to the vision process an external consultant who was previously unfamiliar with the school was invited to spend a few days observing life in the school and to prepare a report on the observations. The report concluded:

> I found [the pupils] open, expressive, friendly, and very easy to speak with about a variety of school topics. They have good relationships with their teachers and are well looked after and cared for. They were serious and attentive when asked to help me with my work and were very willing to engage in discussion and to dialogue. They spoke of the difficulties in their

communities and about personal difficulties with bringing their school friends home . . . Some senior students I spoke with were very reflective and articulate and any school would be proud of them.

In relation to its academic profile, Noreen Campbell likes to think of Hazelwood as an improving school. The very high attainment level achieved in 1992/93 (see Figure 8.4) could have been dismissed as a statistical blip. Noreen Campbell eschewed such a simple explanation, however, and indicated that the drop in the GCSE level had been devastating for the school and was a pattern they had subjected to close examination. A part of the explanation appeared to be that the coursework component of a series of core GCSE subjects was steadily reduced. Notwithstanding this, the school initiated a series of additional measures to support teaching and learning among pupils. These included an after-school study centre, revision classes for pupils up to public examinations and the introduction of a thinking skills programme from Year 8. In addition, the new building has allowed the school to actively promote the use of College facilities for community and adult education. With support from the European Commission Peace and Reconciliation Fund, a Community Campus Manager has been appointed to carry this initiative forward. This aspect of the vision casts the school as a learning centre for the whole community, and not just a 9.00 a.m. to 4.00 p.m. resource for children.

Noreen was keen to add that she sees Hazelwood as a successful school in relation to the personal development of its pupils:

Our kids are happy at school; we have very few alienated children; we don't have a big anti-school subculture; and most of our kids think in terms of education to 18. So, in that respect I would say we are successful, but in terms of actual outcomes, motivation and so on, we are an improving school and we still have a long way to go.[15]

LESSONS FROM HAZELWOOD

So what broader lessons for school improvement can be learnt from the experience of Hazelwood? Perhaps the first and most important lesson is the constant struggle that schools face in trying to sustain a profile of success. In the particular context of Northern Ireland where the negative consequences of social disadvantage are probably reinforced by the operation of a selective system, all secondary schools face a situation of instability which presents constant challenges.

One consequence of this is that schools should not be treated as if they are abstract units in relation to improvement strategies. Changes in one school will have an impact on neighbouring schools as pupils and teachers move around the system. Thus, for example, an improving school may draw in new pupils, thereby affecting the intake of a neighbouring school. The potential of this problem is more acute in a system that is characterised by a diversity of school types where catchments are not necessarily locally based. In some circumstances schools demonstrate success simply by holding their ground in increasingly difficult conditions. This reminds of us not only of the interdependence of schools as social institutions, but also of the practical limits to autonomous action they have at their disposal.

Arguably, schools in Northern Ireland have been subject to a somewhat 'lighter touch' in relation to accountability and external scrutiny. In part because of different ownership arrangements, there are no 'fresh start' procedures, no OfSTED,[16] limited political dispute in local authorities[17] and a public climate which tends to hold schools and teachers in fairly high regard.[18] Furthermore, the New Labour version of school improvement was not pursued with the same degree of publicity as occurred in England.[19] On the other hand, the problems over devolution have left something of a policy vacuum in recent years as key decisions on strategy and funding were put to one side until the political parties could agree a basis for governance. Whether or not the lighter touch in Northern

Ireland has been to the benefit of pupils must remain moot. The policy vacuum has created problems in the lack of joined-up thinking and policy. In this respect Hazelwood represents an example of a school that appears to have pursued such joined-up thinking regardless of the silence from the centre.

This links to another lesson from the Hazelwood experience. In England a lot of political debate has focused on the role of the local authorities. Hazelwood has not enjoyed a particularly strong or positive relationship with the local authority in whose area it resides. However, part of the basis of its success can be related to the degree of autonomy it has enjoyed as a self-governing school. Indeed, as we noted above, the role of external organisations has sometimes been to constrain and limit innovative thinking from the school.

In 1994/95 among the most striking features of Hazelwood were the degree of energy and commitment among staff and pupils, and the extent of forward-thinking that seemed to be pervasive throughout the school. If the years since have been rocky for the school, then the extent to which Northern Ireland has changed, largely for the better, is also quite remarkable. Throughout this period the fortunes of Hazelwood have ebbed and flowed, but the challenge to succeed has always been maintained. The sense of energy, commitment and forward-thinking remains strong. Assuming the peace process in Northern Ireland continues to deepen then it is likely that the integrated sector will continue to expand. Given the number of schools that continue to demonstrate persistent problems of low achievement, one wonders whether aspects of the Hazelwood experience might be transferred onto other schools and how that might be achieved.

NOTES

1 It is perhaps noteworthy that five of the schools are in Belfast, the sixth being in Derry/Londonderry. Northern Ireland is no different from other jurisdictions in that social disadvantage tends to be concentrated in inner-

city areas, but the educational impact of this is probably exacerbated by the selective system, as it can combine the impact of social disadvantage and low ability in some of the secondary schools which serve these inner-city areas. The most socially disadvantaged parts of Belfast are the inner-city North and West areas from where Hazelwood draws a significant proportion of its intake (four of the schools mentioned above are in this area). Not only is this an area of high social disadvantage, but also approximately 40 per cent of all the deaths associated with the Northern Ireland conflict occurred here. (For social data on the area, see Gaffikin and Morrisey (1996).)

2 Other differences not discussed in the body of the text indicate the limitations to some of the comparative data with the other *Success against the Odds* schools. Although schools in Northern Ireland are funded on a formula basis with pupil enrolment being the predominant component, there are several different formulae in operation. Thus, the five Education and Library Boards (or local authorities) operate their own formulae for the primary, secondary and grammar schools for which they have responsibility. The Department of Education operates a sixth formula for voluntary grammar schools and a seventh formula for grant maintained integrated schools (including Hazelwood). Not only do elements of each formula vary, but so also does the amount retained at the centre. Thus, at the moment it is problematic to compare recurrent funding levels for schools within Northern Ireland, never mind between Northern Ireland and other parts of the UK. An additional difference deals with the arrangements for Key Stage Assessments. The implementation of the assessment arrangements is some years behind England and Wales. On the other hand, Northern Ireland has the 11+ Transfer Tests which provide a form of baseline measurement for post-primary schools.

3 Under the 11+ transfer system pupils take two tests during their final year in primary school. The top 20 per cent of pupils in the cohort are awarded an A grade, the next 10 per cent are awarded a B grade, the next 10 per cent are awarded a C grade, and the rest of the pupils taking the test are awarded a D grade. For the last few years the B and C grades have been further subdivided into B1, B2, C1 and C2 bands, with each grade being allocated to 5 per cent of the cohort. In order to maintain consistency over the years Figure 8.2 provides data on the 10 per cent B and C bands. Please note also that about a third of each Year 7 cohort opt not to take the tests and transfer to secondary schools. In effect these pupils are treated as if they were D-grade pupils, but this may or may not reflect their actual level of ability.

4 This is equivalent to Year 11 in England and Wales.

5 These were the only two years for which school and system data on gender patterns were available. The Northern Ireland School Performance Tables published by the Department of Education do not include gender breakdowns on attainment data.

6 The level for all secondary schools on Figure 8.4 is based on the median level for all schools with Year 12 pupils in each year.

7 In 1997/98 there were 21 single-sex boys' and 21 single-sex girls' secondary schools with pupils in Year 12. The remaining schools were co-educational, with the percentage of girls in Year 12 ranging from 25 to 56 per cent. The overall median for the proportion of girls in Year 12 was 45 per cent. The proportion of girls in Year 12 in Hazelwood in the same year was 41 per cent. For a discussion on gender patterns in performance in Northern Ireland, see Gallagher (1997a).

8 It is recognised that the aggregate school-level data available for this analysis are extremely limited and probably do not meet the technical requirements of the multi-level modelling used within the school effectiveness tradition. In effect, however, they were the only data available and any conclusions derived from the analysis need to be set in the wider context provided by the range of data presented in the paper.

9 This is the area where the feud between Loyalist paramilitary groups erupted in summer 2000.

10 At interview the principal suggested that Hazelwood could now run a bus route to collect its pupils that would run through a range of sectarian interfaces in West and North Belfast. Due to the sectarian geography of Belfast most bus routes radiate from and to the city centre, and none follow tangential routes through interfaces, not least because this would involve passing through Belfast's ubiquitous 'peace-lines'. For the moment no bus company is prepared to provide a vehicle for Hazelwood to run its, potentially unique, cross-community service.

11 It was widely believed that some of these 'spontaneous' protests had been encouraged by members of one of the local political parties.

12 There is also a strong case to suggest that the people in inner-city North Belfast have probably seen little tangible evidence of the economic benefits of the cease-fires and peace process. This may have been one of the factors contributing to the violence between Loyalist paramilitary groups in 2000.

13 A number of factors have contributed to this pattern. Under open enrolment each school is given an intake number and must accept pupils up to this number. The only exception is that a grammar school can decline a place to a pupil who it feels is not capable of the academic

curriculum of the school, although in practice this rarely, if ever, happens. When schools are over-subscribed they must select from amongst applicants on the basis of published criteria. Only grammar schools are permitted to use academic criteria, i.e. Transfer Test results, as a selection criterion, and they must use this criterion ahead of all others. An immediate consequence of open enrolment was that all grammar schools took in pupils up to their intake number. This resulted in an increase in the proportion of each cohort entering grammar schools. Over the next few years the total size of the transferring cohort is expected to fall, so the proportion entering grammar schools will increase still further. In addition, in the 1990s two new Catholic grammar schools were opened in response to debates over equality in educational provision (see Gallagher *et al.* 1994).

14 For a discussion on this, see Gallagher and Smith (2000).

15 The last year for which school leaver destinations were published in School Performance Tables was 1996/97. In that year Hazelwood was one of only 34 secondary schools (out of 156) which offered A or AS Levels to pupils. Hazelwood also offered some GNVQ Level 3 provision. The proportions of leavers from Hazelwood who entered higher education (13 per cent) or further education (29 per cent) were comparable to the average for this group of secondary schools.

16 The Education and Training Inspectorate (ETI) operates as a professional branch within the Department of Education and has never acquired the reputation of controversy generated by OfSTED.

17 Although there are local politicians represented on the Education and Library Boards, they hold only a minority of positions, and policy is determined by the Department of Education in any case.

18 See Gallagher (1997b).

19 For example, the schools that were required, due to low achievement levels, to participate in the School Support Programme were never 'named and shamed' in the way that occurred in England. In addition, it seems likely that the Department of Education will issue a consultation paper proposing that it cease publishing annual School Performance Tables.

REFERENCES

Department of Education (2000) The Effects of the Selective System of Secondary Education in Northern Ireland. Research Papers Volumes 1 and 2. Bangor: Department of Education (also available at www.deni.gov.uk).

Gaffikin, F. and Morrisey, M. (1996) *A Tale of One City? North and West Belfast*, Belfast: Urban Institute, University of Ulster.

Gallagher, A. M. (1997a) *Educational Achievement and Gender: A Review of Research Evidence on the Apparent Underachievement of Boys*. Research Report No. 6. Bangor: Department of Education for Northern Ireland.

Gallagher, A. M. (1997b) Attitudes to education in Britain and Northern Ireland. In: L. Dowds, P. Devine and R. Breen (eds) *Social Attitudes in Northern Ireland: the Sixth Report, 1996–97*, Belfast: Appletree Press.

Gallagher, A. M., Cormack, R. J. and Osborne, R. D. (1994) Religion, equity and education in Northern Ireland, *British Educational Research Journal*, 20, 5, 507–18.

Gallagher, A. M. and Smith, A. (2000) The Effects of the Selective System of Secondary Education in Northern Ireland: Main Report. Bangor: Department of Education.

9

ST MICHAEL'S ROMAN CATHOLIC COMPREHENSIVE SCHOOL

Billingham, Stockton-on-Tees

Gerald Grace

THE REGIONAL CONTEXT

Billingham lies to the north of the River Tees in what was the former north-eastern county of Cleveland. St Michael's School is now within the jurisdiction of the new unitary local education authority of Stockton-on-Tees and it is also located within the Roman Catholic Diocese of Hexham and Newcastle. In economic terms the region has experienced a decline in employment in manufacturing industries but Billingham has a relative advantage in the continuing presence of ICI as a major employer and also from some new industrial development. This can be seen in the unemployment figures of the 1991 census which showed an overall rate of 12.1 per cent for Stockton-on-Tees compared with 10 per cent for Billingham.

THE HISTORICAL CONTEXT

St Michael's School was chosen for inclusion in the original study, *Success against the Odds* (1996), because with the help of strong

Table 9.1 St Michael's Roman Catholic School, Stockton-on-Tees

	1995–96	1999–2000
Type and status	Voluntary Aided (RC) 11–16 (Mixed)	Voluntary Aided (RC) 11–16 (Mixed)
Pupil roll	849	919
Headteacher	Tony Maxwell (apptd 1995)	Tony Maxwell
% white pupils	99.5	100 *English average: 88.5*
% pupils with English as an additional language	0	0
% pupils eligible for free school meals (FSM)	17.2	13.3 *English average: 16.9 (1)*
% pupils with special educational needs, incl. Statements	15.0 *English average: 15.2*	11.3 *English average: 22.0 (1)*
Pupil/teacher ratio (incl. head)	17.7 *English average: 16.6*	18.6 *English average: 17.1*
Support staff ratio hours (2)	6.3	9.9
% pupils obtaining GCSE (A*–C grades) 5+ subjects	45.0 *English average: 44.5*	59.0 (1) *English average: 47.9 (1)*
Average GCSE point score per pupil	Not applicable	43.9 (1) *English average: 38.1 (1)*
% year 11 students with no GCSE passes	2 *English average: 7.8*	0 *English average: 6.0 (1)*
Post-16 participation in full-time education or training (%)	74.2 *English average: 70.4*	77.3 (1) *English average: 70.1 (1)*

Table 9.1

OfSTED grade (PANDA) re: GCSE/GNVQ score per pupil in similar FSM school group	Not applicable	A (1) (3)
OfSTED grade (PANDA) re: GCSE/GNVQ score per pupil in similar school group re: prior attainment at Key Stage Three	Not applicable	A* (1) (3)

Key:
(1) 1998–99
(2) Full-time equivalent (f.t.e.) support staff hours per week, per f.t.e. teacher
(3) OfSTED PANDA rubric:
   A* PANDA pupils' results were **very high** in comparison with the average for similar schools
   A PANDA pupils results were **well above** the average for similar schools

parental and community support it had fought off a threatened closure (caused by falling numbers) in 1984–5, and by 1994 was being designated by OfSTED as 'a remarkably effective school'. GCSE results A*–C had risen from a low of 33 per cent in 1990 to a high of 61.4 per cent in 1993. Although the results for 1994 had dropped to 49.7 per cent these were still above local and England averages. Evidence gathered in 1995 from OfSTED and Diocesan reports, from local education authority statistics, from Teeside Training and Enterprise Council and from interviews and observations within the school led the present researcher to conclude that St Michael's School had achieved

> a comprehensive effectiveness . . . its most visible achievements were demonstrated in exceptionally good GCSE results . . . [but] it was clear that the school was also successful in the areas of personal and social education, the generation of community responsibility and an awareness of Christian values.
>
> (NCE, 1996: 233)

The school, having been on the verge of closure in 1984–5 with a falling school roll and with leadership problems, had been turned around so that by 1995, St Michael's School was highly regarded by Catholics and non-Catholics in the local community. As a result of its reputation the school now had a rising school roll and had achieved an oversubscribed intake status. In seeking to explain this transformation in the school's profile, the research team of 1995 (consisting of an educationalist, a community development manager and a local businessman) came to the conclusion that the key building blocks of the school's success were:

- *A strong community support network:* constituted by parents, community members and parish agencies which had formed a significant alliance with the teachers in the struggle to save the school from closure.
- *The school's reputation as both a caring and an ordered community:* a strong pastoral care system facilitated by the effective use of the house/year blocks as social units, a steady insistence upon standards of personal appearance and of courtesy and politeness and an ethos in which the principles of the school's mission statement were constantly aspired to, generated a school climate which was ordered, calm and caring.
- *Staff quality and staff commitment:* quality staff in this context implied teachers and other support workers who demonstrated high levels of conscientiousness and commitment to the interests and welfare of the pupils. Teachers took seriously the principles of comprehensive schooling, equal opportunities and of the comprehensive recognition of achievements, academic, social, sporting, artistic/creative and community-related.
- *Headteacher leadership and management:* the headteacher had played a leading role in the campaign to save the school from closure and he was well known and respected in the local community. He was responsible for widening the conception of the school's mission and purpose so that it had come to serve

other Christians in the local area and those in sympathy with its aims, rather than only the young people of the Catholic community. The headteacher was widely commended for his policy of enabling and empowering others to work more effectively for the good of the pupils. He was seen to be politically shrewd and skilled in human relations and his practice of 'being about the school' and of being involved in classroom teaching, gave many teachers confidence in his leadership.

- *Teaching and learning environment:* a strong commitment to the idea that every pupil was capable of learning and improving was signalled by the school's use of mixed-ability grouping, to help build self-respect among pupils and to avoid the creation of alienated, low-stream, low-expectation groups among the pupils. A tangible academic work atmosphere existed, maintained by regular homework and monitoring of homework. A 'Home Links' newsletter and regular media coverage of the full range of pupil achievements resulted in a clear sense among the pupils that their school was comprehensively effective.

- *School design and school resources:* the school's design and layout as a modern secondary school organised around house blocks made a significant contribution to the pastoral care system and to the creation of good human relations, among the pupils and between the pupils and the staff. A sense of pupil 'ownership' of their particular house block worked to keep vandalism and graffiti to a minimum. The pupils recognised that the school was well resourced in relative terms. The headteacher, the deputy headteacher and others had been successful in supplementing the basic budget allocation with other sources of revenue.

In the 1995 report the research team took the view that the six factors indicated above had been crucial in the school's 'success against the odds'. However, it was also noted that St Michael's School possessed certain advantages which not every school in the local area enjoyed. These included an exceptionally strong community support network; a loyal, committed and cohesive staff group; a well designed school structure on a greenfield site; and relatively good levels of resourcing and finance. As the school came to achieve oversubscribed status it also benefited from the fact that most pupils wanted to be there and that most parents were ready to co-operate with the school to make the most of their children's secondary education.

SUSTAINING SUCCESS IN THE PERIOD 1995–2000

Peter Mortimore (1998) in *The Road to Improvement* has argued that the challenge for schools such as St Michael's is to sustain their improvement once their initial phase of 'turn-around' is over. Given that exceptional levels of professional energy and commitment have been called for to achieve first-phase renewal, the crucial question is whether or not such effort can be maintained over a longer period of time. This question provided the main rationale for a period of research fieldwork undertaken at St Michael's School in June 2000 by the present writer. The following case study demonstrates that sustained school improvement is possible but that its achievement is the outcome of an interlocking network of support agencies, i.e. a form of *social and pedagogic capital* which is differentially available in different school situations.

The evidence-base for the case study consisted of reading the available documentation provided by the school (including the Governors' Annual Report to Parents), the statistical profile of the school as compiled by the research assistant and other statistics provided by the local education authority and by the joint strategy unit. Research interviews were held with the following members of the school:

- the headteacher (5 years as head/34 years' experience in the school): (male)
- deputy headteacher (10 years): (female)

- deputy headteacher (5 years): (male)
- head of history (29 years): (male)
- head of RE (10 years): (male)
- teacher of mathematics (10 years): (female)
- teacher of RE (1 year): (female)
- teacher of mathematics (1 year): (female)
- head of science (4 years): (female)
- supply teacher (3 years): (female)
- head of SEN (8 years): (female)
- chair of governors (1 year): (female)
- foundation governor (priest) (8 years): (male)
- PGCE student on placement (1 year): (male).

Two focus groups were conducted with Year 10 and Year 11 pupils chosen to represent a cross-section of ability and of attitudes towards the school. Nine pupils were involved in these discussions.

ST MICHAEL'S SCHOOL ORGANISATIONAL AND LOCAL CHANGES

The most obvious change which had taken place at the school in the five-year period under review was the appointment of a new headteacher in September 1995. The previous headteacher had taken early retirement in the summer of 1995, after a ten-year period of service in which the school had been turned around from potential closure to oversubscribed status. Such a leadership transition can be a critical event in any school's development. In the case of St Michael's this transition was mediated by the appointment of the deputy headteacher (pastoral) who was already a long-serving member of the senior leadership term. At the time of the research the headteacher had the advantage of 34 years' service in the school and of being closely associated with the policies that had achieved the school's first-phase renaissance. While there was therefore a strong sense of continuity in leadership, the new headteacher had his own ideas and priorities and plans for building upon and extending the school's development. The abolition of the County of Cleveland and its replacement by four smaller unitary education authorities had not had any major impact upon the school's situation. Within the smaller authority of Stockton-on-Tees, the headteacher took the view that the thirteen secondary schools in the area now enjoyed more relative autonomy and that the secondary headteachers as a group had become relatively more influential in the direction of local education policy initiatives.

In the period 1995–2000 the school roll had risen from 849 pupils to 919 (458 girls, 461 boys) and the number of full-time teachers from 44 to 47. The pupil/teacher ratio (including the headteacher) had risen from 18.1 in 1995 to 18.6 in 2000. Figures for free school meal entitlement (FSM) had dropped from 18.2 in 1995 to 13.3 in 2000 and this appeared to suggest some marginal improvement in the economy of the area and in levels of employment. There had been no significant changes to the admissions policy at the school and it was still the case that the majority of the school's places were filled by children from the five Catholic primary schools in the area: St Joseph's (Norton), St John's, St Joseph's (Billingham), Holy Rosary and St Paul's. There also appeared to be no significant change in the attainment and ability scores of the pupils on entry to the school. In 1995, 11 per cent of Year 7 had reading ages two years or more below their chronological age. In September 1999 the comparable figure was 13.8 per cent of pupils.

The proportion of Catholic pupils in the school was estimated by the headteacher as 77 per cent. Given the school's oversubscribed status the admission of other pupils was based upon 'discussions' (not interviews) with the pupils and their parents to assess the degree to which they were in sympathy with the Catholic and religious aims of St Michael's. It was emphatically denied by the present headteacher (as was the case with the previous headteacher) that any form of covert social or academic selection took place during these 'discussions'. However, it was accepted that these

Figure 9.1 Sport is an important element in this academically successful school

families seeking to obtain a place for their children in an over-subscribed context were likely to demonstrate high levels of partnership support for the school's educational programme.

SUSTAINING AND DEVELOPING ACADEMIC SUCCESS

For almost all the period under review St Michael's School has been able to sustain academic results above local and national averages (see Table 9.2). How has this been possible? The focused academic climate in the school had been established by the hard work and commitment of the teachers, encouraged and empowered by the previous headteacher whose own involvement in classroom teaching had high symbolic value. This policy had been maintained by the present headteacher and to an already strong base further innovations had been introduced with the support of the headteacher. The introduction of an Academic Monitoring Programme had produced beneficial effects for all pupils. Academic monitoring, defined by the school as 'a system of one to one tutorials which help to identify each student's potential, develop individual targets, agree actions to meet the targets and involve parents in the monitoring process', had helped to maximise the realisation of potential among the pupils. To this had been added a Year 8 to Year 11 Peer Mentoring Programme in which Year 11 mentors had been paired with Year 8 pupils to assist the latter with their academic planning and study skills. Defined as a system of 'people helping other people', it clearly had not only academic value but also personal and social value for both groups involved. The introduction of extra classes in certain subjects after the scheduled school day for supplementary teaching and revision purposes had strengthened the academic culture and effectiveness of St Michael's School.

The proportion of the Year 11 cohort proceeding at 16 to some form of further education had increased from 70 per cent in 1994–5 to 77 per cent in 1998–9. To encourage more of its pupils to think beyond further education to higher education, the school had introduced visits to the three local universities of Durham (including the new Stockton Campus of Durham University), Sunderland and Teesside.

In this sector of its operations the school possessed a 'constant improvement dynamic', strongly articulated by the headteacher and

Table 9.2 GCSE results for 1995–2000

School year end	1995	1996	1997	1998	1999
% 5 or more grades A*–C	40 (43.5)	45 (44.5)	46 (45.1)	49 (46.3)	59 (47.9)
% 5 or more grades A–G	97 (85.7)	96 (86.1)	96 (86.4)	99 (87.5)	98 (88.5)

Figures in brackets give English national comparisons

supported and implemented by teachers who showed exceptionally high levels of professional commitment. A school policy of encouraging teachers to attend continuing professional development and research-based courses had been responsible for teachers' suggesting initiatives such as academic monitoring and peer monitoring.

The joint local education authorities strategy unit had undertaken a value-added academic analysis for the secondary schools of the local area. This analysis for the GCSE results of 1999 demonstrated that St Michael's School had the second highest value-added score among the thirteen secondary schools of the Stockton LEA.

With form tutors using Tracking Profiles to overview the progress of individual pupils and to set individual targets for improvement, the possibility of an over-intense academic atmosphere had to be considered. In focus group discussions with Year 10 and 11 pupils no evidence of this appeared. On the contrary, the pupils were in general appreciative of the extra time and effort that teachers were devoting to try to maximise their academic progress.

COMPREHENSIVE PRINCIPLES AND COMMUNITY RELATIONS

St Michael's is a comprehensive school and it acts as a comprehensive school. Despite the centrality of academic achievement and the 'use of talents' commitment in the Mission Statement, there is no sense that academic success has come to displace or marginalise other educational, religious and social outcomes of the school. The determination to provide a comprehensive education with an acknowledged comprehensive range of achievements (noted in the report of 1995), had been maintained and extended in the period 1995–2000. Discussions with pupils indicated that they had a real sense that involvement in sport, drama, music, art, religious activity and liturgies, charitable and community work, student councils and debate and assistance to other pupils was an integral part of school life at St Michael's and received public acknowledgement and praise. This sense of the importance of *comprehensive endeavour* had been strengthened by the introduction of a 'Celebration of Achievement Evening' in which the school's total 'use of talents' was formally recognised. Discussions with the Head of Special Educational Needs (SEN) revealed that pupils on the SEN Register (e.g. 12.8 per cent of the Year 7 entry) were fully integrated as members of the school community and received appropriate care and resourcing of their needs. It is sometimes believed that the constant pressure for improvement in the academic results of UK secondary schools will inevitably lead to the abandonment of a comprehensive, liberal and humane education in pursuit of a narrow, results productivity ethos. This had not happened at St Michael's School. The fact that it had not happened may be seen to be evidence of the commitment of its headteacher and teachers to the fundamental principles of comprehensive schooling and to the Mission Statement principle that the school would seek to enhance 'the dignity of the individual', i.e. every individual.

In the 1995 report on St Michael's it was noted that a 14-year-old pupil had said, 'Our school is like a family community' (NCE, 1996: 251). This strong internal sense of family community was still a very evident feature of the school's ethos. It was constituted by the operation of many factors. Among these was the contribution of the house block system to a humane environment, the personal knowledge of many pupils arising from the long service in the school of the headteacher and some senior staff, the continuous association of many families in the stable community of Billingham (low family and pupil mobility levels) with St Michael's School and the interlocking networks of Catholic organisations and parishes which had an impact within the school. The Peer Mentoring Programme introduced in the 1995–2000 period had added to this sense of family community by involving members of 'the family' in helping each other. It might also be said that the headteacher, whose cheerful and optimistic disposition was universally acknowledged and who undertook a high-profile role in sports organisations in the local area, was 'the father' that some of the children had never experienced.

In addition to a strong sense of community within the school, St Michael's is also characterised by developed links with the external community. St Michael's has the advantages which arise from a strong sense of community within the Catholic Church as realised through the involvement of the local priests (three of whom are Foundation Governors) and the organisations and agencies of the feeder parishes. However, the school is also well integrated with the wider community in Billingham through the activities of its staff and pupils in sporting, social and charitable involvement. In the 1995 report a local education social worker observed 'St Michael's touches all parts of the community from a strong Christian perspective' (NCE, 1996: 255). This larger community impact has been maintained and extended.

The provision of a new ICT suite in the school (with the support of the Tees Valley Training and Enterprise Council) had allowed for the development of more adult and community education classes with an emphasis on information technology. In this way the school had become an important educational resource for the whole community.

The school's community relations had benefited from the liaison work of the Head of History, who in addition to his academic responsibilities was responsible for the 'Home Links' newsletter and involved in the production of the St Michael's School Year Book, which was widely circulated among parents, employers and community members. Focused links with various media agencies in the region also ensured that the comprehensive achievements of the school were widely known. In the period under review this activity has been maintained and developed. At the suggestion of the Year 11 Student Council a new publication had been produced, *The Class of 2000*, including photographs of the whole year group, with a 'Did You Know?' information section, for example:

- Tom saved up £70 for Teesside Hospice
- Nuzha is a member of Cleveland Theatre School
- Terry and Philip are yellow belts in kick boxing
- Adam and Danny are members of the school St Vincent de Paul group
- Carl, Joanne, Tom and Alex were part of the Motorola Youth Parliament team that have won the UK finals
- Marc plays professional football for Sunderland
- Alison has done outstanding work for the student council.

In these ways the wider community in Billingham can learn about the full range of the school's activities, and its reputation has been progressively enhanced as a result of this.

CONSULTATION AND PARTICIPATION

The previous headteacher had practised an 'open door' policy to encourage staff to come forward with ideas for the improvement of the school. He had developed a consultative style of school leadership which avoided, on the one hand, a traditional Catholic sense of hierarchy and, on the other hand, the dangers of modern divisions between 'the senior management team' and other staff members. In the 1995–2000 period, the new headteacher had built on these foundations but also extended them to be even more inclusive and to encourage even more participation in the formulation of school policy. The most notable innovation in this second phase of St Michael's development had been the creation of student councils for every year group and also the creation of a formal Staff Council. The intention here was to take seriously the 'voice' of the pupils, as partners in the school community and in itself it seemed to be a concrete realisation of the principle in the Mission Statement which indicated 'mutual respect' as a feature of St Michael's. The more formal empowering of the staff 'voice' through the operation of their council was designed to facilitate a wider spectrum of staff involvement in policy formation. Further examples of wider participation could be found in the inclusion of school governors and of parents as observers in meetings of both Pastoral Heads and Heads of Department. The school had always had a powerful tradition of dramatic and musical productions involving large numbers of pupils and this, as reported by many local observers, including employers, had engendered a sense of confidence and good presentational skills among the pupils.

This 'public confidence' had been built upon in the period 1995–2000 to bring high levels of national success to the school. In a major project of citizenship education the school had involved 250 pupils each year in learning the skills of parliamentary debate and advocacy. Arising from this project St Michael's School had been national winners of the Motorola Youth Parliament Competition in 1997, 1998 and 1999. For an 11–16 Voluntary Aided school to win in such a competition against schools with sixth forms and also leading independent schools was a remarkable achievement in democratic education which had been formally recognised by the Speaker of the House of Commons, 10 Downing Street and the Department for Education and Employment (DfEE). A DfEE advice circular (ACE, 1998) to all schools involved in citizenship education noted that St Michael's School's success was based upon large-scale involvement of its pupils, the production of a video representing a mock parliamentary debate and performance in a political writing competition.

St Michael's School in the period under review had extended an existing policy of openness and consultation into a more fully developed policy of active participation by pupils, teachers and governors in school life. St Michael's School can now claim to be an exemplar of a more democratic culture in the internal life of schools and also a significant contributor to the formation of 'active citizenship' within the wider society.

CATHOLICITY AND RELIGIOUS ETHOS

As I have argued elsewhere (Grace, 1998) there is a distinctive Catholic concept of school effectiveness which includes, in addition to secular performance indicators, a major emphasis upon the religious, spiritual and moral outcomes of a school. More than this, Catholic schools exist to enhance the vitality of the Catholic faith among young people and to give expression to the primacy of religious and moral values and to conceptions of service for the common good. The St Michael's School Mission Statement proclaims an intention to create 'an overtly Christian environment, where Charity, Forgiveness, Use of Talents, Mutual Respect and the Dignity of the Individual provide the impetus for all endeavour'.

The Catholicity of the school, understood to be the realisation of religious, spiritual and moral principles and action within the traditions of the Catholic Church had been a strong feature of the school from its foundation in 1964. The celebration of Mass in the small school chapel, the provision of Confessions for all year groups, the Lourdes Pilgrimage and the extensive involvement of staff and pupils in charitable and community-related activities were indications of the school's religious life. Some observers of contemporary Catholic secondary schools have suggested that their religious culture is weakening over time as the schools give more attention to league-table academic success in a competitive market-driven educational environment (see Arthur, 1995). This was not true of St Michael's School. In fact, the contrary situation was the case. There was considerable evidence that the Catholicity and the religious ethos of the school had strengthened in the period 1995–2000 and was a very distinctive feature of its contemporary culture. A number of developments had contributed to this stronger religious profile. The relocation of the school chapel to a more central and accessible site had been functionally important as well as symbolically significant. However, the single innovation which, by general consent, had made the largest impact on the school's religious life, had been the appointment of two women lay chaplains to the staff. The lay chaplains (one full-time and the other part-time) were paid for out of the school's budget and they represented a powerful addition to the school's spiritual resources. They were available for consultation by the pupils (and the staff) and, as a result of their activities the school's Catholicity had been strengthened. Two 'Mission Weeks' in 1996 and 1999, organised by the Sion Community, had made a considerable impact within the school, as had the introduction of prayer intention cards in the chapel, the formation of lunchtime prayer groups and the extension of charitable activity through the school's St Vincent de Paul group. The introduction of in-school 'retreats' (one day's break from routine) had made a contribution towards a stronger prayer and reflection ethos in the school.

The strengthening of the school's religious culture in the period 1995–2000 was commented on by almost all the teachers interviewed during the fieldwork and the impact of the lay chaplains was widely acknowledged. The vice-chair of the governors (a priest) observed that this appeared to be a way forward for the religious life of Catholic secondary schools. With the decline in the number of priests and with the many other responsibilities carried out by priests, traditional conceptions of the priest school-chaplain had to be supplemented in a major way by the appointment of lay school-chaplains. St Michael's was an exemplary case study of how effective they could be.

THE 'VOICE' OF THE PUPILS

Two focus-group discussions were held with five Year 11 pupils (15–16 years: 3 girls, 2 boys) and with four Year 10 pupils (14–15 years: 2 girls, 2 boys). The purpose of these meetings was to encourage the pupils to reflect upon the extent to which the practice of St Michael's School lived up to its stated Mission principles. In addition to this the nine pupils were asked to reflect upon their positive and negative experiences at the school. One group of pupils could be identified as ideal pupils (IP) and the other group as less ideal pupils (LIP).

Some extracts from the reflections of the IP group are given below:

> In the use of talents, St Michael's scores highly as the talents of the pupils are spread widely across various activities such as productions.
>
> (Pupil: age 15)

> Mutual respect: the teachers understand and work with you on an equal level. Through the student council they listen to what you request.
>
> (Pupil: age 16)

> Charity: since joining the school I have witnessed many events, sponsored and fund-raising to give donations to charities and also the formation of the SVP.
>
> (Pupil: age 15)

> There appears to be a great deal of discipline within St Michael's.
>
> (Pupil: age 16)

> It is a highly Christian community, although it lacks somewhat on the 'dignity of the individual' statement.
>
> (Pupil: age 16).

As might be expected from an IP group, there was large-scale endorsement that the school lived up to its Mission Statement principles. The last two observations related to the disciplinary practice of the school in relation to personal appearance and 'presentation of self'. It was suggested here that the school's policy of very strict enforcement of its 'presentation of self' rules could, on occasions, compromise its position on 'the dignity of the individual'!

The LIP group took up this theme with some vigour:

> I think the school helps with many different charities . . . but I don't think the school is as forgiving as it should be. If you make a mistake it won't be forgotten about and if an incident happens, you will get the blame as you have already made one mistake.
>
> (Pupil: age 15)

> The worst thing about St Michael's is the rules, some of them are absolutely pathetic, e.g. absolutely no makeup.
>
> (Pupil: age 15)

> The teachers sometimes judge you, even if you have not given your side of the story.
>
> (Pupil: age 15).

While there was some feeling among the LIP group that there was too much regulation of personal appearance and, in their view, not enough forgiveness (as promised by the Mission Statement), even this group of school critics recognised that St Michael's was a school with a good reputation, good facilities and good results. There was no sense that they would have wished to be at another school and, when asked, all said that they would send their own children (in the fullness of time) to St Michael's School.

Discussions with only 9 pupils out of 919 can only have an indicative status as evidence. Having said that, the indications are that the pupils of St Michael's School believe, to a large extent, that it is a school that lives its Mission principles. It is also clear that they value being members of the school community and that their positive experiences in the school outweigh their negative experiences.

AN OVERVIEW OF EFFECTIVENESS

In a major research study into the effectiveness of Catholic schooling in the USA reported in *Catholic Schools and the Common Good*, Tony Bryk *et al.* (1993) highlighted a number of factors which helped to contribute to Catholic school success even in the face of difficult local circumstances. Chief among these was what the researchers called 'an inspirational ideology' derived from a Catholic/Christian view of the purposes and values of education. Such an ideology was clearly present at St Michael's School, expressed in its Mission Statement and lived in its pedagogical and social practice. Bryk *et al.* also found exceptionally high levels of dedication and commitment among the school principals and teachers whom they studied. Once again, the parallels with St Michael's are obvious. The school's first-phase renaissance and its second-phase achievements had been accomplished by levels of headteacher and teacher commitment which were nothing less than a manifest professional lay vocation. If to these advantages are added the strong community and family ethos within the school, its caring yet ordered environment and the possession of an external community education network involving the support of parents, community members, parish agencies, priests and local employers, then St Michael's School was well resourced for success. The conjunction of all of these factors has provided St Michael's School with forms of *social and pedagogic capital* which help to explain its continuing success. In making any comparative judgements with any other secondary schools in the locality it is only right to point out that schools vary in the amount of such capital which is available to them. This is not to minimise the outstanding achievements of St Michael's staff and pupils but it is to guard against current simplistic policy and political assumptions that 'if St Michael's School can do it – any other school can do it'. The explanations for individual schools' 'success' or 'failure' are far too complex to be accounted for by easy slogans. Nevertheless, the value of case studies of this type is that some useful lessons can be derived from them which will help other schools to improve their present educational practice.

REFERENCES

Advisory Group on Citizenship (1998) *Education for Citizenship and the Teaching of Democracy in Schools*, London, DfEE/QCA.

Arthur, J. (1995), *The Ebbing Tide: Policy and Principles of Catholic Education*, Leominster, Gracewing Publications.

Bryk, A., Lee, V. and Holland, P. (1993) *Catholic Schools and the Common Good*, Cambridge, MA, Harvard University Press.

Grace, G. (1998) 'Realising the Mission: Catholic Approaches to School Effectiveness' in R. Slee, S. Tomlinson and G. Weiner (eds) *School Effectiveness for Whom?*, London: Falmer Press.

Grace, G. (2000) *Catholic Schools and the Common Good: what this means in Educational Practice*, London: CRDCE/London Institute of Education.

Mortimore, P. (1998) *The Road to Improvement*, Lisse, Netherlands: Swets and Zeitlinger.

National Commission on Education (1996) *Success against the Odds: Effective Schools in Disadvantaged Areas*, London: Routledge.

10

SELLY PARK TECHNOLOGY COLLEGE FOR GIRLS
Birmingham

Tim Brighouse

End of term report – Summer 2000

The process map of school improvement is being used at Selly Park, but there is a differential value on the processes, with the highest value being placed on teaching and learning and staff development. It was unsurprising to discover that the school intends to take on 'Investors in People' not as a panacea, but as another device to strengthen yet further the development of all staff.

To the observation by one member of the research team that the experience of visiting Selly Park had been really interesting, another replied: 'Yes, future perfect'. The school would not claim for itself perfection, now or in the future, because it would know that it had lost the zest and intellectual energy which has brought it so far. Subliminally, however, the phrase captures the school's contrasting past, its present achievement and the certainty of its future success.

It is of course dangerous to make predictions about where a school might be in two, three or four years' time. Nevertheless, there is sound evidence that Selly Park Girls' School may well be continuing to make astonishing progress in achieving success against the odds. That success will increasingly touch all of its pupils.

(Success against the Odds – Effective Schools in Disadvantaged Areas, National Commission on Education, Routledge, 1996, p. 309)

HIGHER ACHIEVEMENT FOR ALL

The behaviour of the youngsters in this school has changed remarkably. Peer-group pressure towards achievement is now so great that pupils ask teachers in the corridor if they can lay on extra tutorials or revision classes, and as the softly spoken Irishman who is part of the senior management team says, 'How can anyone say no when asked? It is flattering and it would be mean of anyone to say no.'

This coaching, which is extra to the timetable, covers all the year groups and is so widespread that there have to be some negotiations to fit in the requested session to the already busy extra-curricular range of activities.

The youngsters all seem to benefit from the 'many projects' which take the youngsters beyond the school, either literally or virtually. So far as the latter is concerned, the pervasive and rooted use of information communication technology means that the opportunities are extensive for e-mail correspondence, video-conferencing and links to businesses and other schools. As for the 'real' opportunities, the school has gone way beyond the normal 'work experience', 'day visits' and 'field trips'. Youngsters frequently take part in teachers' conferences at the great exhibition and conference spaces both in Birmingham and elsewhere. The school's leadership seeks out such opportunities. 'It builds their confidence: they come back different people – more confident', is how headteacher, Wendy Davies, describes it as she pauses for breath before illustrating other

Table 10.1 Selly Park Technology College for Girls, City of Birmingham

	1995–96	1999–2000
Type and status	County School 11–16 (Girls)	Technology College 11–16 (Girls)
Pupil roll	617	711
Headteacher	Wendy Davies (apptd 1986)	Wendy Davies
% white pupils	7.0	9.4 *English average: 88.5 (1)*
% pupils with English as an additional language	82.5	79.2
% pupils eligible for free school meals (FSM)	63.4	54.1 *English average: 16.9 (1)*
% pupils with special educational needs, incl. Statements	0.6	17.9 *English average: 22.0 (1)*
Pupil/teacher ratio (incl. head)	15.2 *English average: 16.6*	15.4 *English average: 17.1*
Support staff ratio hours (2)	6.7	15.8
% pupils obtaining GCSE (A*–C grades) 5+ subjects	43 *English average: 44.5*	52 (1) *English average: 47.9 (1)*
Average GCSE point score per pupil	Not applicable	42.8 (1) *English average: 38.1 (1)*
% year 11 students with no GCSE passes	2 *English average: 7.8*	1 (1) *English average: 6.0 (1)*
Post-16 participation in full-time education or training (%)	72.6 *English average: 70.4*	81.8 (1) *English average: 70.1 (1)*

Table 10.1 continued

OfSTED grade (PANDA) re: GCSE/ GNVQ score per pupil in similar FSM school group	Not applicable	A* (1) (3)	
OfSTED grade (PANDA) re: GCSE/ GNVQ score per pupil in similar school group re: prior attainment at Key Stage Three	Not applicable	A* (1) (3)	

Key:
(1) 1998–99
(2) Full-time equivalent (f.t.e.) support staff hours per week, per f.t.e. teacher
(3) OfSTED PANDA rubric:
    A* PANDA pupils' results were **very high** in comparison with the average for similar schools

opportunities which Selly Park Girls takes to grow its pupils' confidence. 'They write to people as a result of what they may have said and been reported as saying in the newspapers. Quite often they are then invited to visit', she goes on with a winning breathless urgency that seems to leave the visitor with no reasonable alternative.

> And of course we invite visitors and arrange for the girls to talk with them and it is quite often the case that when the visitors leave they have kindly undertaken either to invite some youngsters to where they do their business, or to follow-up in some way with a further visit or correspondence. We make sure they keep their promises because you cannot let these pupils down can you?

I could easily believe that it would be difficult to resist her sort of certainty: it brooks no denial.

We are now at the heart of it. Youngsters in this school, almost to a girl, are fully convinced they will achieve success. What started ten years ago as a trickle of conviction among a few girls who were wise enough in the circumstances to link their beliefs with the fortunes of the head and a few others as a guarantee to future success, has now become a flood of achievement widely celebrated and so infectious that everyone feels energetically part of it. Now all the staff are active participants and disseminators of the achievement culture.

As one long-time staff member memorably says, 'The girls have changed. They have much better attitudes towards us, themselves and their work: they are a delight to teach.' The girls in Years 10 and 11 themselves believe the school is now better placed than it was when they arrived – significantly at the very time that the first account of Selly Park was written.

TAKING IT FURTHER: THE PRESS FOR ACHIEVEMENT

'Every year does better and better', they enthusiastically tell me as they take a few minutes out of revision time to explain their view of the school's success. 'For example, we do not take study leave like many in my sister's year did a few years ago. We are here trying to get the last drop of assistance from the teachers, or by using the learning development centre.' Her colleague then quickly takes over the conversation: 'That is brilliant – you can get straight onto your own electronic file from one of the workstations elsewhere, though it is better in the learning development centre'. These are girls who refer to the teachers as 'more like friends', but then get lost in dispute about whether that is an accurate judgement. They agree that it is not, but that there is something recognisably different from what they know or have experienced of other teachers. The girls are both admiring of and yet in friendly magnetic awe of their teachers. 'They talk to you all the time in the corridor. It is always about achievement, isn't it?' 'Yes, but I do not like the way they are always on about their "A*" pupils'. 'Oh, that is all right, it is very jokey – and they have good words for us all'. One is adamant that she would be quite content with a B grade but she does not relax because her teacher is counting on her getting an A or an A*; 'and I cannot let her down', she concluded.

There is now what sometimes is described as a 'press for achievement' right across the school, as evident in the group who have been chosen to talk to me, as it is in the replies of girls I happen to encounter in unscheduled discussions in the classrooms or during short stops and snatched conversations in the corridors.

Of all the new elements of school improvement this almost universal press for achievement, conveyed without a sliver of a doubt by all the staff and so many of the pupils, appears to be the most important.

HEADSHIP – A THIRD CHAPTER

The trajectory of school improvement derives essentially from Wendy Davies's first chapter of headship in her first five years when she was simply making sure she had a school to lead into a future rather than one doomed to close. Mike Miskella, the Irishman she identified early on as a fellow spirit, had commented on it, and Wendy Davies had observed a similar quality in him.

The second chapter in the development of the school had seen it to the point where I observed it in 1995 in *Success against the Odds*. By then the school had set out explicitly on establishing an achievement culture. Most of the staff were subscribing to it and many were successful in convincingly conveying the certainty of this ultimate achievement to the pupils themselves. Now, during this third phase, this same phenomenon is awesome.

Of all the features of school improvement, this utterly convincing 'can do' culture seems to me now much more important and significant than it did then. Indeed, when I analyse the familiar school improvements processes, whether of leadership, management, staff

Figure 10.1 'Euro-classroom' at Selly Park

development, teaching and learning, parental involvement, collective review, or creating an environment fit for learning, I feel that I have underestimated the importance of the overriding 'can do' factor. It is important in any school, but it is especially so in an urban environment where many youngsters' lives outside school may be at worst hostile and more normally neutral to and rarely supportive of such a fiercely advocated 'achievement culture'.

The girls and the staff confessed it was difficult not to take advantage of the Saturday morning voluntary learning sessions when the head not merely volunteered, but actually went out of her way to pick them up in her car if they had difficulty getting in!

In primary schools the achievement culture is much more pervasively and obviously present – whether in advantaged or disadvantaged circumstances, though it is clearly much more difficult to establish in the latter. At the secondary school level, with the diversions of adolescence and the 'counter-to-achievement' culture so prevalent in the world beyond school, the establishment of it is much more difficult.

I am not, for example, familiar with the very best independent schools, where I imagine this achievement culture is easily recognised. In more advantaged social-economic circumstances within the state sector one encounters many comprehensive schools where it has clearly been sustained over a long period. And it is a factor which the Technology College Trust movement takes pride in identifying as one of its contributions towards school improvement since, so the Trust argues, the acquisition of the status can act as a spur to generating energy among staff and pupils alike. Moreover, there are other schools which are not technology colleges in Birmingham where the achievement culture is taking hold and growing to similar proportions to that witnessed at Selly Park. But Selly Park would be a marker. It is fair to say that there can be no more dramatic story than that of Selly Park in the distance travelled in moving from a non-achievement culture to a fully established achievement culture over a relatively short period.

FIVE YEARS ON: FURTHER INITIATIVES

What has happened to the school since the end of the last chapter in 1995 beyond acquiring City Technology College status?

Well, first, the school has become involved in the University of the First Age (UFA) – a cross-city project which has targeted the first three years of secondary schooling with the idea of providing intensive interest-led accelerated learning opportunities in summer schools and 'extra-to-the-school' learning opportunities.

A powerful ingredient of the UFA programme has been a teacher development network funded by the Paul Hamlyn Foundation and run by the UFA. Hamlyn fellows meet with the Principal of the UFA on every third Monday to compare notes, listen to visiting speakers, and take part in practical curriculum-focused workshops where new materials are created and ideas and resources shared. It becomes a catalyst of growing and sharing ideas where the most energetic teachers collectively share the development of ideas. One of the conditions of the schools' receiving the very modest resource their participation in the scheme brings – less than £3000 – is that they commit themselves to taking part in 'Super Learning Days'. On these, the timetable is suspended and students and teachers alike embark on 'accelerated learning' techniques and new ways of learning and teaching. Additionally, the pupils have access to extended learning opportunities through membership of the University of the First Age.

To mention the UFA, however, is simply to pick out one of many ventures that the school has embarked on since the last visit. All are important. The number of internal and external projects listed in the school's own inventory include such ideas as the 'creation of a mural' (involving Years 10 and 11), 'music composition' (Years 9 and 10 with a local primary school), 'gospel choir' and 'day play' (girls plus a local primary school as part of a GNVQ course), 'literacy', 'Brunei garden' (a project linking with a particular school in Brunei and involving each developing traditional gardens for the other), 'a Euro classroom' (involving the EU), 'European high-speed rail links', 'travel and tourism in Europe', 'Challenge 2000+ Millennium competition', 'visible woman', 'Bournville Trust – Selly Manor' (a Tudor garden will be created in the grounds of the manor and the project will coincide with history lessons on the Tudors), 'Singapore health project', 'young engineers', 'pupil research initiative' (which includes a scientist in residence), together with all the usual clubs, careers conventions, work experience, Duke of Edinburgh Awards and other ventures which all schools engage in.

FOCUS ON TEACHING AND LEARNING

The school's focus on teaching and learning is summarised in a booklet as a reference point for themselves and visitors. In some of the school's own words in the booklet, *Teaching and Learning*

Initiatives 1997–2000, it is possible to see 'details of teaching and learning initiatives (whole school and departmental) and strategies for improving pupils' performance' compiled by the 'senior teacher i/c teaching and learning with the help of all staff':

> Over the last few years there has been a revolution of teaching and learning in Selly Park with a considerable increase in the number of initiatives we have become involved in. There are many projects going on departmentally and some cross-curricular initiatives. This booklet attempts to summarise projects and initiatives to support teaching and learning in school. It does not attempt to summarise all projects and initiatives in school, although it recognises that some of the projects not mentioned here will also have an impact on teaching and learning styles.
>
> In the last few years ICT has come to play a very large part in our lives and is at the heart of much of what we do. Opportunities have increased significantly for all of our pupils in our rapidly advancing technological society. Teaching and learning have benefited tremendously. Computers are used extensively and we are now exploring opportunities to incorporate laptops. At present small groups have been targeted to work on a variety of projects. This will be closely monitored in the coming months.

Section One: Whole School Initiatives

Many of the things going on in school have evolved over a period of years. They have been monitored, evaluated and are constantly updated and improved. Each of these is briefly summarised in this section. Some are then expanded upon in the following section.

Personal Academic Tutors [PATs]

- Each girl has a personal academic tutor
- Each group has an experienced teacher to meet the needs of every individual in the group

- The groups meet once a week to discuss work, solve problems and monitor homework and coursework
- In Years 10 and 11 the pupils are in smaller groups to enable the tutors to monitor more closely examination coursework and discuss any points of concern
- KS3 pupils follow the Skills for Life programme
- KS4 pupils follow a Programme of Study incorporating aspects of time management, study skills, ROAs [records of achievement], Careers Education and guidance and revision techniques.

Individual Target setting and Monitoring pupil performance

In all years, but particularly in Years 10 and 11, information about pupil performance is closely monitored and individual targets set based on all available data. Staff work with pupils on a one-to-one basis to achieve targets set in PAT periods and supported study sessions. Learning mentors have been appointed to support work in all years. Assessment results in all years are monitored on a half-termly basis. The Headteacher and senior staff support the work of Heads of Department, subject teachers and PATs in monitoring the progress of homework and course-work. Green reports can be issued by Heads of Year to monitor pupil performance.

Super Learning Days

Each term pupils in Years 10 and 11 have a Super Learning Day. Each day has a different focus. In the last year pupils have been given a range of strategies to help them organise their work, improve their learning, work to deadlines, organise their revision, revise, prepare for exams, cope with exams and develop techniques for answering exam questions. Pupils have also been allowed to work for part of each day on individual targets with the help of senior staff. These sessions have been co-ordinated by the two Hamlyn fellows in conjunction with other senior staff.

There are plans to extend this to Year 9 to help them prepare for SAT examinations.

Study skills

Study skills are also taught in lower and upper school through the PSE [personal and social education] system.

Extra study opportunities

Pupils are encouraged to come into school early in the mornings and remain late into the evenings. Learning mentors have been appointed to support study in the LDC [Learning Development Centre]. A summary follows in more detail later in this booklet. This supports learning in all years.

Many departments run lunch-time or after-school help clubs and revision clubs. There is also a Saturday morning revision club run by the Head and senior staff with opportunities for subject teachers to participate if they request it. This is done on a voluntary basis.

Easter revision programme

This is provided each year for Year 11 pupils. It is organised and run by the Head and senior staff with many subject teachers participating.

Teaching styles

Selly Park has a partnership arrangement with several ITT institutions to train student teachers. Staff in many departments have trained as subject mentors. This is invaluable for many reasons. It allows a constant influx of new ideas, a constant updating of pedagogy and opportunities to share good practice in the departments involved and beyond.

In addition, the induction period for NQTs demands a very organised programme of support. It has necessitated staff training in mentoring skills and lesson observation. In the departments involved this year this has had a knock-on effect within the department as teaching styles have come under close scrutiny.

Teacher self-review is also encouraged, as is the policy of sharing good practice, both within departments and beyond.

Many staff have been trained by the UFA and participate in after-school homework clubs or summer school activities. This has benefited their teaching styles considerably and given them a better understanding of the ways in which pupils learn. This in turn impinges on the work they do in the classroom.

When new staff are appointed it is now school policy to observe a lesson as part of the interview procedure.

So far, this follow-up description of Selly Park has attempted to convey the picture of a school, now a College of Technology, which has spent what new money it has had on:

- improved environment (especially of carpets and of computers and their surroundings), more staff and staff development,
- an extended opportunity for pupils with a clear emphasis (and very focused intensity) on teaching and learning,
- convincing the pupils that achievement is important and within their reach, dependent only on their (i.e. individual pupils') attitudes.

It is a school that started with the threat of closure and tramped its local streets to secure support. Now it has rippled out so that its sense of community, with which it regularly communicates, embraces the nation and all continents of the world.

ASSESSING SUCCESS AND MEASURING UP NATIONALLY

It is easy to measure, as well as to assess the progress, of Selly Park because there is a seam to it that is rich in data. Moreover, it analyses the data to see where its next intervention should happen or an existing practice should be marginally modified.

Because Wendy Davies has been there since the second half of the 1980s it is possible to describe some striking contrasts.

All the Figures 10.2 to 10.6 illustrate a remarkable rise in attainment levels at Year 11. The school has used YELLIS analysis for many years in order to analyse both which departments are adding value and how far the school adds value overall to the pupils' performance.

These impressive rises are reflected both in terms of added value and in rates of improvement in the *Value Added in Specialist Schools – 1999* report of Professor David Jesson (2000) for the Technology Colleges Trust. Such improvement raises the question of 'intake' and whether or not it has changed significantly.

The school is located in the district from which it gets its name – Selly Park. Although it is close to Birmingham University campus, the school itself is in an area of student accommodation provided through older terraced housing and rented out from the private sector. There are, therefore, very few local girls. The school has always taken and will continue to take its pupils from a very much wider catchment area – much wider than the average non-selective Birmingham school. Put simply, the average distance which pupils travel to get to Selly Park is 3.69 kilometres. This is significantly further than the average for Birmingham non-selective schools which is 2.19 kilometres. The median (middle) pupil at the school lives 3.58 kilometres compared to the median pupils' 1.74 kilometres for all Birmingham non-selective schools. Nor is this changing. The average distance for Year 7 is 3.74 kilometres and for Year 11 is 3.36 kilometres. A comparative study by the City Education Service's Research and Statistics Unit concludes:

> Thus this fine grain analysis demonstrates conclusively that whatever the level of deprivation measured at ward level, pupils

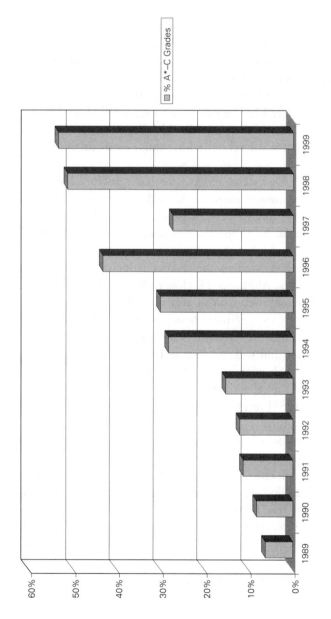

Figure 10.2 Percentage of pupils achieving 5+ GCSE A*–C

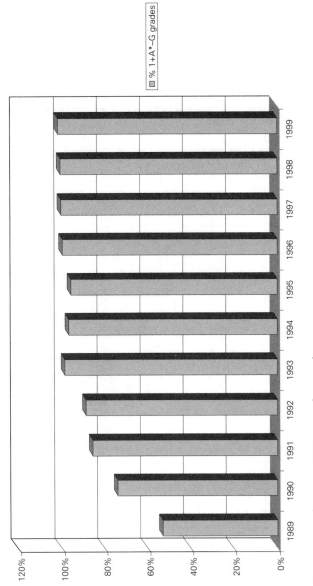

Figure 10.3 At least one GCSE at grade G or above

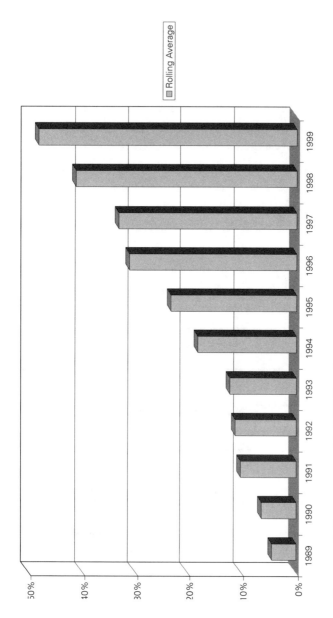

Figure 10.4 Rolling-average 5+ A*–C GCSE grades

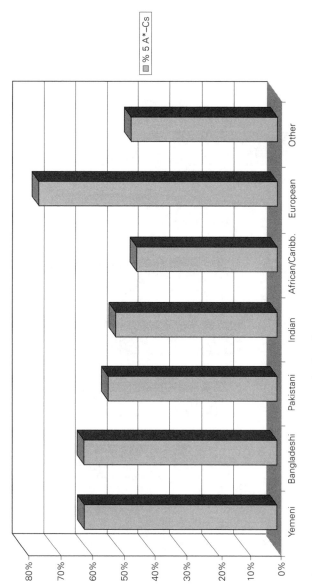

Figure 10.5 Five or more A*–C GCSE grades by ethnic group

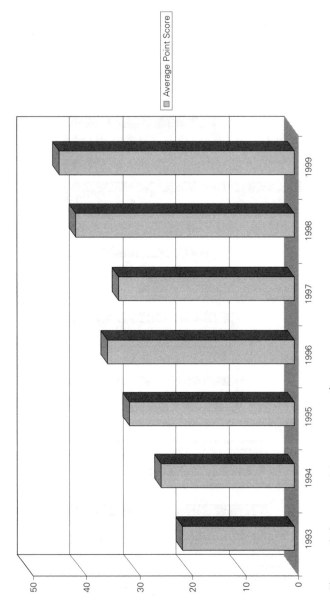

Figure 10.6 Average point score per pupil

in this school are much more likely to come from disadvantaged areas than Birmingham pupils as a whole. Birmingham, we should underline, is much more disadvantaged than the national pattern. These figures are supported by the very high proportion of pupils on free school meals in this school (the criterion for which is a family getting Income Support).

Thus pupils in this school are very likely both to come from disadvantaged neighbourhoods and themselves be economically disadvantaged.

Pupils at Selly Park Technology College travel significantly further to school than is the norm for Birmingham comprehensive school pupils. In essence, the school's catchment area consists of a large cluster, stretching through the Sparkbrook, Moseley and Sparkhill wards. Although these wards vary somewhat in deprivation score, the school's pupils tend to be based in neighbourhoods that are highly deprived.

The number of pupils on free school meals remains at around the 50 per cent level. Since the school operates within the city's overall admission criteria, siblings have priority, followed by a distance criterion. As one can see from the distance analysis, the school's well-publicised success story has not resulted, as one might have expected, in people further away from the school being excluded by oversubscription from those closer to it.

In so far as we can be sure, therefore, what we are witnessing is a school that has raised its five or more A*–C from less than 5 per cent to over 50 per cent, and its points score per pupil from 12 to 43 – both over a ten-year period.

The school's statistical analysis is now extending to Key Stage Three performance, and all is broken down into subject-by-subject and department-by-department analysis. Similar attention has been paid to attendance.

MORE CRITICAL PROCESSES: TOWARDS A SYNTHESIS

To attempt a descriptive introduction to the story of Selly Park and then to provide a flavour of what goes on there by analysis of data is to support the thesis that transformation in the most pressing urban circumstances can happen, has happened and continues to happen.

To comment on the phenomenon is to stimulate the analytical questions, 'Why and how does it happen?'. It is not enough to trace the thread from Wendy Davies's initial brave actions, character and words which conveyed the certainty that she would save the school and anything was possible. *She is* the key and there is no doubt that the issue remarked upon last time of 'not appointing unless someone is absolutely right for the appointment' has remained key in finding a certain sort of staff with character, interest, energy, generosity of spirit and intellectual curiosity. She and the team around her have a 'nose' for charlatans among applicants for posts 'so they do not get to Selly Park'. There is method in their intuition too: they observe applicants teach and take wider soundings. So she has continued to multiply the certainty of girls' achieving by making appointments of people who think from the same principles and are challengingly committed.

But there is more to it than that. The conscious appointment of someone to run projects, the creation and display of targets, the conversation in faculty meetings, the analysis of the data, the sponsorship of activities and projects – all add to the normal rewards/sanctions balance that any school spends most of its time bringing into a painstaking reality. You cannot help thinking that it is the time-honoured comment of reaping what you sow, of only getting out what you put in – and that in Selly Park they put in an amazing amount and are, therefore, reaping all the time. Certainly, two of my witnesses – both as it happens in the first seven years of their career – were remarking on the time they put into their jobs.

They are both Hamlyn Fellows. They both found time for another venture, unconnected with the school, called Ishango. So, in a way – and one was a Head of a Department, the other had a Senior Responsibility Allowance – they were juggling school, Ishango and the University of the First Age. True, they were busy and doubtless they became exhausted, but the overwhelming impression they conveyed was of energetic optimism and certainty that they were involved in something which is only the very beginning of what they thought schools could be like. In short, whereas the rest of us marvel at the extent of the school's climb, each of the comparative newcomers to the school has their sights set on yet-higher levels of attainment.

So, where will it end? I remember writing of school improvement as long ago as 1981: 'I am looking forward to collecting school success stories over the next twenty years as a collector would identify a rare species of butterfly in the wild. I will play mental bets with myself about the height to which such schools might ultimately fly.'

I can equally remember more recently the challenge presented by the original commissioners for the case study in *Success against the Odds* 'Was I sure that Selly Park was a really reliable success story?'.

Not only was I confident, but I knew that its subsequent story would more than justify the choice. The data bears out that judgement. If one were to attempt a 'process of school improvement' end-of-term old-style school report on Selly Park Girls it would look something like the following.

1. Leadership and management

The headteacher has provided continuity in an example of generous energetic expectation. This is reflected in her school improvement team which has replaced the old senior management team. There are many new faces in the team and one gets the impression that all are co-opted to feel they are a 'leading' part of the school. All staff – not just teachers – and pupils are allowed the room to contribute to leadership and management. This is because of the increased opportunities afforded by the multiplying number of initiatives or projects taken on by the school. The virtuous circle thus created derives from the enlargement of the school's community both in staffing and in a wider sense of contacts the leadership of the school has made in industry, the voluntary sector, universities and abroad.

2. Creating an environment for learning

The visual environment of the school reflects the pupils' rising achievements; conversations in carpeted corridors and classrooms revolve mainly around achievement and learning. There is a sense of all being part of a great collective endeavour reflected in the simple illustrations drawn at random from the newsletters of Selly Park. Behaviour and assessment policies accentuate 'appreciative enquiry' (i.e. building on what is good), or celebration of awards, rather than sanctions and problem-solving. Not that this school is soft and does not have its problems, but they are dealt with quietly and quickly rather than magnified by endless replaying of the issues. Use of computers is further transforming the behaviour of all the community.

3. Collective review

The strength of the school is its schematic collection and use of data. All are engaged in monitoring and nobody is excluded from the process of review. But it is accepted that the person who has the leadership role on a particular topic or issue should be the one to have a strong voice in the confirmed, adjusted, or totally new direction decided on after the evaluation is completed.

4. Staff development

It continues to be a feature of the school that it is meticulous about appointments and is unwilling to make one if there is any hesitation about the suitability of a potential post-holder. The school is outstanding in discovering the extensive range of talents which each member of staff brings to the school. Ways are continually sought to find a way of enabling staff to become fulfilled (and tired!) by deploying such skills and interests. Many new support posts appear to have been filled by people with a teaching background, thus strengthening the learning culture and incidentally building in for such staff the chance of overtime by teaching when teachers are away sick or on courses.

5. Parental and community involvement

The school belongs to many communities. By its location and simple gender composition Selly Park is less a part of its immediate locality than some schools. But it contributes to the place where it carries out its mission. It interprets community involvement on a pan-Birmingham, national and international stage. All teachers are encouraged to belong to their own professional communities.

6. Teaching and learning

This is the particular strength of Selly Park. The Judith Little (1993) comment that there are four ingredients present in successful schools, namely:

- (i)   teachers talk about teaching
- (ii) teachers observe each other teach
- (iii) teachers plan, monitor and evaluate their teaching together, and
- (iv) teachers teach each other things

is manifestly present right across the staff at Selly Park.

CONCLUDING REMARKS

This school has already contributed to our deeper understanding of the journey of school improvement in challenging circumstances. Fussiness in choice of staff was manifest in its rigorous system of appointments and described as a feature in the first analysis of Selly Park in *Success against the Odds* (1996). This has continued and is cleverly supported by the imaginative use of support staff. No school has better harnessed ICT in the heart of its learning and teaching mission, nor to motivate youngsters and provide vital access to learning at much more extensive hours.

Five years from now the school will regard its present considerable, and to some, astonishing achievements as but a staging post in showing that schools can transform life's chances in disadvantaged circumstances for all pupils.

REFERENCES

Jesson, D. in association with Taylor, C. (2000) *Value Added in Specialist Schools – 1999*, London: Technology Colleges Trust.

Little, J. W. (1993) Teachers' professional development in a climate of educational reform, *Educational Evaluation and Policy Analysis*, 15, 2, 129–51.

11

SUTTON CENTRE
Sutton-in-Ashfield, Nottinghamshire
Jean Rudduck and Ian Morrison

A school and its community

This study was carried out by Professor Jean Rudduck (who led the 1995 team) and Dr Ian Morrison, both of Homerton College, Cambridge. The extensive documentary database that we amassed (published reviews of good practice, LEA reports, OfSTED reports, school records, notes from governors' meetings, school development plans, etc.) was extended by on-site interviews with the headteacher and the following people (the order is alphabetical by undisclosed surname):

- Non-teaching staff governor (G,nts) (f)
- Parent governor (G,p) (f)
- Key Stage 4 Manager (M,ks4) (f)
- Deputy Head, Personnel (DH,p) (f)
- Deputy Head, Resources (DH,r) (m)
- Head of Community Education (H,ce) (m)
- Leader of the Parents Project (L,pp) (f)
- Key Stage 3 Manager (M,ks3) (f)
- Head of Humanities and Coordinator of Staff Development (C,sd) (f)
- Deputy Head, Curriculum (DH,c) (m)

Table 11.1 Sutton Centre Community College, Nottinghamshire County Council

	1995–96	1999–2000
Type and status	County 11–18 (Mixed)	Community 11–18 (Mixed)
Pupil roll	746	905
Headteacher	Andrew Mortimer (apptd 1992)	Andrew Mortimer
% white pupils	99.7	99.2 *English average: 88.5 (1)*
% pupils with English as an additional language	0	0
% pupils eligible for free school meals (FSM)	32.4	22.3 *English average: 16.9 (1)*
% pupils with special educational needs, incl. Statements	31.0	29.0 *English average: 22.0 (1)*
Pupil/teacher ratio (incl. head)	14.7 *English average: 16.6*	16.7 *English average: 17.1*
Support staff ratio hours (2)	10.6	9.5
% pupils obtaining GCSE (A*–C grades) 5+ subjects	29.0 *English average: 44.5*	33.0 (1) *English average: 47.9 (1)*
Average GCSE point score per pupil	Not applicable	29.5 (1) *English average: 38.1 (1)*
% year 11 students with no GCSE passes	9.0 *English average: 7.8*	4.0 (1) *English average: 6.0 (1)*
Post-16 participation in full-time education or training (%)	45.9 *English average: 70.4*	57.4 *English average: 70.1 (1)*

Table 11.1 continued

OfSTED grade (PANDA) re: GCSE/ GNVQ score per pupil in similar FSM school group	Not applicable	D (1) (3)
OfSTED grade (PANDA) re: GCSE/ GNVQ score per pupil in similar school group re: prior attainment at Key Stage Three	Not applicable	B (1) (3)

Key:
(1) 1998–99
(2) Full-time equivalent (f.t.e.) support staff hours per week, per f.t.e. teacher
(3) OfSTED PANDA rubric:
    D PANDA pupils' results were **below** the average for similar schools
    B PANDA pupils' results were **above** the average for similar schools

Each interview was conducted by either Ian Morrison or Jean Rudduck, and lasted about an hour; substantial sections of the interviews were transcribed. The codes indicate how extracts from interviews are referenced in the text.

The authors would like to thank the headteacher, the governors and the staff for their willingness to talk to us at length and for the openness of the conversations.

THE SCHOOL AND ITS STUDENTS

Sutton Centre Community College opened in 1973. When it was built, a green-fields grammar school was what the community expected – but what it got instead, in the words of a deputy head, 'was the equivalent in terms of schools of a "Spielberg spaceship"' – right in the middle of the town. The picture of the school presented in *Success against the Odds* (Rudduck *et al.*, 1996: 260–1) is still reasonably accurate five years later:

> On arriving at Sutton Centre you don't see the usual institutional trappings of a school. There is no gate to pass through; no iron railings mark it off from its surroundings; no high walls contain the students, or keep local people out. There is no concrete playground, no tarmac drive. It is difficult to know whether you are on the school premises or not. And when you are inside, the windows look directly on to the marketplace, the town library, a newly refurbished shopping centre, a health centre and a pub. Three paths wind through the buildings, taking members of the community across the site or into its buildings, for the school is also the local community and leisure centre [and the] students share the facilities with the . . . adults who come each week to learn, to practise their hobbies, to take part in sports and health activities, or to visit the theatre, which doubles as the school's assembly hall. It is a very accessible site.

There is still no school uniform; the headteacher explained: 'We believe that the responsibility invested in students to dress appropriately is very important'. Again, little has changed in terms of the school's setting although there have been some small changes in the community: benefits policies have lifted the community, and the unemployment that followed the closure of the coal mines and the hosiery factory has given way to more casual employment opportunities. And while drugs problems in the area may have increased they do not come into the school.

The 1997 OfSTED report describes the student intake. This has not changed its character much in the subsequent three years, although the number of pupils has increased, reflecting the community's gradual acceptance of a school that is 'different' – and doing well:

Pupils admitted to the school come from the full range of socio-economic backgrounds but the college's catchment area includes areas of real disadvantage. The proportion of pupils coming from socially advantaged backgrounds is well below average. . . . The school's intake of pupils represents the full attainment range but there is a skew to the middle and lower ranges of attainment with about 20 per cent of pupils admitted to Year 7 having reading ages that are more than two years behind their chronological age.

In 1997 the percentage of students eligible for free school meals was 31 per cent; the LEA's 1999–2000 School Improvement Report gives a figure of 27 per cent (over 200 pupils), compared with an English national average of 17 per cent. The percentage, however, has recently been calculated as 22.3 per cent – to the head's annoyance in that the new figure may give a misleading picture. In fact a very sizeable minority of additional students can be described as being *almost* eligible for free school meals. As the head argues, the new figure is not an indication of an increasingly stable and affluent community but reflects the growth in casual earning.

In the period 1994/95 to 1997/98 the number of pupils with SEN including statements rose from 22.2 per cent to 44.2 per cent, but it has since declined to 29.0 per cent;[1] the England figures rose from 15.2 per cent to 19.0 per cent but they are still lower than those for Sutton Centre. The site has been adapted to receive students, from a wide area, with physical disabilities. (*Sources:* School Statistical Profile and LEA School Improvement Report, 1999–2000.)

The pupil/teacher ratio has worsened from 14.0 in 1994/95 to almost 17.0 in 1999/2000. The comparable England figures for the same period are 16.5 per cent and 17.1 per cent. (*Source:* School Statistical Profile.)

SUCCEEDING AGAINST THE ODDS, 2000

Five years ago the odds against were the ways in which social disadvantage in the community affected students' attitudes to learning and aspirations for the future; now the odds are to do with teachers' stamina and a financial situation which does not make the task of sustaining improvement any easier.

The social disadvantage is still there but the staff think they understand the problems for young learners well enough now to work on them constructively. They remain, however, cynical about public pronouncements that appear to underrate the constant effort and resources needed to sustain commitment and progress in difficult circumstances:

> All those unhelpful comments about being poor is not an excuse – you have to struggle more [in areas like this].
>
> (DH,p)

In the community, attitudes to learning and to getting qualifications are at last catching up with the reality that you can't any longer leave school at 16 and walk straight into a job. The school has had to struggle – perhaps a bit less each year – to create with each new year-group a 'readiness to learn' and a recognition that doing well at school is a foundation for the future.

The demands on staff are often social as well as academic and they come from parents as well as from students who 'see this place as central to the community and as a place where help is available' (DH,p); the staff accept this as one of the outcomes of being a community school: 'We don't walk on water [here], we just want to teach the kids, but if you're [in trouble] then we will tell you where to get help' (DH,p).

The deputy for resources sums up the situation:

> We understand the social context that we work in now, we've got the systems in place . . . and we can work with some very difficult

students. We've got a lot of expertise now in getting parents on side, getting students on side, working together as a team to manage learning difficulties, behaviour difficulties . . . What we lack . . . is the (material) support to underpin it all – and to find the time to be able to do it.

(DH,r)

A very early inspection report (in 1978, a few years after the school first opened) warned that the pace and multiple demands on staff would be difficult to sustain. The report was right; the pace and the multiple demands on the staff are still there – but the commitment carries the school through. As the head says, 'in order to teach effectively here you have to be very, very active as a teacher'. Staff turnover is running at about 7 per cent; 'This', said the head-teacher, 'is a crucial factor in maintaining the momentum and seems at about the right level to balance out experience and youthful energy.' Promotion is the main reason for leaving.[2]

When student numbers were lower, the staff decided to make as few redundancies as possible and to use the 'extra' person-power for various forms of essential student support. Now that student numbers are higher, the staff are trying to maintain at least the same levels of support for more pupils with the same staff complement. As a consequence, in the last three years, the pupil/teacher ratio has gone up from 15 to 17 and class sizes are scheduled to increase next year from 26 to 30; non-contact periods are now fewer and these are often used for counselling individual students: 'By spreading the jam a little bit thinner and people taking the odd extra period' (DH,r), money can be used to sustain the initiatives that matter to the school.

As an example of the difficulty of sustaining successful externally funded initiatives the staff still refer to the project which started some years back, with a 2-year grant of just under £30,000, to find ways of raising attendance. The strategy involved telephone pagers, clerical assistance and additional help from the educational welfare office. Attendance went up beyond the threshold of 90 per cent (if a school falls below 90 per cent attendance special measures can be implemented). After two years the expectation was that the activity would be self-sustaining but the telephone bills of £4000 to £5000 a year and the need for dedicated assistance didn't diminish and the money had to be found from somewhere else in the school's budget.

Then, of course, the presence of some reluctant students requires another level of support:

> You've cajoled and persuaded them and shall we say delivered them to school in some instances and once they are there you need the support systems to actually begin to turn them round. . . . I mean improving your attendance figures is the tip of the iceberg really.
>
> (DH,r)

Another area which takes scarce resources is the sixth form. Local proposals to set up a sixth form centre are still in the air and Sutton Centre lives with the threat of losing a sixth form which has made a difference to staying-on rates and to raising aspirations post-16. A sense of security matters to Sutton Centre students; some are not adventurous: 'If we closed the sixth form and there was a sixth form centre opened up somewhere, a lot of our students would say "Oh well, I'm not going there, no" and we'd lose a lot'. The costs of trying to raise aspirations and encourage young people to continue with their education and training are high here: the shortfall between income and expenditure for each Year 12 or 13 student is about £1200; the money has to be found somewhere. The investment is seen by the staff as worthwhile – and in line with government policies:

> In this area there is, traditionally, a very, very low staying-on rate. We are beginning to actually cut into that now. We are getting significant numbers of students who are opting to stay on who

wouldn't have done before [and] if they can get over that hurdle they tend to do quite well.

(DH,r)

Recruiting up to target offers the school a longer-term financial perspective than when the numbers were uncertain – and it also means that Sutton Centre will not need to take in, because it no longer has spare places, students who are transferred from other schools and who inevitably bring with them a raft of problems that make heavy demands on staff.

The financial situation is complicated by the fact that the school, as a Community College, is joint-funded. Pressures have developed in relation to issues of wear and tear on the buildings. 'Problems of ageing buildings continue' (1998), 'maintenance money is inadequate' (1999), say the reports to governors.

Raising achievement here is a slow, incremental process; it is an achievement in some years not to slip back, says the head, and additional effort is always needed to move forward, step by step. And yet this is what the school has done.

EVIDENCE OF PROGRESS OVER THE LAST FIVE YEARS

This is a school that used to get the worst exam results at GCSE level and that blighted the view of the community. In the last 4 years they have been the best, for 3 out of 4 years, in the local coalfield community.

(Head)

We had to sell ourselves and now that has gone away.

(M,ks3)

Evidence of progress has to be looked at in the context of information about the school and its pupils' prior attainment.

Figure 11.1 Design technology at Sutton Centre

Recruitment and roll

The total *number of pupils* on the register has grown steadily from 738 in 1994/95 to 905 in 1999/2000. The standard number has been 167 since 1997/98; the number of new admissions to Year 7 has grown from 122 in 1995/96 to 187 in 1999/2000. The intake is now 12 per cent above the standard number. Transfers out have remained level at an average of 6 per year. (*Source:* School Statistical Profile.)

Attendance and exclusions

The *attendance rate* among pupils of compulsory school age, at just above 90 per cent, is very close to the English national average of 91 per cent. The percentage of authorised half days missed – under 8 per cent – is at or a little below the national average. The Sutton Centre percentage of unauthorised half-days missed is 1.6 per cent, while the national average is 1.1 per cent. In most years the percentage of permanent exclusions, at 0.36 per cent, has been close to the national average of 0.34 per cent. The number of fixed-term exclusions (3.93 per cent) is low and well below the Nottinghamshire average (5.47 per cent). (*Sources:* School Statistical Profile and LEA School Improvement Report, 1999–2000.)

Outcomes 11–16

The Local Authority 'Tracking Project' data show *attainment on entry* to be well below average; percentages of pupils (both boys and girls) in both the medium and lower ranges of ability are high. Trends in pupils' attainment by the end of Key Stage 3 show a marked improvement over recent years, in English in particular, but with positive trends in other subjects too. Nottinghamshire LEA has developed, over a number of years, its own 'value-added' system of analysis which takes account of parental occupation as well as free school meals. The summary of the 1999–2000 Report says:

The vast majority of pupils come from significantly disadvantaged backgrounds. They demonstrate poor standards of attainment on entry and by the end of Key Stage 3 improvements in performance merely represent a catching up in respect of a previous lag in attainment. In Key Stage 4, although attainment is below the national average, the improvements shown by the value-added data indicate a phenomenal level of improvement and particularly high standards in some areas of teaching and learning.

The percentage of pupils with 5 or more grades A*–C has risen from 16 per cent (1994/95) to 33 per cent in 1998/99 with a high of 36 per cent in 1997/98. During this period the English national percentage rose from 43.5 per cent to 47.9 per cent. (The projection for the 2000–2001 cohort is high but for 1999–2000 the projection is less good.) Staff are optimistic about reaching 40 per cent in the next couple of years. The percentage of pupils with 5 or more grades A*–G rose from 74 per cent (1994/95) to 84 per cent in 1998/99. During this same period the national percentage rose from 85.7 per cent to 88.5 per cent. The percentage of 1+ A*–G, at 96 per cent, is above the national average.

The LEA's value-added figures show that the percentage of pupils attaining 5+ A*–C grades is well above average for similar schools in the county. (*Sources:* School Statistical Profile and LEA School Improvement Report, 1999–2000.) The school feels that the PANDA calculation of free school meals (it shows a 10 per cent drop since 1995–6) does not reflect the reality of the intake. Because the free school meal percentage is used as the basis for comparing the school's GCSE/GNVQ outcomes with those of 'similar' schools, the PANDA grade of D (see Table 11.1) is contested; the LEA judges the school much more positively.

Outcomes 16+

Statistics indicate that the school is raising pupils' academic expectations. In 1998–9, 48.1 per cent of students stayed on in the sixth form (Years 12 and 13). The percentage in full-time education in FE colleges has risen from 7.2 per cent to 9.3 per cent. Figures for employment without training have fallen over the period.

The average points score per candidate taking 2+ A-levels or AS equivalent has remained at about 13 while the English national comparison has grown from 17.5 to 18.2, but the combined GCE A/AS and Advanced GNVQ average points score per candidate is 16 while the national figure is 17. Even at A-level, says the LEA report, students' attainment is better than might reasonably be expected and the figures do not indicate the considerable range in attainment achieved by A-level students, nor the considerable achievement made by some individuals. (*Sources:* School Statistical Profile and LEA School Improvement Report, 1999–2000.)

The LEA report concludes that the school is doing well for its pupils and that results reflect a continuing improvement trajectory since 1995. The LEA recognises the effort that lies behind the improvement figures and offers praise: 'Sutton Centre provides good value for money. . . . The effectiveness of the school's head teacher and the collegial approach of its senior management team have a very positive and considerable impact upon school improvement and the raising of standards' (*Source:* LEA School Improvement Report, 1999–2000). The 1997 OfSTED report arrived at similar conclusions, noting 'the high standards achieved in teaching, behaviour and educational provision for the full range of young people'. A visit by two HMIs in 1998, in the wake of the LEA inspection, focused on performance management; notes taken on the oral feedback suggest that the inspectors thought that performance data were being well used to support overall planning and that planning was effectively followed through to departmental level.

Changes in the way the school is perceived by the community have made a big difference to the school's sense of progress:

> The old fears about the school uniform, about the playground, the first-name terms, they are dying away. Certainly, as parents we are not required to defend the place.
>
> (G,nts)

The coverage of the school's achievements in the local press (such as the following item in 1997) may well have contributed to the school's acceptance by the community.

Top marks for Sutton Centre from OfSTED inspectors

> The quality of teaching at Sutton Centre has gained top marks from education watchdogs. In one of the highest awards in the country for a secondary school, 93 per cent of all lessons observed . . . were judged to be sound or better – a figure which is well above the national averages. . . . The inspectors praised the hard working staff who 'provide a very broad range of opportunities for all pupils'. . . . The report says pupils' attitudes are positive and they behave well.

The achievements of individual students are also noted in the local paper – for instance, this item in 1998:

> Rebekah Williamson, 18, scooped five A-levels – and said she owed it all to her teachers. The youngster achieved grade As in English literature, general studies, German and history and a grade B in French.

The account of Sutton Centre five years back (see Rudduck *et al.*, 1996) shows a lingering suspicion of a school which was 'different' in style and appearance and where every small incident was seen as confirmatory evidence of its strangeness. As the head said, confidently but wryly, 'I don't get the feeling any longer that everyone's waiting for Sutton Centre to trip on a banana skin'.

INITIATIVES DESIGNED TO SUPPORT ACHIEVEMENT

The head explained that progress is about keeping effective current initiatives going, while judiciously introducing new ones. The school has managed to hang on to all the earlier initiatives that were expressive of its concern to support the achievement of the wide range of students. For instance, the eleventh session (an early and pioneering form of what might now be called 'study support' or 'homework clubs') continues (see later); the work on the Local Business–Industry–School *Compact* continues to support the school's concerns about attendance and punctuality and has opened up the possibility of business mentoring for students who are vocationally oriented and who lack a positive sense of future. The yearly Activity Week continues, with cross age groupings that allow students to sample and succeed in a range of different activities. The attention to transfer has been sustained, with Year 10 students visiting pupils in primary schools and Year 12/13 pupils acting as mentors to Year 7s. There is better use of primary school performance data and is involved the transfer liaison teacher in primary school literacy and numeracy programmes. As the head said, 'Everything that has been achieved in the last 5 years has been on the foundation of the previous 10 years. There has been a sense of growing confidence in the place.'

Work on teaching and learning continues to evolve and at the same time some major initiatives have been taken in relation to:

- raising expectations, monitoring performance and mentoring support;
- parental involvement in learning;
- adult and community education.

The non-teaching staff governor explained, with some pride, that in her view the school was 'usually in front of initiatives rather than grasping them as they are presented to us: the eleventh sessions – we have been there, done that, long before homework clubs [were thought of]; we have worked with disaffected students. We are going down the vocational field now, and have been for a little while.'

RAISING EXPECTATIONS, MONITORING PERFORMANCE AND MENTORING SUPPORT

> What we've tried to do since 1995 is be quite systematic about our use of data and about really raising expectations and aspirations with the students and also, within the community, with parents.
>
> (M,ks4)

Raising expectations has been a continuing commitment at Sutton Centre and the portfolio of strategies has expanded in the last five years. The introduction of data management systems – recommended by OfSTED in 1997 – has enabled staff to build coherent monitoring and support systems. It also feeds into and strengthens work at departmental or 'area' level. All students have a tutor that they stay with from Year 7 to Year 11, but the tutor's role is being redefined as a 'learning manager' who is 'familiar with all the data on individuals and is better placed at Year 9 to help them with choices about the future' (DH,c). The performance tracking system supports the tutor in this role. And, again, the personalised Year 7 data on students' social skills allow staff to pinpoint and work on behaviours that, if they became intensified, could lead to exclusion in later years.

The management team has a formal dialogue with teachers in each subject department twice a year; one meeting focuses on a review of progress and the other on planning in the light of the review. There is also a system for looking at samples of students' work across subjects. Departments are now asked for targets for each pupil: 'We've gone from looking at predictions to looking at targets: a target is a prediction plus challenge.' Where there appears to be a risk of under-achievement, then a mentoring system comes into play. Various systems of mentoring have been tried but they proved very demanding of staff time. As a consequence, students who are under-achieving are now invited to nominate a mentor and teachers give up their own time (lunch breaks or after school) to provide the necessary support. There is also subject-related mentoring for students in Years 10 and 11 who are finding some aspects of the course difficult. The system of 'buddy' pairings between Year 12/13 and Year 7 students continues; a parent governor talks about her son's experience as a mentor:

> My son in Year 12 goes swimming with Year 7s and I do know that he has made some quite good progress with a very difficult student in Year 7 that we very nearly excluded permanently. Often this student cannot behave [but] he has been able to go swimming and achieve. That is what is brilliant about this place.
>
> (G,p)

One important dimension of building students' academic confidence is that they know that they will be entered for every subject that they study – a strategy that has paid off in terms of the percentage of 1+ A*–G grades.

The school is also trying to raise expectations post-16. For the first time a group of students was taken to visit the university at Humberside; in this locality there are few families where anyone has enrolled for higher education and the students are not well informed:

> They were asking questions like 'Do you stay there, do you sleep there?' They wanted to know how much you have to pay to go to

that particular university so money was an issue. . . . When they talked about grants they all said 'oh I can't get into debt' – that's the [family] perspective and that came up in parents' evening. Getting into debt isn't on. So some of them are saving now to go [to university].

(M,ks4)

Both students and parents 'are [now] looking at [continuing] education as the next step rather than stopping education'. The staff are consciously trying to use a language of continuity: 'Even from Year 9 when they come in for their option evening we talk now about the next *four* years – we don't talk about the next *two* years'. Of course, a more realistic understanding of the limited possibilities of the local labour market supports staying on, but now a wider range of parents is coming to the prospective sixth-form evenings: 'If you were looking at similar students a few years ago those parents wouldn't have been coming in' (M,ks4).

PARENTAL INVOLVEMENT IN LEARNING

'Parents-as-Co-Educators' has been a major initiative for the last three years. It reflects the view that 'if only parents and children could work closely together and if parents could support children and knew how to do so, then this would help to raise their achievement' (L,pp). NFER test data on measures of social skills among Year 7 pupils indicated that many had difficulty in relating to others 'in a calm and rational way' (Head): many of the new students 'do not know how to listen, they can't join in games without trying to push in; they take other people's things without asking, they can't control their anger when someone upsets them' (L,pp). The project team thought that by working with parents the parents might be able both to model appropriate behaviours in their interaction with their children and to help with their learning. Workshops were held for groups of interested parents in 1997–8 and the explicit focus was on helping children to achieve more in school. There were four topics: helping with reading and writing, helping with number work, using the computer and the library, and managing behaviour – including reluctance to do homework.

The LEA offered support for a project assistant and the team won a millennium award to supplement the handbook with a video: 'We are hoping to do role play in [difficult] situations showing the wrong way and the right way to react'. The project links with the school's commitment to helping Year 7s to be more confident and purposeful about learning. A parent who successfully participated in the project is going to talk to the new Year 7 parents next academic year. The emphasis on homework is seen as an important part of establishing study skills early on in pupils' school careers: 'We are looking at homework as a distinctive issue, particularly the American notion of interactive homework which allows parent and child to work much more together' (L,pp).

In short, 'What started as a raising achievement of children project has become, because of the nature of the place, a community project: we are raising the achievement of all learners here and that includes parents as well' (DH,c).

ADULT AND COMMUNITY EDUCATION

The main changes in the past five years reflect a stronger principle of responsiveness. This has meant:

- taking learning into the community rather than expecting adults to come to the provider. Courses are now run in primary schools, church halls, clubs, community centres, old people's homes and social services day centres;
- flexible timing, morning, afternoon, twilight and evening sessions geared to the habits of possible users (e.g. parents who are dropping off or picking up children from school);
- marketing programmes in accessible and everyday settings such as the shopping centre, the super-store, local bingo halls;

- basing provision on needs analysis (interest in training in ICT emerged, predictably perhaps, as the priority across groups; with support for basic skills training from the 'Laptops' project 37 parents moved from the exploratory work to enrol on accredited courses);
- targeting discrete sections of the local community and designing tailor made courses for particular groups.

Courses are also planned so that they provide progression routes, taking into account the anxiety and uncertainty that many adults (many of whom had not done well at school) feel when they contemplate 'returning to learning'; for instance, it is important that the first steps are non-threatening, without pressure, and lead to an experience of success. In many ways the principles that underpin adult learning reflect the principles that operate in school for the younger members of the local community.

It is relevant to discuss the new initiatives in adult education because, as suggested above, the more members of the community value and participate in learning beyond school the more likely it is that young people will see learning as important and as a pathway to constructive futures.

CURRICULUM, TEACHING AND LEARNING

A sustained emphasis in recent years has been on progress at Key Stage 4 and it is now shifting to progress at Key Stage 3. The work with the older students paid off. The school has built up a wide variety of courses to capture the imagination of its pupils. OfSTED (1997) praised the 'breadth and balance' of its programme. Developing the credibility of GNVQs in a community which has traditional values is important:

> Early suspicions about GNVQs being a 'Mickey Mouse' course as opposed to GCSEs, that is beginning to change because the

parents are beginning to do NVQs. They are finding out there are routes which can enable them to develop as individuals. They therefore see them as appropriate for their children. In a sense they have to live through it themselves.

(DH,c)

Some students go to the West Nottinghamshire College for taster vocational courses: 'We particularly identify students who may disappear from the system and it's an excellent course for them'. And in Years 10 and 11 the youth award scheme endorses the sense of steady continuity and progression that the staff are trying to engender in their students; and then there is the National Record of Achievement which can be continued at College. The staying-on rate, now at 58 per cent, is among the highest in the area.

An important learning-support initiative which the school has managed to sustain is the 'eleventh hour sessions' (see Rudduck *et al.*, 1996). The title is a hangover from the past when each week had ten half-day sessions – and the eleventh session was voluntary work that went on in the evening. The sessions still run from 6.30 to 8.30 four days a week and there are on average between 600 and 700 attendances per week – including some adults who are following part of the adult learning programme.

Which students attend, and for what?

Those students who find a bit of difficulty during the day but are willing participants – they come back in the evening and iron those difficulties out. . . . You actually get to marginal students who you can affect.

(DH,c)

There can be a multiplier effect: if popular peer leaders – the 'social pivots' – decide to try the eleventh sessions and judge them to be all right, then others will follow. The situation can require delicate handling because a lot is at stake in terms of the students' self-image:

You just say, 'Well, you know, you can do this. Come back and try it again tonight 'cos you made a bit of a mess up of it today', and they would come back and they would do it and you wouldn't put any pressure on. You'd say, 'That's really good. Do you want to write it up? I'm here next week and I'll give you a hand to write it up'. And they come back and their camp followers see that these significant people were coming back in the evenings and a critical mass then starts to roll.

(DH,c)

These evening sessions allow students to sort out difficulties they have in class, or catch up with work they have missed or not understood; but for others it is an opportunity to start something different. And there is the added advantage that they see adults from the community learning for pleasure and a purpose:

The younger students are constantly exposed to role models for life-long learning: they are able to see learning as . . . a process in which their elders in the community are engaging voluntarily.

(H,ce)

At the moment, 'teaching approaches' do not have such a prominent profile in the school as other initiatives. There are two reasons. First, as was made clear earlier, the OfSTED report judged 93 per cent of lessons observed to be 'sound' or better; earlier staff development work is paying off. There is no complacency here – only a belief that since many Year 7s do not have a predisposition to learn, the priority has had to be in establishing a firm foundation of both social and study skills early in students' school careers. However, with so much of the underpinning now in place, classroom teaching and learning will be, once again, high on the school's agenda.

HOLDING ON TO THE VISION

Part of the explanation for the progress that Sutton Centre has made is the continuing centrality of the founding principles: these provide a vision which acts as a kind of mountaineering rope – staff have something to hold on to in difficult times and they stay together.

When the school first opened in 1973 the values that defined both its social and academic aims were developed by the staff and there was, in a sense, no need for them to be formally written down. HMI, inspecting the school in 1978, made explicit the aims after talking with staff (see Rudduck *et al.*, 1996). The aims are summarised below:

- To teach a common, balanced curriculum, which will provide an appropriate education and an equality of esteem for all students.
- To teach so as to meet the individual needs of the diversity of students.
- To integrate educationally with the community by providing opportunities for adults and adolescents to work and learn together.
- To maintain a system of pastoral care of each individual student which enables the development of self-discipline, personal development and consideration for others as the basic principle of conduct.

It is clear that the 'multiple intelligences' of the students are respected and catered for (DH,c) and that different talents are recognised alongside conventional academic achievements. The school continues to go about its everyday business quietly and consistently: 'We don't create confrontation and conflict. We try to do everything gently and fairly. Children respect "fair". They understand "fair" and respond to "fair"' (M,ks3). In short, the values that give the school its identity remain strong:

The ethos is still the same. This is a unique school; it is for the staff and for the children their place of learning and their place of work. . . . Staff may come and go and children pass through but the ethos always stays constant.

(G,p)

It is difficult to document something that permeates so much of the thinking in the school but two quotations from senior staff suggest the continuing strength of the commitment to the original values:

Foremost in the school it's the individual student that matters and it's the individual student that is at the centre of everything that we do. If we've got children who are leaving as confident students and confident learners and wanting to carry on with their learning and to bring something to the community or to the wider society then I think we have achieved quite a lot – in addition to getting five GCSEs.

(M,ks4)

It's not just senior staff, it's staff at all levels who are rock solid people and who have committed themselves not to easy careerism, fast tracking – they've made personal sacrifices because they have, for a variety of reasons, committed themselves to this institution because it's that kind of place.

(DH,p)

Teachers also understand the importance of holding on to the values while allowing the school to move forward.

In order to maintain places like this people have to be visionary, they have to have a historical sense: they have to see what formed [this school], what brought it into being. The core values are what we have to maintain and [the challenge is] how you can do that within a very different historical situation.

(DH,p)

If there is a change it is that the academic now has pride of place alongside the social and pastoral. As the head said, 'We can be caring but our prime purpose is schooling'. There is widespread pleasure in the school's academic progress and enthusiasm for taking the next step:

I think the 40s [i.e. 40 per cent A*–C passes] are within our grasp. I'm determined that we'll get there and it's the work that ensures that but at the same time . . . not to focus over much on that because it's the whole experience in school [that matters] – to keep that.

(M,ks4)

The school's academic results may not yet be at the national average but they are a good deal closer than they were five years ago and the staff do not think they have sacrificed too much of the original vision on the way.

SUSTAINABILITY, RESPONSIVENESS AND CHANGE

Five years ago Sutton Centre earned its place as a school beginning to 'succeed against the odds' but the foundation of its claim to the label was still emerging. It was able to demonstrate 'success' on several fronts and those who knew the school believed in its potential as well as the early evidence of its formal performance. The staff knew then that the only prospect was to move forward slowly and steadily and learn to manage new initiatives without jeopardising hard-won achievements; as we said five years ago, 'there are no short cuts, no quick fixes' (Rudduck *et al.*, 1996).

Philip Runkel (1984) said that an innovative school is one that tries one thing after another without getting any of them right. Sutton Centre can't afford the luxury of wastefulness. New initiatives are identified in part through the school's self-monitoring procedures: the school identifies priorities which are worked on and evaluated over a three-year period. Importantly, the school has learned the prudence of making use of mandated changes to serve its own purposes rather than waste time and energy in whinging:

> I suppose from day to day it might seem as if it will get you down when you are getting so much paperwork to do and so many new initiatives but it's trying to bring the positive out of them, what's positive for the students, and not see them as a negative experience.
>
> (M,ks4)

On potentially divisive issues the staff seek to arrive, through consultation and discussion, at a 'position'; for instance, even performance-related pay, which many staff were opposed to in principle, was openly discussed and an agreement to proceed without rancour was accepted and respected. Task groups are regularly called on to map out the implications of new external requirements and their conclusions are then presented to the whole staff and staff development programmes set up as necessary:

> We try to manage those initiatives in ways that (1) help us to deal with the potential overload optimistically and (2) help to ensure that they work for us and help us to keep our particular ethos and keep our particular set of values as a community school.
>
> (C,sd)

The benefits of the data management system – the school is very appreciative of the guidance and support from the LEA for this – are widely recognised. For instance, in the current academic year the tracking procedures have allowed teachers to target a group of high-achieving boys – 'which is unusual because it's usually the other way round' – and make sure 'that they don't become an underachieving group of boys'.

The kind of headteacher that features in school improvement fairy stories is usually a high-profile 'miracle grow' person who gets quick results – and then moves on. Andy Mortimer is not like that and he has a different perspective on change. His patient, quietly assured style, together with the loyalty and commitment of the staff, is what has kept the school moving steadily forward. Teachers understand the significance of the consultative approach for Sutton Centre:

> Anything that would leave a significant proportion of staff behind would give him nightmares, I know that. He's very careful to sound out the staff on ideas and he will not only talk to the teaching staff, he will go and talk to the technicians, to the office staff downstairs and if we are doing anything significant, he will go and say, 'Well, what implications do you think there are for you?'. It's not the autocratic 'This is what we are going to do'. He won't be rushed into doing things. He will listen for a long time. It's frustrating sometimes, I have to say, . . . particularly where you are working in a culture of table bangers.
>
> (DH,r)

The head has been there eight years now – a successful and satisfying but tiring innings. He uses the image of the 'virtuous circle' to explain why he thinks things have gone well:

> I'm very interested in the notion of a virtuous circle, and when good things start to happen in the school that then creates more people feeling good about the place, which then makes it better, which then makes more people again feel good about the place. The challenge is not to slip back.

Having an effective data management system underpins the 'feelgood' factor; it has provided the staff with evidence that their strategies are having an impact as well as guidance on what they need to be better at. But above all it has given them confidence – and external recognition, from OfSTED, from the LEA, from various published accounts of aspects of the school's work: 'If you are demonstrably doing well then you can cope with anything that's thrown at you, can't you?' – the virtuous circle again. But the head is also warily realistic: 'I would say just keeping it together is a challenge, just keeping it together in this open environment is a threat. I mean the threat of the wheels coming off is always there, I think, bearing in mind what happened to the school in its previous history.'

The head offered his own comment on school improvement strategies: 'I actually think we need quiet, hard-working, determined heads who will show that they are with their staff and they are not trying to do it for themselves, they are doing it for the place'. He went on:

> It's like building an engine, isn't it, with all the different bits that intermesh and work together and it will run independently of any individuals. . . . I mean, if you build successful schools around individuals what happens when they go? I mean, what has anybody achieved if, when they go, the good goes with them? *If there's a worry* at the moment, it's about the workload that the staff carry and whether they can, for all their spirited support for the school and each other, sustain such arduous schedules.

If there's resentment, it's about the way that some heads and some schools become overnight media stars, and the nagging feeling that slow progress in difficult circumstances goes unrecognised: 'What matters is sustaining the changes and that is the kind of process that doesn't make it into the press'. *If there's a question*, it's how far beyond 40 per cent A*–Cs you can aspire to without losing out on the other things that are important for the young people in this community.

ENDNOTE: REFLECTING ON SCHOOL IMPROVEMENT

The story of Sutton Centre challenges some recent orthodoxies about school improvement which centre on rapid 'turnaround' and charismatic headship, and which take improvements in test scores as the only key criterion for judgement. Some of the things that we learned from our contact with Sutton Centre suggest other ways of thinking about school improvement:

- Improvement strategies need to be constructed to reflect the particular conditions and histories of individual schools and their relationship with their communities.
- Lists of discrete factors conducive to school improvement are not always a reliable guide for action: what matters is how coherence is understood and managed.
- Coherence is more likely to be achieved when policies and their daily enactment in practice are consistently informed by a clearly defined set of principles and values.
- External requirements can sometimes be acted on in ways that serve the principles and values that the school holds dear; in this way the intensification of work that they represent can become more acceptable.
- Improvement can be a slow process: changing the culture (or 'ways of seeing') of members of the school or the community is a pre-condition of progress.
- Sometimes, for schools that work in difficult circumstances, sustaining progress at the new level may itself be an achievement – and can take constant vigilance and energy. (Each new cohort can bring new challenges but cumulative experience of dealing with the problems enables more robust and reliable strategies to be developed.)
- Despite the 'ever onwards, ever upwards' motto of policy makers, schools may need to pace themselves. (Meteoric rises are what

meteors have – and meteors burn out pretty quickly. As the headteacher said, 'The bedrock of our progress is the centrality of unspectacular, unmeteoric and unremitting graft'.)

- Many schools seem to experience 'blips' in the smooth pattern of progress (these are most apparent in records of year-on-year exam passes); we need to know more about the source of these blips, what the early warnings are and what interventions schools might make to keep on track.

- Constraints on how far a school's aspirations can reach – and how quickly they can be realised – may be set by its 'capacity'; capacity seems to be an amalgam of staff commitment and understanding, resources, and local conditions and traditions.

- Stardom at the level of the school tends to highlight the dramatic, the rapid, the spectacular and ignore the quiet and steady progress of schools where conditions, short of seismic changes in catchment and intake, do not lend themselves to glitzy make-overs.

- The system, at the moment, celebrates 'stars', but the principle of stardom – at the level of the headteacher and the classroom teacher – can be at odds with the collegial spirit that fosters mutual support and shared commitment to improvement.

Freeman (2000) says that how schools discover the will to improve, and at what cost, and with what implications – these are the genuine unknowns of education. What the study of Sutton Centre reveals is the importance of staff commitment to the students, to the community and to the principles which have helped the school to navigate the stormy waters of local controversy and national debate about success and failure. Commitment is transformed into effective action by the capacity for institutional self-knowledge over time. As Richardson says in her classic case study of Nailsea School (1973: 67; cited in Freeman, 2000), 'in evaluating the process of development in a complex setting, the success–failure dimension is meaningless. The later stages could not have happened without the experience gained from the earlier ones.' But, as Freeman also says (discussing the work of Barth), the important questions now are about the nature of collegiality: 'What is collegiality? It's difficult to spell, hard to pronounce, harder to define. It's hardest still to establish in a school. . . . It is the flip side of parallel play.' The sense of collegiality and common purpose is an extremely important dimension of Sutton Centre's profile.

Finally, in the text of the chapter, we quoted a teacher who talked about the importance for pupils of the principle of 'fairness': 'Children respect "fair". They understand "fair" and respond to "fair".' We think that the principle should be strenuously upheld in relation to judgements about schools' achievements. For schools like Sutton Centre, the only fair approach is to use a 'value-added' measure and to compare schools with their own previous achievements and with the achievements of schools that are like them in terms of levels and kinds of social disadvantage. It is also important to take into account what pupils are gaining at school in addition to grades and points scores; most schools have an agenda that goes well beyond – and properly so – what they continue to be judged on.

NOTES

1 The number of pupils with Statements at Sutton Centre has remained constant at about 1 per cent while the English national average has risen from 1.9 per cent to 2.5 per cent. The school believes that it has more pupils who deserve to have Statements (there are of course financial implications). Within the LEA decisions are made by a number of Mainstream Support Groups and these divide the funds available on a local basis. The money is used to give support to a wider range of pupils with problems and there may be, as a consequence, fewer pupils with formal Statements of educational need.

2 Since 1996, there have been 4 staff departures each year, 16 in all; of these, 13 were for promotion, 1 for ill health and 2 were resignations for personal reasons.

REFERENCES

Freeman, D. (2000) *The Socio-Political Construction of School Failure*, draft PhD thesis, University of Sheffield.

OfSTED (1997) Sutton Centre Community College Inspection Report (ref. 122841).

Richardson, E. (1973) *The Teacher, the School and the Task of Management*, London: Heinemann.

Rudduck, J., Clarricoates, K. and Norman, R. (1996) Sutton Centre. In National Commission on Education, *Success against the Odds*, London: Routledge.

Runkel, P. J. (1984) Maintaining diversity in schools. In D. Hopkins and M. Wideen (eds) *Alternative Perspectives on School Improvement*, Lewes: Falmer Press, pp. 167–87.

FURTHER LESSONS IN SUCCESS

Margaret Maden

Compared with the first set of case studies in 1995, these appear to offer much greater certainty about both success and the odds against which such success is won. There is now much more statistical information available and there is a strong government view about what constitutes success. This is based primarily on knowledge about school effectiveness drawn from a massive database of school inspection reports held by OfSTED. It is also driven pro-actively through many government programmes with associated earmarked funding to schools, as well as to local education authorities.

The sense of urgency on the part of a New Labour government is palpable; short timescales are set for the delivery of specified improvements. Invocations such as 'poverty is no excuse' ring loud across the staffrooms and council chambers of England. (In Wales, Scotland and Northern Ireland, such prescriptions are more muted, but mounting.)

Beyond the bailiwick of education, government actively pursues policies aimed at reducing the odds against which the pupils in these schools struggle. Social Inclusion is a key New Labour objective. Setting up neighbourhood zones – focusing on education, health or employment – and other area-based interventions seek to complement a raft of national strategies, particularly those represented in the overarching concept of Welfare to Work. These measures suggest that even though 'poverty is no excuse' when schools appear to fail their pupils, government nonetheless recognises that poverty is disabling at both a personal and a societal level.

And yet. Is the knowledge about successful schools as clear as we are urged to believe? Are the measurements of school and pupil achievement adequately illuminating? Are the indicators of disadvantage sufficiently robust? How much do we really know about sustaining improvement – as opposed to a series of 'quick fixes'?

John Gray, in his introduction to these case studies, has mapped out the knowledge base which can be used to explore the journey travelled by these schools in the past five years. The landscape has been marked by a vast range of government requirements and initiatives and by some advances in academic and theoretical knowledge. This book doesn't aim to challenge that knowledge, but the testimony of heads and teachers in eleven schools is itself valuable and is, perhaps, a refreshing antidote to a recent surfeit of more mechanistic, predominantly statistical, analyses of the inner lives of schools.

School 'success' is not the same as 'effectiveness' or 'goodness'. Neither can these be automatically aligned with 'improving', although it is difficult to see how a school – or any organisation – can be described as a success if it isn't, year on year, improving and actively finding ways to do just this. Our original choice of the term 'success' was conscious. We wanted to bring together the criteria and concepts of 'school effectiveness', developed during the previous two decades by scholars in the United Kingdom and elsewhere, with older and broader understandings of 'good schools' which teachers, pupils and parents continue to work towards and frequently live to enjoy.

Not surprisingly, the less obvious, as well as the more obvious, qualities that combine in a school to bring about its success feature in these case studies. Just as success invariably includes aspirations and strategies for achieving better outcomes, especially academic results, it also includes wider and deeper versions of success. Beyond measured outcomes, whether or not 'benchmarked' to take account of quantified 'odds', there is a range of less easily measured success criteria. The energy of parents and pupils, as well as of teachers and other staff, in providing wider educational experiences – beyond the National Curriculum – is one example of these. Another is the quality of human relationships and conversations, between pupils and pupils, pupils and teachers, teachers and parents. In 'business-speak' these are both inputs and outputs, as well as process factors in maintaining the momentum of successful schools.

Searching for success in all pupils and staff, and building on this, isn't particularly easy, especially in these schools which serve, as Tim Brighouse observes, 'an urban environment where many youngsters' lives outside school may be at worst hostile and more normally neutral to . . . a fiercely advocated achievement culture'. What has happened to the eleven schools in the past five years reveals significant variation in the amount and kind of success and improvement experienced.

Some schools have experienced a kind of 'lift-off' to a level and quality of higher achievement which seems to render them unassailable. Other schools maintain hard-won improvement, but are still acutely aware of the struggle and exceptional human effort needed for this. In the Hazelwood study, there is a kind of success characterised by 'simply holding their ground in increasingly difficult circumstances'. In one school, Fair Furlong, the breakthrough chronicled in 1995 was lost and is only now being recaptured.

CONTEXT IS ALL

The importance of context is perhaps more strongly evident than when these narratives started in 1995. The contexts of policy, of organisational structure and of local community markedly affect the schools. The 'odds' against which schools wrest their success are invariably part of this wider context. The relationship and tension between the characteristics of the wider context and those of the school's internal world are significant matters. These case studies deepen our understanding of the dialectic between a school and its setting; for, of course, no school is an island unto itself.

Push and pull

Sometimes, there are contextual factors which support the forward movement of the school, such as lower unemployment rates, more determinedly ambitious parents (as appear to exist amongst the ethnic 'minorities' in Burntwood and Selly Park) or the Catholic Church in St Michael's. Less supportive contextual factors are well described in the Hazelwood study where sectarian anger and volatility persist, in spite of the Northern Ireland peace process. In Tower Hamlets, at Columbia Primary School, health problems and concerns about increased religious fundamentalism in the local Bangladeshi community, as well as the greater emotional turbulence of families and children, stand out. In Manchester, at Crowcroft Park, the shifting population with its increasing range of languages and nervousness on the part of recent immigrants and refugees adds to the complexity of the educational task.

The huge boulder of community and parental scepticism and unfamiliarity about education as a personal good, emerges in the accounts of Haywood High in the Potteries and Sutton Centre, Nottinghamshire, both being located in former coalfield areas. The persistence of effort required to shift such a boulder comes through more strongly in 2000, even though a lot of progress has been made since 1995. In Sutton Centre, there is a 'back to the future' movement, with lifelong education being encouraged: a return to its origins as a community school in the 1970s – another time, another place.

OfSTED and all its works

Government policy represents a further contextual factor that is frequently raised in these case studies, sometimes positively, sometimes not. The presence of OfSTED is keenly felt, with predominantly positive inspection reports not doing much to raise the spirit of teachers at several schools, many having found the inspection experience diversionary and professionally depressing. The long post-inspection recovery time is also commented on in several instances. 'Very anxious, still anxious' at Crowcroft Park, 'wasteful and inaccurate' at Columbia Primary. The head at Haywood High observed that 'It set us back a year, no question. It drained me and it drained the staff. Everybody was exhausted. At the end, I just felt I had to go away and mourn privately'. However, early warning signs were flagged up in a 1997 OfSTED report on Fair Furlong. Perhaps this is OfSTED's main value: identifying problems and weaknesses. How these are then acted on is, rightly or wrongly, a separate and critical issue.

More recently, OfSTED has provided schools with annual PANDA (Performance and Assessment) reports which set out the school's main outcome data, including SAT and examination results, against not only national averages, but also 'benchmark' schools of a similar kind. For this latter purpose, schools are grouped according to Free School Meal entitlement and, separately, in relation to pupils' prior attainment. In primary schools this compares Key Stage One with Key Stage Two performance, and in secondary schools GCSE scores are graded relative to other schools with similar Key Stage Three SAT scores. These gradings of school performance represent an attempt to consider the context within which schools operate and are therefore particularly relevant to the schools in these case studies.

The more analytic objectivity represented in PANDAs should be commended and these schools are, in any case, 'data-hungry', using statistical evidence as one of several means of understanding more about themselves. However, each report is at least forty pages long, packed with dense text and figures – not very user-friendly. Of more concern is the generation of resentment and anger caused by OfSTED's choice of statistical measures and their cut-off points. The latter, for example, include the grouping of all schools, undifferentiated, where more than 50 per cent of pupils are entitled to free school meals. More substantively, free school meals is a less and less satisfactory proxy indicator of disadvantage as more parents move into low-paid jobs and claim Working Families Tax Credit. This stops their entitlement to free school meals for their children. Meanwhile, many such families retain other characteristics of disadvantage, including poor housing conditions, high mobility or English as an additional language. At Crowcroft Park, for example, the percentage of children entering the school with minimal prior attainment in English has increased, since 1995, from 6 to 21.

An associated concern is the ascription of blame or praise to a school for pupils' academic progress when the school hasn't been responsible for its pupils' prior attainment. More than 30 per cent of Key Stage Two pupils at Crowcroft Park were not attending that school at Key Stage One and most new enrolments have limited knowledge of English. There is also considerable evidence in several secondary schools that attainment levels before Key Stage Three are lower than five years ago. In any case, the attainment of pupils at the end of Key Stage Two, just as they enter secondary schools, is not the responsibility of the latter and clearly affects the Key Stage Three 'baseline'. Of course, what everyone should concentrate on is diagnosing the individual pupil's performance at different stages and act accordingly, whatever needs arise. Most teachers do this, but, unfortunately, the whole published system of 'league tables', inspection reports and centrally driven targets seems to conspire to drive teachers and schools into defensive behaviour. 'Watching your back' is how a teacher at Lochgelly North School puts it.

Tackling the odds

Other government policies are more readily embraced by several schools in a spirit of positive realism and a continuing determination to 'colonise' (a term initially coined at Columbia School, Tower Hamlets) external initiatives and shape them to their own ends. A wide range of government schemes are targeted at disadvantaged communities and under-achieving pupils and it is not surprising, therefore, that many have been taken up by these schools. They represent a major policy shift in the context of the schools since 1995.

Excellence in Cities is one such instance, constructed on the basic understanding that educational under-achievement is multi-dimensional in its origins – and isn't simply a matter of good or bad teachers. Under this programme, four schools (Haywood High, Burntwood, Columbia and Crowcroft Park) are being supported in their work, sometimes with children who are more difficult to teach, and in other cases with more able pupils. At Burntwood, Wandsworth, and Selly Park, Birmingham, specialist school status has been granted, with its associated requirement that some of the additional resources and expertise acquired must be shared with neighbouring schools.

Under this same policy, one of the primary schools – Columbia – is at the receiving end of the programme, with a small group of pupils attending an ICT workshop at a local specialist school on two afternoons each week. This isn't entirely satisfactory to the 'donor' school and it points to the relative lack of knowledge about how best to organise such collaborative schemes.

The *New Opportunities Fund* and *Single Regeneration Budget* zones are further instances of government policies aimed at improving the social and physical environments within which these schools work, as well as raising educational standards as a key component of a neighbourhood's 'cultural capital'. Noticeable improvements to the neighbourhood's physical environment are welcomed at Crowcroft Park, Manchester, and Fair Furlong, Bristol. Opportunities are being expanded for school pupils in and out of school, as well as for pre-school children and adults. It is to be expected that these schools, with their 'can do' approach to problem-solving make the fullest possible use of such initiatives – as well as those emanating from European Union, local authority and charitable sources. Selectively but keenly scavenging all available initiatives and funding opportunities appears to be the name of the game.

Cries and Whispers

It is surprising that some of these schools and their teachers do not feel entirely at ease with the changed policy context: 'bafflement and bitterness', 'accountability gone mad' and a sense of 'more work, less trust' at Columbia; anger and frustration at the bureaucracy overload at Blaengwrach and Crowcroft Park; dismay at the consequences of a short-term bidding culture at Sutton Centre. Reacting to some of the sound-bites and rhetoric from government ministers and the Chief Inspector of Schools, Sutton Centre staff also express a general fed-up-ness with the heroes-and-villains drama unfolding around them, replete with 'super-heads' and 'glitzy make-overs' for failing schools and teachers. Their alternative to this is the reality of 'rock-solid people' with a carefully thought-out educational philosophy and a patient, but firm, way with some difficult pupils, many with a chronic lack of self-esteem.

Sutton Centre staff are not alone in feeling that their knowledge and convictions about the demanding nature of their educational task are neither comprehended nor appreciated by government or OfSTED. Such a context, with its atmosphere of teacherly scepticism and surprised disappointment is an unexpected drag-factor on an otherwise dynamic momentum towards further improvement.

The 'Celtic lands'

In Scotland, Wales and Northern Ireland, there is not yet the same degree of government intervention in the detailed work of schools, benign or otherwise. However, there are signs that the English model is spreading to these more devolved parts of the kingdom. In the Scottish case study, the pressures emanating from the new Scottish Executive, 'with a determination not to be left behind nationally or internationally', have led to a requirement that particular targets be applied to pupils with complex learning difficulties. This is described as 'daft' by one teacher. MacBeath observes that the requirement has 'diverted energy into the formulation and tight specification of detailed behaviours', and whilst this has 'immensely increased staff skills in target writing', it has 'contributed little to the achievement of those targets'.

In Northern Ireland, a quite different policy context applies: a 'policy vacuum', following decades of political attention being paid to other, more pressing, problems of a non-educational kind. Such a 'silence from the centre' (Gallagher) is probably worse than the English sense of 'policy overload'.

Structural shifts and tensions

In several schools, there are other dimensions to the context in which they operate. Structural shift, with the increased number of integrated (Catholic and Protestant) schools in Northern Ireland represents both a success and a threat to Hazelwood College. Success, because imitation is the sincerest form of flattery, and threat, because Hazelwood already operates within a competitive marketplace with the continued existence of grammar schools. In Scotland, another kind of integration is being promoted by the Scottish Department of Education: that which expects children with special needs to be educated alongside their 'normal' peer group in mainstream schools. For Lochgelly North, this produces an ever-present uncertainty about its own role and future existence as a Special School.

A further variation on this theme of a school's place in the larger school structure is at Sutton Centre where its sixth-form unit costs are higher than its funding formula provides. With the onset of a new Learning and Skills Council in September 2000, both the funding and continued existence of the sixth forms are in question. Of the six secondary schools in these case studies, only two have sixth forms, with Burntwood probably large enough to be safe from further threats.

The schools without sixth forms, Haywood High, Hazelwood, St Michael's and Selly Park, do not appear to be concerned about this lack of post-16, often high-status, work on their premises. At St Michael's, contacts with three local universities provide opportunities, before students leave school at 16, of seeing higher education as an aspiration for many. Sutton Centre, however, argues that unless they retain their own sixth form, then many of their students will not continue their studies beyond the end of statutory schooling. We need more evidence about this, about the factors which encourage students, especially those from disadvantaged backgrounds, in schools with and without sixth forms, to continue their education.

Getting and keeping teachers

A further contextual threat, made explicit in the Columbia case study, is that of a worsening position in relation to teacher retention and recruitment. Throughout these studies, both in 1995 and now, is the critical importance of the commitment, stability and quality of teachers. It is tempting to suggest or infer that the existence of such teachers is due solely or mainly to the leadership and ethos of schools succeeding against the odds. However, as the Columbia study suggests, there are sometimes larger forces at work, such as a booming central London economy (and high housing costs), which threaten this essential component of successful schools. For rather different reasons, we are told that staff recruitment is now more difficult at

Lochgelly North, the reason cited being the government's requirements for more monitoring, accounting and recording by teachers.

However, that the majority of these schools buck a worsening national trend is remarkable. How they do this is well worth examining, but it cannot be assumed that high-quality and plentiful teacher recruitment and retention are simply down to a school's own efforts.

The local context

The local support structure is a contextual factor which has been reconfigured in several cases in the past five years. In five schools (Blaengwrach, Fair Furlong, Haywood High, Lochgelly North and St Michael's), the LEA has changed, following local government reorganisation. The net result has been some disruption and considerably smaller LEAs, with fewer specialist advisers available to the schools. None of the schools is reported as feeling unduly affected by this change, although reference is made to a smaller, less expert 'canvas' at Haywood, including a smaller and less varied group of local headteachers with whom to exchange ideas. In primary schools, the local education authority (LEA) remains an important source of advice and knowledge. At Fair Furlong, Bristol, the LEA has been particularly important in 'holding the ring' and steering the school through difficult times, following the headteacher's resignation in 1996. However, the LEA structure changed at the very time the school most needed its support. None was immediately available and a thriving 'cluster' of local primary school headteachers wasn't an appropriate 'back stop' when help was needed.

The capacity of a local network or agency to provide intellectual and professional stimulus and thereby 'add value' to school improvement is hinted at in two schools.

At Selly Park, Birmingham LEA, with its innovatory University of the First Age and Second City vision, is enriched by the creativity of Selly Park, whilst the school also gains from being part of these thriving 'can do' city projects. At Haywood High, the local university appears to perform a similar function, with the Keele Improving Schools Network, Kisnet, providing a range of professional opportunities which help to extend and enlarge the school's own aspirations and knowledge.

Mental maps: the school in its larger system

At Burntwood, the head's 'state of the nation' address to colleagues at the start of each school year is a further variation on this theme, as is the Hazelwood governors' review of the college's basic values and purposes, through employing an external consultant as a facilitator. In each case, a conscious effort is being made to think about and shape the larger 'mental maps' carried around in the heads of teachers. These maps of the larger context in which teachers – and schools – work are an essential component of teachers' classroom interactions with students. Context may not be quite all, but the way teachers and heads conceptualise their place and role within the larger setting – organisational, political and philosophical – is a critical part of their effectiveness.

The interaction between a school and its context is clearly an important dimension to our fuller understanding how these eleven schools have progressed, or not, over the past five years. In some cases, reports of worsened or more complex environments represent a fundamental component in evaluating rates and kinds of progress and 'success'. Against this backdrop, the particular strategies and tactics adopted by the schools need to be considered.

LEVERS OF CHANGE AND IMPROVEMENT

Teachers, teachers, teachers . . .

Perhaps the battle cry 'Education, Education, Education' should be replaced by 'Teachers, Teachers, Teachers'. In these schools, the attention paid to the appointment, induction and further development of teachers is all-pervasive. It is tempting to dwell solely on the headteacher as a kind of miracle worker, but these heads know that, above all else, securing improvement comes through the hearts and minds of teachers. That is why so much time and effort is spent on the selection and appointment of teachers. At Selly Park, we are told about the prior observation of applicants' teaching ability and the insistence that unless someone is 'absolutely right' for the school's ethos and values – quite apart from their technical competence – then no appointment is made. At Blaengwrach, as much attention is paid to applicants' educational philosophy and community involvement as to their professional skills. At Haywood High, the 'cream' of trainee teachers from Keele University is targeted whilst they are on teaching-practice there, and the recently appointed headteacher was himself impressed by the quality and detail of his own interview process, including the two focus groups of pupils.

Teachers are also given both support and continuing stimulus in these schools. Apart from structured, more formal in-service training events and programmes, they are encouraged to keep on learning through their day-to-day encounters with each other and with pupils. At Burntwood, the headteacher talks about the school 're-inventing itself' so that teachers never get bored or are tempted to believe that the school's success means they can stand still. Here, and at Lochgelly North, reference is made to the importance attached to making mistakes and learning from these. A teacher at Burntwood says, 'you have to make mistakes, you learn from them', and at Lochgelly North emphasis is placed on teachers' ability to 'persevere, to cope with failure, to take risks'. Risk taking is an intrinsic part of moving forward and an organisation's culture or 'capacity' is critical to this being possible.

Other forms of professional development also arise in the accounts of Blaengwrach, Sutton Centre and Haywood High. For these developmental strategies to operate successfully, i.e. leading to better practice, teachers have to feel supported within the larger school system; 'you never feel alone' is how a Burntwood teacher expresses this. In a more systematic and material way, the head of Lochgelly acts to protect her staff from unfair exposure when teachers are 'very upset' when they are trying to calm and re-engage a 'kid who is effing and blinding and barging their way down the corridor . . . everyone has a strategy that's been discussed and approved by me'. At Fair Furlong, a widespread sense amongst staff of not being supported, and not being part of a 'shared leadership', is identified as the most important factor in the school's slippage in the 1996–8 period. Neither is it surprising that deteriorating pupil behaviour prevented teachers from moving forward professionally.

Ethos, culture, capacity

John MacBeath alludes to the 'inner, more deeply hidden culture' at Lochgelly North. Kathryn Riley and her colleagues, at Burntwood, distinguish between the 'surface' and 'subterranean' features of the school's daily life, and in all cases, there is an attempt to analyse 'atmosphere', conversations and the 'buzz' of the place. At Crowcroft Park, Manchester, the extremely low teacher absence rate, through a winter term of flu epidemics, is almost certainly explained by a school culture which supports and values teachers as well as pupils. At Burntwood, 'pupils and teachers exude confidence and self-worth', and at Selly Park, Tim Brighouse believes that 'this utterly convincing 'can do' culture' . . . is 'much more important and significant' than he acknowledged in 1995. In this, and most other cases, the 'can do' relates to what Brighouse calls a 'press for achievement', to what Gerald Grace describes as the 'constant improvement dynamic' of St Michael's and to what MacBeath calls the 'focus on learning' at Lochgelly North.

It is probable that 'school capacity' is the single most important matter in trying to identify how and why some schools maintain and sustain improvement. This must be the aim of all schools, especially those – like Fair Furlong in these studies – which have moved ahead impressively from a weak position, and then slipped back again. In the first part of this chapter, the importance of context was spelt out: both local and in terms of national policy. The interaction between contextual and internal processes is not well understood, but, in the meantime, heads, teachers, pupils, parents and governors want to do all they can to create an organisational capacity – or school culture – which secures continuous improvement. The characteristics of such a culture have already been touched on, but others are worth outlining.

The spelling out of values and core beliefs is important. This isn't the slick business model of a touchy-feely 'mission statement' – even if this latter term is deployed. Rather, it is a clearing-out process, of all the inessentials and diversions which clutter up the works and are sometimes imposed from elsewhere. There's a lot of talk about values, vision and ethos reported in these accounts. These are live matters; they are not simply warm words in some abstract mission statement. Once the requisite technical proficiency has been validated, it is the values and philosophy of teachers that matter when new appointments are made. Time and again, the extreme care taken in the selection of staff returns to this, perhaps most explicitly at Blaengwrach and Selly Park. Once appointed (or, for pupils, once enrolled), the values which underpin the school's ethos and its daily routines are seen and felt to be important. Such values are the school's 'cultural glue', without which individual empowerment and diversity would not be possible. Some will acknowledge the paradox in this.

The quality of relationships

Michael Fielding (2000) has recently reminded us that 'education is immediately and ultimately about becoming more fully human' and that the 'fundamental importance of purposes' needs to acknowledged in all schools, colleges and universities. This is why the centrality of teaching and learning, in and out of classrooms, is given so much attention in these schools. It also explains why there is so much attention paid to the quality of relationships between pupils and pupils, pupils and teachers, teachers at different levels of seniority, teachers and parents, and so on.

At Lochgelly North, there is 'something special' about the 'way people speak to each other'. It is therefore not a matter of chance that headteachers are sharply conscious of their duty of care towards staff as well as pupils. At Haywood, the leadership is described as 'shared and collective' and a colleague says of the recently retired head, 'all her geese are swans'. Here, as at Selly Park, it is the insistent 'press for achievement', combined with respectful relations between people of whatever age, that seems to make all the difference. The three 'core beliefs' at Burntwood apply equally to staff and pupils, 'Everyone is valued', 'Everyone can succeed' and 'Everyone is entitled to an equal opportunity to succeed'. We are also told that the 'recognition of individual strengths and an appreciation of diversity stems from the headteacher'.

More energy is found to work even harder – and this applies, again, to staff and pupils – when fundamental purposes and values are clear and shared. The governors at Hazelwood understood this truth when they led a school review of core values and objectives, following a dispute with the previous headteacher. The recovery of St Michael's, following its threatened closure over a decade since, has been secured and sustained as much by its religious ethos as by its technical strategies. Its 'social and pedagogic capital' is what makes the difference, the social and the pedagogic being equally important and mutually reinforcing. With its huge diversity of languages and national and ethnic heritages, Crowcroft Park secures its continuous progress through 'a strong commitment to shared aims and values'.

At Sutton Centre, staff are quite explicit about the personal being educational. In this case, social skills tests show that students are held back by their 'difficulty in relating to others in a calm and rational way'. Quite properly, therefore, a lot of time and creative energy is spent on personal and social education – the kind embedded in the detail of student–teacher relationships. At Fair Furlong, the apparent loss of balance between rewards and sanctions led to negative relationships between staff and head and between staff and pupils, with a predictable loss of progress on the teaching and learning front. At Lochgelly North, the close interdependence of the personal and the educational is expressed by a parent when she says her son 'has been driven on' and 'is much happier here'. Both are needed, in any school at any time.

Permeating the explicit value systems of these schools then, is the way people treat other people. Schools exist to educate children and young people and their single most important resource for achieving this is the teacher. Teachers assemble and deploy other resources, including other people, books, computer programmes and so on, and work out – with pupils – how their education may be best organised. It is hardly surprising, therefore, that the human angle looms large in these accounts.

More 'adults other than teachers' (AOTs)

At Columbia Primary School, a counsellor and a home–school liaison worker have been appointed, in response to growing concerns about pupils' more complex social and personal problems. At St Michael's there are now two lay chaplains, and at Lochgelly North three therapists now work closely with teachers and directly influence individual curricula and pedagogic strategies. At Selly Park, many of the classroom assistants and other support staff are former, mainly retired, teachers. Each of these developments represents an increase in the adult resource available to pupils and teachers. A dual point is being made. First, these developments confirm that education is an intensely personal business. Second, these and other schools have become smarter and more 'customised' in recent years. An aspect of this is the more widespread use of adults other than teachers in supporting the educational task.

The tables at the start of each case study show a 'support staff ratio' and how this form of learning resource has, in almost all cases, increased. What isn't shown is the parallel increase of voluntary parent assistance, particularly in primary schools. Apart from carrying out tasks which do not require qualified teachers, except in a co-ordinating and supervisory role, the increased number of support staff and parent–helpers is also part of a marked development of out-of-classroom opportunities for students.

Value-added curricula

Boosting the learning of pupils beyond the National Curriculum is certainly a significant feature of schools which are determined to succeed against whichever odds are there. These case studies are strewn with examples, from the importance of exploiting visitors at Selly Park, Hazelwood and St Michael's, to the sending out of students as emissaries in these and other schools. The development of study and homework centres, not necessarily on school premises, is being actively encouraged by government, but many of these schools have already got these – and more besides. At Sutton Centre, Crowcroft Park and Haywood, the encouragement of parents and other adults to join in classes and ICT workshops, often in the evening or at weekends, strengthens the message about education being for everyone, not just children. At Lochgelly North, the school is part of a local schools' consortium, bidding to be one of the Scottish Executive's 'full-service' community centres. Through the European Commission's Peace and Reconciliation Fund, Hazelwood College in Belfast is enlarging its community education programme – for its own students and for their relatives and friends. With young people and families who are at least sceptical about the benefits of education, whether personal or economic, these advances are of great importance. Sutton Centre identifies the 'social pivots' amongst its students and their importance in influencing their less engaged peers in the Centre's 'eleventh hour' activities. A less usual marker of education's ubiquity and importance, beyond the school's perimeter fence, is the 'learning packs' and accelerated tutorials at Crowcroft Park for pupils who make extended family visits to Bangladesh or Pakistan.

Independent schools, charging high fees, have always stressed the 'added value' of opportunities and experiences beyond the formal curriculum. The further acquisition of skills and knowledge is even more important for students in schools facing complex and sometimes deep-seated odds. The headteacher at Blaengwrach is especially convinced that spotting aptitudes and enthusiasms in this way has a beneficial spillover effect on 'mainstream' schoolwork. Additional resources are available in most cases so that classroom teachers do not have to carry the full workload involved. Some resource shortfalls persist, however. At Crowcroft Park, some families cannot always find the money to pay for school journeys to the Lake District.

In three primary schools and in Lochgelly North Special School, concern is also voiced about the reduction of hours spent on a sufficiently broad and balanced curriculum, following a government-led need to emphasise literacy, numeracy, science and ICT. In England, the national literacy and numeracy hours are not resisted or resented, but quite properly, are seen to be inadequate if they are not augmented by wider and more creative learning experiences.

Alternatively, a further reason for making a special effort on the extra-curricular front arises in the Fair Furlong study. 'Keeps the rogues off the playground', says the acting head as he worked with staff to reconstruct the school.

Personalised pedagogies

In 1995, the case studies revealed a marked advance in how pupils' progress was being monitored and promoted. In all schools, nationally, it is now less unusual to have this amount of focus and targeted specificity in relation to individual pupils' learning. Nonetheless, a lot of further development and knowledge continues to be generated in the case study schools. There is a heightened consciousness about pedagogic skill, and many of the teachers interviewed, as well as students, appear to talk about this, largely unprompted. We hear of 'deep target processes' at Haywood High and the evident advances made in their academic mentor system. Peer mentoring is now more common than in 1995, sixth-form (Years 12 and 13) mentors for new intake 'Y7s' at Sutton, Year 11 students supporting Year 8 students at St Michael's, 10-year-olds helping 7-year-olds at Crowcroft Park, and a 'Friendship Squad' at Columbia.

The 'coaching' concept denotes a more particular form of teaching identified skills at Selly Park, with a wider, more defined range of teaching and learning methods explored and developed in the Birmingham UFA 'Super Learning Days' with Hamlyn 'Teacher Fellows' acting as transmitters of good ideas. The existence here, too, of individual student files on the ICT database, for students to access, exemplifies a welcome co-existence of modern technology and personalised learning programmes. Hazelwood also fought for intranet connections, again to empower its students and teachers to access knowledge and each other more systematically and usefully. 'Catch-up and Keep-up' classes and tutorials also feature here.

Active learners: owning their learning

A major success criterion which emerges from this explosion of more individualised support systems is that of student ownership and empowerment. At what point and how do students take charge of their own learning – or at least, feel they do? This is difficult to achieve, especially where, traditionally, there are few role models available to show them what this might look like. The sense of a continuing struggle to achieve this is well described in the Sutton Centre study, and there is a rather special version of what personal independence means in the Lochgelly North chapter. One parent says her daughter is now able to 'sleep in her own bed', whilst another child, with steady support, is able to attend, one day a week, the local FE College.

The extensive survey of student, parent and teacher perceptions at Burntwood bears testimony to an advanced sense of these three 'players' sharing a 'common understanding' of the school's basic educational purposes. Tim Brighouse appears to have been literally overwhelmed by enthusiastic and loquacious students as they tell him how they learn and, within a decimal point, their next learning target. Self-conscious learners, whether amongst pupils and students or teachers, appear to mark out the most successful schools.

Headship and leadership

Qualities and dimensions of headship and leadership insistently recur in these accounts, as they did in 1995. Effective headship seems always to include the nurturing of leadership opportunities for teachers, but also, in the case of Selly Park, for pupils. Capacity building, in this sense, is both a condition and an outcome of raising aspirations and achieving yet more success. In two cases, Selly Park and Sutton Centre, this process is described as a 'virtuous circle'.

Who are these paragons of headship ? Can they be spotted early on in their careers or, indeed, by the DfEE when it is involved in the opening of another 'Fresh Start' school, reconstructed after years of apparent failure?

First, there is no identikit style. The 'breathless urgency' of the Selly Park head is light years away from the 'patient, quietly assured style' of the Sutton Centre head. Neither does the length or type of experience suggest a template for policy makers or those who appoint headteachers. Of the eleven heads here, two have been in post less than a year, four for more than twelve years, with the remaining five between one and eleven years. Six are women; five are men. In total, they have 286 years of experience working in schools, with the length of such experience, excluding their current headship, ranging from 29 years (St Michael's) to 10 years (Fair

Furlong). Two have had previous headship experience (Burntwood and the new head at Haywood).

What might be significant is the amount of experience outside schools. In six cases, this includes LEA advisory or developmental work which provided access to a wide range of schools and teachers from a different angle. Working abroad, teaching in a Further Education college or working in the voluntary, charitable sector also feature in four cases. Two have acquired a Master's degree and two of the women spent eight and twelve years at home with their own children.

It isn't possible to infer too much at all from these outline features. I am especially conscious of the head of St Michael's having had no non-school experience and, indeed, now being in his thirty-fifth year in the same school. Perhaps, in this case, the catholicity of the Catholic Church, plus his earlier experience as an art teacher, make up for any deficiencies implied in my tentative theory?

Personal and virtual networking

In any case, more important than the breadth of past experience is the way these heads now cultivate and exploit networks of people and organisations which might help their schools. This can be 'virtual', via the internet, personal through the encouragement of visitors as a living 'learning resource' for students, professional and micro-political in the local community, or in headteacher arenas at both local and national levels. But in all these wider connections, the possession of finely tuned sensors or antennae is a necessary attribute of headship, as important within the school as without.

Thus we are told that the head at Crowcroft Park is 'a respected member of her local school cluster' and that she speaks as its representative in several city-wide forums. The head of Columbia is 'an important opinion former within the education community in Tower Hamlets' and, across the Thames at Burntwood, the head 'nurtures outside contacts' and undertakes 'a number of roles with local education groups and in higher education'. It is clear that a seeking-out of wider opportunities for further learning amongst staff and pupils is a key characteristic of these heads.

Reference has already been made to the related importance of extra-curricular activities. Heads set a high standard in this, believing that the National Curriculum isn't enough for pupils and the statutory five 'training days' are, likewise, insufficient for teachers' growth and development. In all kinds of ways, the best of these schools are creating their own 'knowledge society', based on increasingly fuzzy boundaries. The world is in the school; the school is increasingly out there engaging with the larger world.

Honing judgements

The heads are constantly selecting from and distilling this wider bombardment of knowledge. This is an important part of the job. Such filtering of information and the 'judicious selection of initiatives' (Haywood) and a belief that the school 'interprets national policies, rather than being governed by them' (Burntwood) run alongside less positive feelings about too much bureaucracy, described earlier. The persistent sense of being 'in charge', when combined with a clear articulation of values and core beliefs, provides a sound base for a school's vision – a vision which answers the questions, 'For what and who are we striving and why?'.

These heads also make sure that they keep in touch with their colleagues, both teachers and support staff, as well as with pupils and parents. This helps the head in the exercise of judgement and decision-making. At St Michael's, the head has extended and formalised consultation processes through the establishment of staff and student councils, whilst at Sutton Centre we are told that 'anything that would leave a significant proportion of staff behind would give him [the head] nightmares'. This and other heads are noted for their high visibility around the school; 'omnipresent' is the term we used in our original study.

Conversely, at Fair Furlong, a new headteacher in 1996 seemed not to fully communicate her priorities with colleagues, who felt disenfranchised and, observed the acting head, were badly 'de-skilled' as a result.

Identifying success = energy fission

A final characteristic of these successful heads and schools is their energising capacity. The head at Haywood, appointed in 1989 with an unpopular school amalgamation to manage, says, 'I was always energised by what was going on in the school'. Her colleagues say, 'the team is so strong – it pulls you along', and the author suggests that the school's 'momentum, energy and commitment seem not only to have been sustained, but also increased'. This matches the observation at Selly Park that the staff 'put in an amazing amount and are, therefore, reaping all the time'. Again, the virtuous circle, which not only demonstrates that nothing succeeds like success, but that success – and its identification – is like a fast breeder reactor of energy fission.

Such energy creation at first appears to be almost mystical, or restricted to an elite group of people and circumstances which cannot be replicated. It is undoubtedly true that a particular configuration of odds, against which some schools struggle, results in their own sense of success being comparatively limited. This is especially marked when 'success' is defined solely by measurable academic outcomes and national 'norms'. Nonetheless, extra mental and emotional energy seems to be triggered off by a shared sense of achievement, particularly when this is the result of the real efforts of staff and pupils. But, still, the nature of the achievement affects the degree of celebration and, therefore, energy boost.

Does Andrea's successful progression from her 'bum shuffle and roll' at Lochgelly North count as much as the publicly acclaimed GCSE scores, above the national average, at Burntwood, St

Michael's and Selly Park? A less extreme case is the gradual and hard-won rise in the post-16 educational participation rate at Sutton Centre, but still significantly below the national average. There is also the difficult and threatening work at Hazelwood where the decision of a high-profile Loyalist politician to enrol his child there is identified as a palpable hit. Perhaps these less easily measured or non-normative successes are not such powerful energy creators?

What is undoubtedly the opposite of an 'energy boost' is the experience of staff at Fair Furlong: following a diffficult two or more years of uncertainty and conflict, 'we felt vulnerable, felt we were total failures, all of us'.

All these headteachers know that academic outcomes matter hugely in their schools' success, publicly and personally for pupils and teachers. At Lochgelly North, the increased independence of students is an equivalent success criterion. But the head's vision is also profoundly concerned with other social and spiritual outcomes and these are expressed in the school's ethos and stated values. Not surprisingly, the heads combine what is variously described as 'sound common sense' (Crowcroft Park) or 'pragmatism' (Haywood and Lochgelly North) with 'real vision' (Burntwood) or the school's 'founding values' (Sutton Centre).

Walking alone

Sometimes, we sense a certain reluctance on the part of staff to fully embrace new requirements or ways of working. In at least two of the primary schools, the National Literacy Strategy was greeted initially with a degree of scepticism, but the heads had already established a constructive evaluative approach to such initiatives. At Blaengwrach, the head has always emphasised an openness to new ideas amongst his colleagues, with an emphasis on dis-passionate evaluation. In such schools, there is neither automatic absorption nor rejection of new ideas and practices, whether enshrined in government policy or not.

At Lochgelly North, it was the head who acknowledged the potential value of the government's 5–14 curriculum framework for children with special educational needs, even though several of her staff felt otherwise. She says, 'it puts us in the continuum of provision. We're part of the link. It has given us credibility – it's good for the kids.'

This is one of the less comfortable parts of leadership and least easy to judge: deciding when your colleagues' instincts or prejudices should be resisted. The head at Hazelwood, in a similar way, wouldn't accept an easy explanation of the school's exam results. Instead, she embarked on a rigorous analysis of these, and this led, in turn, to a range of new systems aimed at better performance. But how, then, should we interpret a new head's decision to change the school's pupil behaviour strategy at Fair Furlong? Was she wrong to try? Was it simply the way she did it? Either way, it led to a sharp decline of morale and performance.

An insufficient knowledge base

There remain several unanswered questions about headship in these, and other, studies. For example, when and if the generic skills and attributes of effective heads have been identified, is there then a residual issue concerning the matching of a particular kind of head to a particular kind of school? 'Particular' might include the personality and life history of the head and the school's history, location and configuration of staff, pupils and parents. Would the heads of Selly Park and Sutton Centre, or Blaengwrach and Crowcroft Park, be able to swap jobs without too much difficulty? Would a successful headteacher of a top 'public school' slip comfortably into headship at Haywood High, or vice versa ? Our whole system of governing-body interviews, with LEA or other expert advice, rests on a belief in a more customised 'matching' of head to school. In other countries, this is not so. In recent years, central government or national 'headhunters' have been involved in the appointment of 'Fresh Start' school heads, not always with great success, and apparently based on a concept of 'good heads' being universally transferable. This represents an important gap in our knowledge.

A second question arises in the matter of 'succession' and the difference made to a school when one head leaves and another takes over. This is explicitly raised at Burntwood where it is believed that when Brigid (who, for many, *is* Burntwood) leaves, 'the fundamental ethos of the school will be saved'. At Fair Furlong, Haywood, Hazelwood, St Michael's and Lochgelly, new heads have been appointed since the schools were last studied. In the last three cases, the heads were appointed from amongst existing staff, with the explicit intention of upholding the school's essential values and spirit. At Haywood, an outsider has been appointed, but with a strong commitment to developing the practices and philosophies overseen by the previous head.

However, at Fair Furlong, there was also a powerful commitment to the practices and beliefs of the previous head and her colleagues, fully documented in *Success against the Odds* (1996). When that head left the school in 1996, following a celebratory visit by the then Opposition Education spokesman, David Blunkett, there was a widespread assumption that the school's successes would continue. It appeared as though robust systems were in place, for monitoring pupils' work, for reviewing and developing teachers' practice, and for securing regular and constructive dialogue with parents. The Fair Furlong case study, on this occasion, provides an important commentary on the robustness of succession and progression. It also raises questions about the 'downside' of headteacher autonomy – a valuable antidote, perhaps, to the 'upside' versions elsewhere in these studies.

A third question is about the special nature of leadership and management in schools, as distinct from other kinds of organisations. It is sometimes suggested that a 'good manager', irrespective of professional background and experience, can run a successful school. Conversely, most – perhaps all – of these eleven heads could run most organisations very effectively. Indeed, the complexities of headship are invariably underestimated. However, it is at least helpful if the top man or woman knows something about the organisation's 'core business' and preferably more than theoretically. The core business of schools is teaching and learning. It is this that comes through so powerfully in each of these accounts of both headship and school leadership in all its forms and at all levels.

Another organisation which is complex, person-centred and dependent on its key staff being both technically competent and creative, is the BBC. Recently, its Director General, Greg Dyke, described the characteristics of a successful BBC. He said that 'organisations only work when there is a common belief in what you're trying to achieve' and that 'You're not going to get talent to work here if they don't like the place – if they think it's vicious or unpleasant or bureaucratic'. He added that 'if you want organisations to change, you have to carry the staff with you. If you can't do this, you can't change it.' He also criticised an inherited 'report mentality' which seemed to lead to a belief that 'having written the paper, that's the end of it' (Gibson, 2000). These injunctions apply equally to schools, including the importance of an essentially oral culture. However, they do not imply, necessarily, that Greg Dyke knows enough to lead any one of these schools.

SUSTAINABLE SCHOOL IMPROVEMENT?

Most of these schools demonstrate the 'deep-coping strategies' (Louis and Miles, 1992), referred to in John Gray's opening chapter. These strategies are intrinsically connected to regular thinking about – and acting out – basic values and visions. The latter are focused on a fairly wide view of teaching and learning, beyond the National Curriculum for pupils, and placing high value on teachers as agents of change and of good-quality learning. John Gray also presents evidence about *building the capacity to improve*, including the way some schools recognise that developing such capacity is an 'extremely complex and long-term enterprise' (Stoll, 1999). He points out that 'the long haul' doesn't exclude spotting the value of short-term tactics. These case studies confirm such observations.

What exactly constitutes 'long-term' needs to be thought about, especially when the dynamics of changing contexts and expectations are so rapid. Any idea of *stasis* is not possible and so it is the human, as much as the structural, capacity to understand this that matters. The ability to thrive in circumstances which constantly challenge pupils and teachers – and which constantly throw up new opportunities – is needed. At the same time, schools need to offer elements of certainty, reliability and routine. A fusion of dynamism and calm order seems to characterise most of the schools in these case studies.

School improvement studies and strategies, not surprisingly, concentrate on what schools can do for themselves. But in using the term 'success against the odds', these case studies are also looking at the dialectic between schools and their wider environment. Heroic heads and heroic schools exist here and more widely. However, one thing that is more sharply defined in these eleven schools in the year 2000, compared to 1995, is the wider environment's contribution to the school's successes. 'Odds' are usually associated with poverty and lack of area (or parental) social and cultural 'capital'. This is not a wholesale condemnation of values and behaviours in disadvantaged areas, but it recognises, rather, the time and thought needed in schools where, traditionally, many parents have not had strong reasons to stick with education, especially when education never seems to have done them any favours.

There is reference to the benign effects of a small middle-class influx to Columbia School in Tower Hamlets and the same in Blaengwrach, West Glamorgan. Parents of girls whose original heritage is amongst ethnic and linguistic groups in the Indian subcontinent, at Burntwood and Selly Park, could possibly be added to such a broadly pro-education grouping. The extent to which a school has a 'critical mass' of more engaged, broadly 'pro-school', children to start with is touched on in these case studies.

A related matter is the wider school system: how many children are being selected by other schools and whether, because of this, the work of some schools is more difficult than others. The impact of school systems on children's self-esteem should be examined. Amongst the schools featured here, Burntwood, Selly Park and St Michael's, wittingly or otherwise, have acquired a degree of 'place advantage' in their local school systems. This probably adds to the sense of self-worth amongst pupils and staff equally, although the forms and degrees of 'selectivity' confirm and strengthen, rather than create, such a sense.

Alternatively, at Hazelwood College and Lochgelly North, there is some evidence that the local 'pecking order' of schools has a depressing effect (perhaps only marginal) on the schools. In the case of Lochgelly North, from a well-intentioned policy comes an un-intended consequence: children with complex learning difficulties can't cope in 'mainstream' schools (and probably vice versa) and thus 'downshift' to Lochgelly North, where they invariably flourish.

But equally important in these re-visits is the effect of wider political and social turmoil. The sectarian conflicts of West Belfast condition the definition of 'success' at Hazelwood, as does the rapid ebb and flow of recent immigrants and refugees in central Manchester at Crowcroft Park. The regeneration of former coalfield areas for Sutton Centre, Haywood and Lochgelly North seems to be a longer, more complex process than envisioned in 1995. The Fair Furlong study also reveals deep-seated problems in its local area which cannot be solved overnight – or within the lifetime of a parliament or single cohort of children passing through school.

In 1995, we asked if 'the odds against which schools succeed need be so great' (NCE, 1996: 357). At that point, the 'odds' were mainly social and economic. On this occasion, there is abundant evidence that the government is actively pursuing strategies aimed at reducing such odds. Likewise, it actively pursues policies aimed at pushing all schools towards a more rapid rate of improvement. Some of these case studies suggest that some of the means adopted in the latter now count amongst the 'odds' to be confronted. The promised 'light steer' is certainly needed, with less paper . . . and fewer bytes of electronic data. Additionally, government's increased differentiation and 'layering' of secondary schools supports, rather than creates, the successes experienced in some of the schools featured here, but might produce an undue concentration of 'hard-to-teach' children in other schools.

Amongst the real successes in these schools are the 'hard-to-teach' children who gradually become 'a pleasure to teach' (Selly Park teacher) or, at least, make the kind of progress they would be unlikely to make in less successful – or effective – schools. The head at Sutton Centre talks of 'unspectacular, unmeteoric, unremitting graft' being the bedrock of that school's success. Such 'graft' exists in all these schools, as well as the pleasures and fun of achievement.

The cautionary tale of Fair Furlong points to the importance of knowing more than we do about school or organisational 'capacity'. Overdependence on a particular headteacher probably militates against such strength and consistency, although these qualities are more likely to be sustained when the head has built up a shared leadership in a school. Agnes McMahon's distinction between 'teamwork' and 'shared leadership' is interesting in this respect.

A related issue is the speed at which city life, in particular, changes. 'Cities are fantastically dynamic places', wrote Jane Jacobs in *The Death and Life of Great American Cities* (1961), and her account of continuous decay and regeneration remains germane to our understanding of urban policy. The 'odds' encountered by seven inner-city schools in these studies are intrinsically part of such dynamism (but so, also, are many positive and creative opportunities). We do not know enough about sustaining and maintaining school success and 'capacity' in such settings. Is Valerie Hannon correct in her ascription 'unstoppable momentum' to Haywood High School in Stoke-on-Trent? Does this belief minimise or sideline the school's interaction with its larger context, its ecology? Does an urban ecology make succession, progression and sustainable growth more difficult to achieve than in a more stable, more homogeneous ecology?

It would be surprising if any eleven schools continued to perform and maintain their successes at an equivalent level over a five-year period. The fortunes of these schools demonstrate different kinds of journeys, including the rates of officially measured improvement provided by OfSTED in their PANDA reports. The value of case studies lies in the fuller account of the how and why, as well as the who. The lens through which such accounts are viewed – eleven different authors – adds to the variability of evaluation, as do the narratives provided by eleven headteachers. None of this need detract from the insights and pointers to policy appraisal or development. Quite the reverse. The authenticity and directness of these chronicles help to ensure that more qualitative, open-ended analyses are available for practitioners in schools, local authorities and government.

Lessons in further success abound. These include fuller definitions of success and of leadership. 'Success' is intimately bound up with a school's interaction with its wider community, locally and nationally. Structures matter, as well as standards. Unanswered questions, requiring further investigation, include how best to secure succession and progression, particularly when there is a change of headteacher. Part of the answer lies in a clearer understanding of 'school capacity' and its contributory elements, including shared leadership and a high level of consciousness, amongst staff and pupils, about the school's essential values and purposes. When staff and pupils feel positive about their work and this, in turn, centres on a 'press for achievement', then it is more likely that all kinds of success will be celebrated.

REFERENCES

Fielding, Michael (2000). The person centred school, *Forum*, 42, 2, 51–4.

Gibson, Janine (2000) Article in *Guardian* Media Supplement, 21 August, pp. 3–4.

Jacobs, Jane (1961) *The Death and Life of Great American Cities*, London: Penguin.

Louis, K. and Miles, M. (1992) *Improving the Urban High School: What Works and Why*, London: Cassell.

National Commission for Education (1996) *Success against the Odds*, London: Routledge.

APPENDIX A
Methodology and Guidelines for Authors

THE PROJECT

Overall, the project focuses on how eleven successful schools, originally identified in 1995 as facing a range of 'odds' and serving disadvantaged communities, have – or have not – maintained and sustained their success over the five years, 1995–2000.

Following the publication of *Success against the Odds* (1996), Reynolds and Stoll (1996: 102) observed that:

> In the UK for example, we still have no in-depth, qualitative portrait of the effective school equivalent to Louis and Miles 'Improving the Urban High School' [1990] which provides excellent case studies of process variables, although the National Commission on Education (1996) examination of eleven schools which were successful 'against the odds' has encouraged a start in this area. The absence of rich case study explanations reduces the practitioner relevance of the effectiveness research and makes the transfer of knowledge to improvement programmes difficult.

Mortimore (1998) later observed that:

> The work on school improvement and, in particular, the case studies of schools working against the odds or recovering from failure have shown how academic research can inspire practice-based projects.

Mortimore also cited an observation from the conclusions of *Success against the Odds* (1996), 'the nature of school improvement . . . has yet to be thoroughly understood and measured in a sensible and sensitive way', adding that 'Researchers [have] expressed real doubt about whether such schools would succeed in the long term' (*The Guardian*, 14 September 1999).

Whilst the 'long term' is rather more than five years, this project seeks to establish whether and, if so, how the eleven schools in *Success against the Odds* have maintained their 1995 position when, between them, they demonstrated differing degrees and kinds of improvement, secured during the previous three to six years.

The project is a contribution to a literature of 'in-depth, qualitative portrait(s)' sought by Reynolds and Stoll (1996), and it again aims to address, in a scholarly way, important questions of practice. In particular, its central focus is on factors and processes which appear to secure the maintenance of school improvement and development over a period of several years.

The lead authors of the eleven case studies, which featured in *Success against the Odds* (1996), were asked to re-visit the schools in the early summer of 2000. All, bar two, accepted the invitation and all the schools agreed to be involved.

In 2000, there were much greater amounts of statistical and inspection report data available on schools than was the case in 1995–6 and it was therefore decided that authors would be provided with a summary of these for their schools. This, in particular, led to a proposal being successfully submitted to the Nuffield Foundation for a research grant so that data could be collected and tabulated by a research assistant.

Another difference from the original 1995 study, at least as a matter of emphasis, was the growth of research and other documentary evidence about school improvement, as distinct from school effectiveness. However, both remained important areas of interest in this project. This led to an invitation to Professor John Gray, an acknowledged expert in both these fields of scholarship and research, to write the Introduction.

RESEARCH METHODOLOGY

In *Success against the Odds* (1996), no claims were made about 'scientific' objectivity but, rather, that the case studies represented a way of exploring and illuminating some of the key propositions concerning school effectiveness and school improvement which had emerged over the previous two decades. The same applies to these follow-up studies. Likewise, the observational and interpretative skills provided by the lead authors, combined with the depth and breadth of their knowledge about school effectiveness and improvement, probably represent the project's chief asset.

School Statistical Profiles (SSPs) were constructed for each school. These are now available on the RoutledgeFalmer website, www.tandf.co.uk

Data were collected and collated by the project research assistant. Data sources included OfSTED inspection and PANDA reports, Form 7 statistical return (January 2000), DfEE Annual School Census (1999–2000), LEA financial returns, Audit Commission Annual School Expenditure Reports, DfEE Statistical First Releases, Local Careers Offices, and LEA/LA statistical services. Advice and further data were provided by the Scottish Executive, Welsh Assembly and Department of Education, Northern Ireland. Headteachers checked the SSPs, as well as the summary table which is provided with each case-study chapter.

Authors and headteachers were asked to examine the School Statistical Profiles for their schools and to identify key changes and trends in relation to contextual factors, input factors and performance trends over the period 1995–2000.

In a note to authors, the editor asked that they should include the following matters in their examination of the SSP, in identifying questions arising from the data and in acquiring additional data, not available from published sources:

- Any marked changes in the 1995–2000 period in the socio-economic or ethnic composition of the neighbourhood(s)

from which pupils are drawn. (NB: the government data we have collected are mainly variations of 1991 Census returns and, therefore, more local perceptions and observations will be useful. We do have Form 7 data, however, incl. Free School Meals take-up.)

- Staffing issues: If the headteacher is the same person as in 1995, how has s/he maintained or revived their professional skills, creativity etc? (CPD, incl. TTA NPQH? Job swaps? Secondment or a Sabbatical ? . . .)

  or, if a new headteacher, how long in post? 1st or 2nd headship? Background in similar or different schools?

  Any significant staffing changes IN/OUT? Easier or more difficult staff recruitment?

  Role and number of support staff – significant changes, 1995–2000?

- Pupil turnover. Any figures for this? (LEAs have been asked to help, but their practice varies a lot.) Percentage of pupils per year group who (i) leave, (ii) enrol . . . this may not be a significant issue, but recent research shows it to be important in some inner-city schools.

  Any change in the school's admissions policy? If so, why and how has this changed?

  What is the overall effect on the school?

- Impact of wider policies on the school.

  Any particular views about how these have affected the school?

  e.g. OfSTED inspections, 'New Labour' initiatives (new school types, EAZ, social inclusion constraint on pupil exclusions, Excellence in Cities, National Literacy Strategy/Numeracy, The Standards Fund, Advanced Skills Teachers, pending Fast Track teachers and PRP/threshold determination, etc.).

- Finance, School budget and other revenue, in real terms, more, less, the same? Any Capital spending (Buildings/computers/equipment)?

  NB: We are collecting statistical data on finance, but these are difficult to compare over the past five years because of changed formulae, especially in the elements making up the school's budget.

  However, the most important line of enquiry remains that of determining how a trend of improved performance (broadly defined) and morale are maintained over a reasonable period of time – five or more years.

  Alternatively, if such a trend hasn't applied and the school has had a bumpy ride since 1995, then why? What could or should have been done to help the school maintain its momentum?

  These obviously need to be considered within the context of local and national changes and developments which impact upon the internal world of the school.

  (Letter to authors, April 2000)

Authors were asked to visit their school at least once and to interview the headteacher, two or more other members of staff, and, wherever possible, representative pupils, parents and governors. In each case study, authors were asked to provide an outline of their own schedule of interviews and discussions, as well as other means of conducting their enquiry.

SCHOOL EFFECTIVENESS, SCHOOL SUCCESS

Authors were again asked to refer to the National Commission on Education's ten postulated features of school success. These had been compiled for the Commission by research staff at the University of London Institute of Education, under the guidance of Professor Peter Mortimore in 1993.

The ten features of school success are;

1. Strong, positive leadership by the head and senior staff.
2. A good atmosphere or spirit, generated both by shared aims and values and by a physical environment that is as attractive and stimulating as possible.
3. High and consistent expectations of all pupils.
4. A clear and continuing focus on teaching and learning.
5. Well-developed procedures for assessing how pupils are progressing.
6. Responsibility for learning shared by the pupils themselves.
7. Participation by pupils in the life of the school.
8. Rewards and incentives to encourage pupils to succeed.
9. Parental involvement in children's education and in supporting the aims of the school.
10. Extra-curricular activities which broaden pupils' interests and experiences, expand their opportunities to succeed, and help to build good relationships within the school.

HEADTEACHERS

The editor also asked headteachers of case study schools to provide additional information about themselves. The questionnaire included the following items:

- Number of years in current school (a) as Head . . . . (b) other post(s)*. . . . . . .

  *if applicable, please give further detail. . . . .

- Previous headships? Yes/No. If 'yes', please give brief details of number of years, type(s) of school and community served, etc.

- Previous school experience.

  No. of years in schools (excl. headship) . . . .

  No. of years in posts mainly in subject leadership role . . . .

  No. of years in posts mainly in pastoral/admin. role . . . .

- Range of school types (eg: Primary/Sec/Special, Co-Ed/Single sex, County/VA/GM, Denominational . . .)

- Range of community types served (e.g. rural/urban, affluent/ poor)

- Non-school experience.

  Please outline/list work NOT in schools, incl. LEA secondments /posts or those in FE/HE and in non-educational occupations. Please include time spent as a 'homeworker' or in studies beyond initial university or college study.

REPORTS

Authors were asked to write an account of between 5000 and 7000 words. Final drafts would be checked for factual accuracy with headteachers. Authors' own reflections upon factors affecting the maintenance of success, effectiveness and improvement were sought in relation to the particular school, as well as more generally.

REFERENCES

Mortimore, P. (1998) *The Road to Improvement*, Lisse, Netherlands: Swets and Zeitlinger.

Reynolds, D. and Stoll, L. (1996) 'Merging school effectiveness and school improvement: the knowledge bases'. In D. Reynolds *et al.* (eds) *Linking School Effectiveness and School Improvement*, pp. 94–112, London: Routledge.

APPENDIX B
Terminology used in Case Studies

ACHIEVEMENT ON ENTRY

See **Statutory Assessment**

BASELINE ASSESSMENT

See **Statutory Assessment**

CPD (CONTINUING PROFESSIONAL DEVELOPMENT)

Development of a teacher's skills and abilities to enhance their performance. As part of its Teaching Reforms programme the government intends to improve the provision of teaching and management training for teachers. The term is beginning to replace INSET (Inservice Training) which covered both school-based activities and external courses.

DEPARTMENT FOR EDUCATION AND EMPLOYMENT (DFEE)

Formerly the DES (Department of Education and Science). Government department responsible for all education and employment policies in England.

EDUCATION ACTION ZONE (EAZ)

Clusters of schools working in partnership with the LEA, local parents, businesses and other organisations to take innovative action to raise standards and overcome disadvantage in urban or rural areas of educational underperformance. Some may have links to Health or Employment zones or with projects under the Single Regeneration Budget. The zones are given priority in government initiatives such as establishing specialist schools and excellence centres, summer schools, out-of-school hours schemes and access to computers. Twenty-five zones were in operation by 1999 and over 50 by 2000.

EXCELLENCE IN CITIES (EIC)

A government strategy, introduced in 1999, to raise educational standards and aspirations in inner cities. It draws together several government initiatives such as learning centres, opportunities for gifted children, measures for failing schools and access to computers, and gives them a particular inner city focus. The initiative started in Manchester/Salford, Liverpool/Knowsley, Birmingham, Leeds/Bradford, Sheffield/Rotherham, Inner London.

FREE SCHOOL MEALS (FSM)

The provision of a mid-day meal for children whose parents are receiving Income Support or an income-based Jobseeker's Allowance.

GCSE (GENERAL CERTIFICATE OF SECONDARY EDUCATION)

Examinations usually taken by pupils in the year in which they are 16. Pass grades are A–G with an A* grade introduced in 1994 for outstanding achievement.

GNVQ (GENERAL NATIONAL VOCATIONAL QUALIFICATIONS)

Examinations with a technical and vocational bias, introduced to provide a link to the knowledge, understanding and skills needed for the world of work. They can be studied at Foundation, Intermediate or Advanced level.

GRANT MAINTAINED SCHOOLS (FORMER)

These schools were funded through the Funding Agency for Schools after parents had voted for the school to opt out of LEA control. The governing body then became totally responsible for the school, including its admission arrangements. Under the School Standards and Framework Act of 1998, this arrangement was discontinued. Most Grant Maintained Schools then opted to become Foundation Schools.

ICT (INFORMATION AND COMMUNICATION TECHNOLOGY)

ICT is one of the subjects in the National Curriculum. It is concerned with effective ways of finding, storing and presenting information using computers and other electronic communications media.

ITT (INITIAL TEACHER TRAINING)

The course of training required to obtain Qualified Teacher Status (QTS) for which there are now national standards. Training may be provided by colleges, universities or a consortium of schools but must now conform to national curricula for ITT.

KEY STAGE (KS)

See **National Curriculum**

LEA (LOCAL EDUCATION AUTHORITY)

Part of the local authority structure responsible for the provision of Maintained Schools in a particular area. In 2000, there were over 150 LEAS in England and Wales. In Northern Ireland, where they are referred to as Education and Library Boards, there are 5.

LEARNING AND SKILLS COUNCIL (LSC)

These were established in 2000 in 47 sub-regions of England. They are responsible for all post-16 education and training provision in their areas, except higher education (universities). Further Education Colleges and school sixth forms are funded, and where necessary, re-organised by these Councils.

MAINTAINED SCHOOLS

Types of schools maintained by the LEA are:

Community Schools

Schools funded by the **LEA** which is also responsible for admission arrangements. The LEA owns the site and buildings and is the formal employer of staff. In September 1999 this term replaced the former term, county schools.

Foundation Schools

A new category of school introduced in September 1999. They are funded by the LEA but the governing body has control of admissions, owns the site and buildings in trust and employs the staff.

Voluntary Aided Schools

A school established and owned by a voluntary (usually religious) body but largely maintained by the **LEA**. A majority of the governors are appointed by the foundation body (Diocesan Authority for denominational schools) and are responsible for admission of pupils, employment of staff and, in denominational schools, religious education.

NATIONAL CURRICULUM

Sets out what pupils in maintained schools should be taught. It was introduced in 1988 and its latest revision came into effect in September 2000. It is divided into four key stages (KS) that end at age 7, 11, 14 and 16. For each key stage in each subject there is a Programme of Study which sets out what should be taught and Attainment Targets (ATs) describing the standards which pupils are expected to reach. The targets are divided into 8 levels plus a description of 'exceptional performance'. The expected levels of performance at the end of the first three key stages are levels 2, 4 and 5/6. By law, children's progress must be assessed at the end of each key stage. (See **Statutory Assessment**)

NEWLY QUALIFIED TEACHER (NQT)

A teacher in their first year in the profession. This now implies a period of induction consisting of mentoring and support to continue the development of their knowledge and skills. Their teaching timetable is reduced to allow for this to happen. At the end of this period they must be able to demonstrate that they have been able to perform at the nationally determined standards for QTS in the school situation.

OFSTED (OFFICE FOR STANDARDS IN EDUCATION)

Established in 1992 to replace the duties of Her Majesty's Inspectorate (HMI), OfSTED determines the framework for inspecting schools, LEAs, ITT and Early Years education. It appoints and trains private teams to carry out a regular programme of inspections. Their reports are publicly available and, for schools, all parents receive a summary of the report. School governors must draw up an action plan to address any failings indicated in the report.

PANDA (PERFORMANCE AND ASSESSMENT REPORT)

A report issued annually to each school in England by OfSTED. It provides a detailed analysis of the school's results in Statutory Assessments in the context of national performance and also 'benchmarked' against the performance of similar schools. There are also indications of trends over time. The reports are not made public but are intended as a management tool for use within the school.

PERSONAL, SOCIAL AND HEALTH EDUCATION (PSHE)

A programme of study to teach the life skills needed for children's safety and confidence and for a healthy and fulfilled life in the future. Although there is a national framework for this subject it is not part of the statutory National Curriculum.

PGCE (POSTGRADUATE CERTIFICATE IN EDUCATION)

A postgraduate course of training through which graduates can obtain Qualified Teacher Status (QTS).

PRIVATE FINANCE INITIATIVE (PFI)

Introduced by the Conservative government in 1993 as a means of using private finance to fund capital works in the public sector.

PUBLIC PRIVATE PARTNERSHIP (PPP)

Introduced by the Labour government in 1997, and closely related to the PFI to provide new or improved buildings, facilities and services. It includes some projects started under the Private Finance Initiative (PFI).

QUALIFIED TEACHER STATUS (QTS)

See **ITT**, **Newly Qualified Teacher** and **PGCE**

REGISTER OF SPECIAL EDUCATIONAL NEEDS

See **SEN**

SATS (STANDARD ASSESSMENT TASKS)

See **Statutory Assessment**

SEN (SPECIAL EDUCATIONAL NEEDS)

Various types of difficulty in learning requiring additional or specific help. Since 1993, the provision for these children has been governed by a **code of practice** established by the Department for Education and Employment (DfEE). The code suggests a 5-stage process for meeting these needs. Schools keep a Register of Special Educational Needs children. Children at the later stages are assessed by the **LEA** which may decide to compile a Statement of Educational Needs. This specifies in writing the child's needs, the educational provision he/she should have and which type of school he/she should attend.

SMT (SENIOR MANAGEMENT TEAM)

A term usually used in secondary schools for a management group comprising the headteacher and 3–4 other senior staff.

SRB (SINGLE REGENERATION BUDGET)

Introduced by the Conservative government in 1993 for multi-agency regeneration projects which will improve employment prospects, the physical environment and public services, including education, in disadvantaged neighbourhoods. Continued by the Labour government, they are administered by the Regional Development Agencies, under the control of the DETR (Department of Environment, Transport and the Regions). This Department also produces regular updates of the Index of Local Deprivation, which is used in deciding the allocation of the SRB.

STANDARD NUMBER

This is the number of pupils a school enrols in each of its year groups/cohorts. It has to be approved by the DfEE. Parents are entitled to appeal against the school's Admission Authority (LEA or governing body) if their child's application to enrol has been turned down. In more popular schools, the Standard Number is thus exceeded, following successful appeals.

STANDARDS AND EFFECTIVENESS UNIT (SEU)

A unit in the DfEE, established in 1997, concerned with a range of government initiatives aimed at raising standards in schools. National Numeracy and Literacy Strategies are administered by the SEU, as are LEA Educational Development Plans.

STANDARDS FUND (SF)

Direct grants from the DfEE's SEU to schools for the improvement of educational standards, with a particular emphasis on literacy and numeracy, social inclusion and GCSE. They are distributed via the LEAs which, for some grants, also make a 50 per cent contribution.

STATEMENT OF SPECIAL EDUCATIONAL NEEDS

See **SEN**

STATUTORY ASSESSMENT

National arrangements require the following assessments to be made:

Baseline Assessment/Achievement on Entry (AOE)

Within 7 weeks of entering a reception or Year 1 class, 4/5-year-olds are assessed in language and literacy, mathematics, and personal and social development.

STANDARD ASSESSMENT TASKS (SATS)

National Curriculum tasks or tests in English and maths at the end of Key Stage One and in English, maths and science at the end of Key Stages Two and Three. There is also teacher assessment in English, maths and science at the end of Key Stages One and Two and in all National Curriculum subjects at the end of Key Stage Three.

At the end of Key Stage Four, GCSE examinations are used as the method of assessment.

SURE START

Initiative to improve services to families and young children under four in areas of need, as a means of combating social exclusion, raising educational standards and reducing inequalities in health and opportunity. It aims to promote the physical, intellectual, social and emotional development of children in readiness for their school life. Sixty 'trailblazer' areas started in 2000 and at least 250 programmes throughout England are proposed by 2002.

INDEX